African Christology

African Christology

Jesus in Post-Missionary African Christianity

CLIFTON R. CLARKE

PICKWICK *Publications* · Eugene, Oregon

AFRICAN CHRISTOLOGY
Jesus in Post-Missionary African Christianity

Pickwick Publications
An Imprint of Wipf and Stock Publishers
199 W. 8th Ave., Suite 3
Eugene, OR 97401

www.wipfandstock.com

ISBN 13: 978-1-60899-433-5

Cataloging-in-Publication data:

Clarke, Clifton R.

African Christology : Jesus in post-missionary African Christianity / Clifton R. Clarke.

xiv + 190 p.; 23 cm. Includes bibliographical references and indexes.

ISBN 13: 978-1-60899-433-5

1. Theology, Doctrinal—Africa. 2. Jesus Christ—Person and offices. 3. Christianity—Africa. I. Title.

BT205.C55 2011

Manufactured in the U.S.A.

To
Marcia, Joel, and Jessica
and
Hilda and Kenweline Clarke

Contents

Foreword

IN THIS ORIGINAL, FIELDWORK-BASED study of the Christology of some Akan independent churches in Ghana, Clifton Clarke has broken new ground. He comes from a unique perspective as a Black British Pentecostal bishop who spent several years living and working as a mission partner of the Church Missionary Society. It was my privilege to work with him supervising his doctoral research at the University of Birmingham. His work indicates how much times have changed. Young English CMS missionaries humiliated the elderly first African bishop Samuel Crowther and wrested power from African leaders in West Africa in the late nineteenth century. Secession was inevitable and the first African independent churches (AICs) were often a reaction to that western missionary control that lasted well into the twentieth century. In the 1920s a new form of resistance to western cultural hegemony emerged in AICs that were founded as a result of healing and revival movements. These originated in grassroots movements throughout the continent, but especially along the West African coast, East Africa and Southern Africa. The Gold Coast (Ghana) was one of those centres of AIC activity, partly initiated after 1915 by followers of the famous Liberian prophet William Wade Harris. These churches that preferred to be called "churches of the Spirit" were more African in orientation, seeking to answer questions that Africans were asking and catering for the whole person and not just the dichotomized "spiritual" person. Although many of these AICs today do not refer to themselves as "pentecostal", the differences are not as significant as is often claimed, and their pentecostal character is recognized by scholars.

These AICs are African-initiated churches that, in common with Pentecostalism, emphasize the working of the Spirit in the church with ecstatic phenomena. They are widespread across a great variety of Christian churches in Africa, including the vast majority of the several thousands of AICs thought to be in existence today. They practise gifts of the Spirit, especially healing and prophecy, and they also speak in tongues. Because of their Spirit manifestations and pneumatic emphases and experiences, earlier studies of these churches misunderstood or generalized about them and branded them "syncretistic," "post-Christian" and "messianic." Western observers saw these churches of the Spirit as accommodating the pre-Christian past, and being linked with traditional divination, ancestor rituals and the like. More recent studies have shown this to be an erroneous view. In particular, as this study shows, they have a Christological focus. The Spirit churches do differ from western pentecostals in several ways, and the passing of time has accentuated these differences. They differ in their approach to African religions and culture, in liturgy, in healing practices and in their unique contribution to Christian theology in a broader African context. Their innovative approach often differs sharply from those African pentecostals who are more heavily influenced by western Pentecostalism, and this creates a certain amount of tension.

The pentecostal missionaries that came to Africa from western countries in the early twentieth century also came from the margins and were doubtless influential in popularizing the new message of the power of the Spirit with accompanying spiritual gifts. But the message was about Jesus Christ. This message with its accompanying democratization of charismatic leadership in turn created space for the new African missionaries who arose in different parts of Africa in the early twentieth century. They were catalysts of a new ingathering of Africans to Christianity on an unprecedented scale, and for which western missions were totally unprepared. But it was also the precedents laid down by African charismatic leaders, pioneers largely untouched by western Pentecostalism, that had possibly the most lasting effect on the shaping of African Christianity in the twentieth century. Pentecostalism is a polycentric phenomenon that had different beginnings in Africa, just as in other continents. It is also a movement that is constantly reinventing and reinvigorating itself in the multitude of different expressions that exist in African Christianity today and in the forms of African Christianity that are now being reproduced in Europe and North America. It remains to be seen whether these vigorous expressions of Christianity in Africa will find each other and acknowledge both their inter-relatedness and their mutual indebtedness.

Although these forms of African Christianity emphasized the working of the Spirit empowering the powerless and marginalized in the oppressed social and political order of European colonialism, they were not exclusively pneumatological. In the analyses that have been made of these churches, the equally significant Christological emphases have often been obscured. Dr. Clarke sets out to rectify this imbalance. Members and leaders of African Spirit churches, classical Pentecostal and new Charismatic churches often exclude each other from their self-imposed categories of "authentic" Christian and even demonize the others, but the unmistakable links that bind these movements to each other cannot easily be denied. In their inculturation of Christianity, they have a distinct and considerable contribution to make to African Christian theology. This inculturation has been done in an intense and far-reaching way. In a 1996 article on "AIC Contributions to the World Church", the Kenya-based Organization of African Instituted Churches said, "We may not all be articulate in written theology, but we express faith in our liturgy, worship, and structures".[1] Theology is our human response to God's word in Christ. The African pastors, bishops, or prophets who lay hands on the sick and lead their congregations in rituals of worship are enacting theology. Significantly, they do this in decidedly Christocentric ways. Members of AICs have responded to God's word in Christ to them in a particular way. In this respect they have an extremely significant part to play in formulating African theology. If, as Ukpong suggests, the main goal of African theology is "to make Christianity attain African expression", then "Christianity must be made relevant to and expressive of the way [Africans] live and think."[2]

This is precisely what the AICs strive to do. Probably more than any other form of Christianity in Africa, the "Spirit" AICs have given a uniquely African character to their faith. In certain respects, they have attained the goals towards which formal African theology still struggles. Because theology is our human response to God's word, Christianity must be expressive of everyday life or be in danger of becoming inconsequential. Not only must the Christological contribution of African Christians be recognized by the wider community of theological scholarship, but its practical consequences for daily living in a marginalized continent that has suffered so much oppression and deprivation must be appropriated also. Clifton Clarke's study focuses on one aspect of this innovative approach to African theology, that of Christology. He sets out for posterity

1. Quoted in John S. Pobee and Gabriel Ositelu II, *African Initiatives in Christianity: The Growth, Gifts and Diversities of Indigenous African Churches—A Challenge to the Ecumenical Movement* (Geneva: WCC, 1998) 70.

2. Justin S. Ukpong, "Current Theology: The Emergence of African Theologies," *Theological Studies* 45 (1984) 520.

the Christological focus of the AICs he studied and worked with. I believe that this book will change the way we think about Christology in Africa and I commend it to you for your careful consideration.

Allan Anderson
Professor of Global Pentecostal Studies and Head of the School of
Philosophy, Theology and Religion, University of Birmingham, UK

Acknowledgments

I AM FIRSTLY GRATEFUL to God for His boundless love and grace upon my life and for enabling me to complete this book project. I want to acknowledge the support and understanding of my wife Marcia and children Joel and Jessica, who gave me the room to complete this volume. "Hey guys, I'm back!" I also want to recognize the encouragement and support of my wider family and friends.

I want to thank Dr. Allan Anderson for sharing his enthusiasm for African Pentecostalism and African Indigenous churches. A debt of gratitude is owed to the Rev. Dr. Trevor Grizzle (my brother-in-law) for coaching and encouraging me along this journey and taking the time to read through this work in spite of his own grueling schedule, and to Dr. Selwyn Arnold for his inspiration and moral support.

I would like to thank the faculty and students of Good News Theological College and Seminary in Accra Ghana where I taught for ten rewarding years. Thanks guys for your friendship and insights. Thanks to Rev. Dr. Thomas Oduro, Dr. Abraham Akrong, and Professor Kwame Bediako for sharing with me their insights into African Indigenous Christianity. I would also express my appreciation for all the AICs pastors and church members interviewed for this research. Thanks for opening up your churches and ministry to me.

I am thankful to the Church Mission Society (CMS) for sponsoring this study during my tenure as a Mission Partner to AICs in Ghana. I am also indebted to the New Testament Church of God in England and Wales, particularly the Church of God in Nottingham, for teaching me the value of education and the pursuit of excellence.

Abbreviations

AIC	African Indigenous Churches
CMS	Church Mission Society
GNTCS	Good News Theological College and Seminary
MDCC	Musama Disco Christo Church
NT	New Testament
OAIC	Organization of African Instituted Churches
OT	Old Testament
TEE	Theological Education by Extension

1

Introduction: The Quest for an African Christology

IN 1967 JOHN MBITI, a Kenyan theologian, made the remark: "an African concept of Christology does not exist."[1] Seven years later at a consultation of African theologians in Accra, Ghana, Dr. E. W. Fashole-Luke of the University of Sierra Leone announced that "there are no signs that Christological ideas are being wrestled with by African theologians,"[2] and urged the delegates to make fulfilling this need a top priority. In 1977, ten years after Mbiti's statement, Kofi Appiah-Kubi of Ghana despairingly observed that very little literature on African Christology was available. Two years later, Gabriel Setiloane of Botswana announced that the "task given to African theologians is to work hard and thoroughly at such a Christology, exploring who Jesus is and what Messiah or Christ means in the African context."[3]

On one level this "crisis of Christology" is somewhat a "storm in a tea cup," perhaps nothing more than a crisis amongst the theological elite, many of whom have been educated in the west. The rapid growth of Christianity could point to the fact that Christ is "alive and well" in Africa. It could be argued, therefore, that this obsessive call for a seemingly "African Christological definition" is more a case of African theologians seeking to replicate the western Christological definitions they themselves were taught. However, this has very little to do with the way Christ is experienced by African Christians on a daily basis. The approach to theology taken by the Council of Nicea, AD 325, which declared that Jesus was *homoousios* (one in being or one of substance) with the Father, and the Council of Chalcedon 451 statement that the two natures of

1. Mbiti, "Some African Concepts," 51.
2. Fashole-Luke, "Quest for African," 110.
3. Appiah-Kubi, "Jesus Christ," 56.

1

Christ (the divine and the human) are without division or separation, is not an African approach to theology. The importance of a defined African Christology or even an African theological paradigm could be challenged on the basis that Christianity in Africa is not primarily an intellectual pursuit, conforming to western logic and discursiveness, but rather a "lived" experience in which Christ is a part of everyday life for an African believer. However, on another level, there is an important role for intellectuals (theologians or otherwise) to assess and define national phenomena and socio-cultural as well as theological significance of faith in Jesus, in order to gain a deeper understanding of the working of aspects of society as well as to have the capacity for self-definition.

The impact of African theologians responding to the challenge of constructing an African contextual Christology has been impressive. Over the past thirty-five years or so, African Christian theologians have had to search for an authentic African response to the Christ event. Since then the quest for an authentic African Christology has been the subject matter in many international conferences as well as personal research. It has gone through many phases involving definitions and redefinition, out of which some key concepts emerged. The situation in regard to Christology in Africa has changed to such an extent that Nyamiti claims, with some degree of caution, that Christology is the most developed subject matter in African theology today.[4] The Christian religion revolves around questions concerning the meaning and identity of Jesus, and so Christology is perennially at the center of the quest to understand any particular expression of Christianity in an African context.

One indication that Christology in Africa is now coming of age and is perhaps more prominent today than ever before is the fact that African Christology itself is now being critiqued from within. There are two areas of which that critique is pertinent to this research. First of all, it reflects failure to break free from the "umbilical cord" of western mission Christianity. African Christologies have not been sufficiently related to Africans and the missionary responsibility of the African churches. This shortcoming was highlighted by John Mbiti who maintained that although African theologians have written a great deal about the role of foreign missions in Africa—particularly pointing out the biasness of

---

4. Nyamiti, "African Christologies," 3.

a western Christology—there is almost nothing written about ways in which the African church is engaging in homeland.[5]

The other critique levied against African Christologies is that they are mainly systematic academic reflections on the mystery of Christ in the midst of African realities which need to be complemented with Christologies that really function in the life of African people.[6] This position demands a greater dialogue between African academic Christologies and Christologies that are lived out in the everyday lives of African Christians. My observation further reveals an over-dependence on the theological methods adopted by the western theological tradition and an undervaluing of the resources African oral tradition provide.[7]

This research is part and parcel of the ongoing theological reflection on the meaning of Christ for Africans in an African context. It seeks to respond to the critique that African Christologies are constructed using the epistemology or the intellectual framework that is used in western theological reflection. Taking seriously the claim that a greater dialogue needs to ensue between the professional theologian and the local theologian,[8] it seeks to explore ways in which the raw materials of African oral tradition may aid the professional theologian and the local theologian alike to talk about Christ using a language reflective of an African epistemology.

THE SIGNIFICANCE AND AIM OF THIS STUDY

Christians through the centuries have tried to understand and express the meaning of Christ in terms that are meaningful to their culture and worldviews. The New Testament itself is no exception—containing images, titles, and models of Christ, all designed to answer meaningfully the question asked by an emerging generation: who is Jesus Christ? Thus Jesus is presented as the Good Shepherd, Son of God, Son of man, Son

---

5. Mbiti, *Bible and Theology*, 176–227.

6. Marthinus Daneel has argued this position in his book *African Earthkeepers*, 204.

7. The issue of "African oral tradition" will be discussed at some length in chapters 5 and 8 of this work.

8. Schreiter maintained that a professional theologian is one who has been professionally trained in the art of theology as an academic discipline. Local theologians he stated, on the other hand, are the small but condensed groups who have seen the insight and the power arising from the reflections of the people upon their experience and Scripture which has prompted making the community itself the prime author of theology in local context. See Schreiter, *Constructing*, 16.

of David, and Messiah.[9] In spite of the tension that exists in balancing locally constructed African Christologies and simultaneously respecting the universal significance of Christ, the long-term success of Christianity in Africa will ultimately depend on the development of an inculturated Christology.

Christology is, in the final analysis, the most basic and central issue of Christian theology.[10] The faith that Christianity cherishes and bears witness to must have Christ as its foundation and goal. From a Christian point of view, without Jesus Christ as the central cornerstone and final aim, nothing in Christianity counts; nothing in theological thought is of any significance. Mugambi and Magesa place beyond doubt the centrality of Christ to Christianity:

> In fact, to be precise, theology is not Christian at all when it does not offer Jesus Christ of Nazareth as the answer to the human quest, and as the answer to people who ask the reason for the hope that all Christians hold through faith.[11]

The works detailing the development of Christology in Africa are numerous; however, some of the more prominent contributions, as well as the shape the Christological discussion has taken, are compiled in Robert Schreiter's book *Faces of Jesus in Africa*, Mugambi and Magesa's *Jesus in African Christianity*, and John Pobee's *Exploring Afro-Christology* and *Towards an African Theology*. Among those who have examined Christology specifically from an Akan perspective are John Pobee in *Exploring Afro-Christology*, Kwame Bediako in *Jesus in Africa*, and Abraham Akrong in "Christology from an African Perspective."[12] Examining Christology from the perspective of African indigenous churches (AICs) is certainly not a new idea. Existing research from the Akan AICs provided important Christological insights. At the time of this writing, however, this author is unaware of any other research focused primarily on the Christology of Akan AICs in Ghana, as this study is attempting to do.

---

9. For a fruitful discussion on the different titles and models used for Jesus, see F. Hahn, *Titles of Jesus*.

10. Mugambi and Magesa, *Jesus in African Christianity*, viii.

11. Ibid.

12. Schreiter, *Faces of Jesus*; Mugambi and Magesa, *Jesus in African Christianity*; Pobee, *Exploring Afro-Christology*, also Pobee, *Toward an African Theology*, 81–98; Bediako, *Jesus in Africa*; Akrong, "Christology from an African Perspective," 119–36.

The fieldwork for this research has been extensive and utilized three different approaches to information gathering. Questionnaires were used in all ten regions of Ghana; one-to-one interviews were conducted; and focus group sessions were held. Each of these approaches was designed to obtain a grass roots perspective, which is considered to be a significant contribution within this research for the ongoing Christological discussions. Further, it is the aim of this work to examine the Christology of the Akan AICs, drawing upon their sources for Christological epistemology, as well as to discover how their Christology functions in the life of their faith communities.

It is the position of this study that their understanding and experience of Christ, which is appropriated through their view of the world, makes a valuable contribution to the quest for a relevant Christology in Africa as well as providing a critique to the western propositional approaches to Christology. This western approach is also very often adopted by African theologians and writers on religion in African. This work is concerned with how Akan AICs—out of the richness of their symbols, their cultural expressions, their experiences, their hopes, their fears and their daily life in community—articulate faith in Jesus Christ.

CHRISTOLOGICAL CONSTRUCTION

The notion that all Christologies are cultural constructs is today commonly acknowledged, particularly in missiological circles.[13] It is, however, only fairly recently that this essentially contextual nature of the faith has been recognized. For many centuries every deviation from what was considered "orthodoxy" was viewed in terms of "heterodoxy" and even heresy. The apprehension of theological (or Christological knowledge), which was thought to exist in "objective forms," was situated under the tutelage of the Church and was neither open to personal interpretation, nor was it contingent upon cultural, political, and social factors.[14]

---

13. Bosch, *Transforming Mission*, 421. See also Schreiter, *Constructing Local Theologies*, 4–5.

14. The key to Plato's (429–347) philosophy is influential here. His theory of knowledge posited that "knowledge" in the strict sense cannot be obtained from anything so variable and evanescent as sense-perception. He forwarded a view of a transcendent non-sensible world of forms or ideals, which are apprehended by the intellect alone. See Kelly, *Early Christian*, 10.

This generated an attitude of intolerance against other forms of theological or Christological constructs which was particularly evident after Constantine, when the erstwhile *religio illicita* became the religion of the establishment.[15] The Church then adopted the imperial, Roman view of culture, which viewed culture as objective with Christianity as an integral part. In other words, it was assumed that the gospel must be proclaimed everywhere in a single, "perfect," cultural form.[16] Any variation was deemed to be either a deviation or a stage of development towards the, as yet, unrealized ideal.

It was this belief that governed the way the Church authorities handled the Christological controversies that challenged the Church's orthodoxy such as Arianism, Donatism, Pelegianism, Nestorianism, Monophysitism, and numerous similar movements.[17] Such movements were all regarded as doctrinally heterodox, and those who promulgated such views were often very severely dealt with. The ecumenical councils, such as the ones held at Nicaea in AD 325 and at Chalcedon in AD 451, had on this basis of preserving Christian orthodoxy sought to establish a single faith throughout the empire. This, they thought, represented revealed truth and therefore did not recognize how their own cultural, social, and political influence would determine the shape of their Christological construction.[18]

When the classical Greco-Roman philosophy came to be applied to the truths of the Christian faith, the immutability of the Christian cultural ideal was sealed. According to classicist assumption, there was only one culture which could be aspired to through diligent study of the ancient Latin and Greek authors and through the learning of Scholastic philosophy and theology. In Shorter's view, the classicist theologian often assumed therefore that the Church's dogma was permanent, not so much because it represented revealed truths, but because of belief in a universal, permanent culture and in the existence of fixed, immutable substances and meaning.[19]

---

15. Kelly, *Early Christian*, 223.

16. Shorter, *Toward A Theology*, 18.

17. See Kelly, *Early Christian*, 9–17.

18. Ibid., 223–338.

19. Shorter, *Toward A Theology*, 19.

The socio-political philosophers of the seventeenth and eighteenth centuries adopted the classicist universal view of human culture.[20] This classicist normative view of culture permeated the Church's missionary activity, hindered the Church from being self-reflective, and distorted its own understanding of itself. It further led to Christians failing to recognize cultural changes and developments and the ways in which these affected the Church's interpretation of the Christian message throughout history.

To summarize developments briefly, Friedrich Schleiermacher was one of the first theologians to question this "objectivized" paradigmatic approach to theology.[21] He argued that all theology was influenced, if not determined by, the context in which it had evolved. He very convincingly put forward the idea that there was no such thing as a "pure message" (supracultural and suprahistorical), and therefore it was impossible to penetrate to a golden core, the Christian faith, that was not already an interpretation. The object of religion, he believed, was not a particular being or activity above or alongside others. Like the "Absolute Self" of the Idealist and Tillich's "Ground of Being" or "being-itself," Schleiermacher's God was not to be thought of as a self-contained immutable being over and above the world but one that interacted with it. Of particular relevance for Christology was his view of Christ as the mediator between the infinite God and the finite world. The divine God-man of the creeds and orthodox theology is replaced by a figure who illuminates the world and all people with the light of the infinite God. This paradigm shift marked a significant turning point toward theologies that would be shaped and influenced by contexts.

The accomplishments of the eighteenth-century historical-critical method and the early twentieth-century form, and redaction critics through their textual analysis and in their quest for the historical Jesus, further built upon this new paradigm shift.[22] They themselves, however, failed to realize that their own interpretations were as parochial and

---

20. This attitude was epitomized in the Enlightenment approach of Immanuel Kant, who maintained that "pure" and "theoretical" reason may be acquired absolutely independent of all experience, and therefore by implication, religious knowledge and truth could not be gained by engaging with culture. See Kant, *Critique of Pure Reason.*

21. For more on Schleiermacher's influence on theology see Brown, *Jesus in European,* 105–32.

22. See Krentz, *The Historical-Critical,* 6–32.

conditioned by context as those they were criticizing.[23] The more recent hermeneutical approach of literary critics like Paul Ricoeur[24] advanced the view that every text is an interpreted text that "becomes" as we engage with it and is not "out there" waiting to be interpreted. This approach has also been helpful. Still, it did not go far enough toward liberating the text from the hegemony of western dominance.

The real breakthrough came, however, with the advent of Third-World theologies (and implicitly Christologies) in their various forms.[25] Christological perspectives are now constructed from a plethora of theological and socio-political contexts.[26] This essentially contextual approach to Christology represents what David Bosch calls an "epistemological break" from traditional Christological approaches. He states:

> Whereas, at least since the time of Constantine, theology was constructed *from above* as an elitist enterprise (except in the case of minority Christian communities, commonly referred to as sects), its main source (apart from Scripture and tradition) was *philosophy* and its main interlocutor the educated non-believer, contextual theology is theology *"from below"* "from the underside of history" its main source (apart from Scripture and tradition) is the *social sciences* and its main interlocutor the *poor* or the *cultural marginalized.*[27]

Our entire context therefore comes into play when we interpret a biblical text. This was considered such a significant epistemological break with traditional theology that Segundo referred to it as "the liberation of theology."[28]

In line with the Third-world theologies, this study takes the view that Christology is a cultural construct reflective of the cultural, historical, economical, and socio-political context from which it arises.

23. Bosch, *Transforming*, 423.

24. Stiver, *Theology After* Ricoeur; see pp. 56–79 for details on his hermeneutical approach.

25. Bosch, *Transforming*, 423–24.

26. See citations 101–3 in this chapter.

27. Bosch, *Transforming*, 423.

28. Segundo, *Liberation of* Theology; see particularly chapter 1: "The Hermeneutical Cycle."

CHRISTOLOGY AND INCULTURATION

Christology in Africa, as elsewhere, cannot exist meaningfully without a social context.[29] This therefore brings the issue of Christ and culture to center stage, once again highlighting the creative tension between the particularity and the universality of Christ. The complexity of the term "culture" makes it necessary for this study to clarify how the term will be used.[30] The early definition given by Sir Edward Tylor—who coined and popularized the term—as "that complex whole which includes knowledge, belief, art, morals, law, customs and any other capabilities and habits acquired by man as a member of society," in spite of its datedness, is adopted.[31] Culture is thus essentially a transmitted pattern of meaning embodied in symbols that are dynamic and therefore susceptible to development and change.

The foregrounding of culture as the subject matter with which missiologists must grapple has led to an explosion in terminology attempting to name this process. The terminologies include *accommodation, adaptation, incarnation, indigenization, inculturation, interculturation, localization,* and *translation.*[32] Initially *accommodation* and *adaptation* were deemed to be appropriate terminology to express the process of Africanization. However, the term came "under fire" following a shift in theological thinking among African Catholics who began to question the meaning of the concept of theological unity expressed in the term *adaptation,* which Vatican II as well as Pope Paul VI had encouraged.[33] It was felt that the term, which was an invention and imposition of western missionaries, was concerned only with Africanizing superficial and exter-

29. Pobee, *Afro-Christology,* 17.

30. For a number of definitions and different usages of the term "culture," see Shorter, *Toward a Theology,* 4–5; Hesselgrave, *Communicating Christ,* 68; Kraft, *Christianity in Culture;* 46.

31. Geertz, *Interpretation,* 89; Tylor, *Primitive,* 1.

32. For the meaning and relevance of each of these terms, see Schineller, *A Handbook,* 14–24; Shorter, *Toward a Theology,* 3–16; Ukpong, *African Theologies,* 26f; Dickson, *Theology in Africa,* 116; Bosch, *Transforming Mission,* 63–71.

33. See Pope Paul VI's Address to the *All Africa Bishops" Symposium* on July 31, 1969, in which he declared to the bishops that ". . . you may, and you must have an African Christianity," in *AFER,* vol.10, no. 4, 1969, 302–5. Following this address, African Catholic theologians began to explore "ways and means of articulating what this African Christianity is"; Lugira, "African Christian Theology," 56.

nal trappings of African Christianity.[34] Following *adaptation* and *accommodation*, the emphasis then shifted to *incarnation*, which was preferable because it involved "immersing Christianity in African culture"; just as Jesus became human, so Christianity must become African.[35] In spite of the stimulating character of the analogy of *incarnation*, it too was felt to possess serious inadequacies.[36] In Protestant circles the preferred term was *indigenization*, which was particularly championed by Bolaji Idowu in his spirited publication of 1965, *Towards an Indigenous Church*.[37] For Idowu, Christianity was a foreign religion on African soil. The "foreignness" of Christianity in Africa was a fundamental datum and the starting point for an African Christian discourse. *Indigenization* was as much about discarding "foreignness" as it was about rooting the faith in local realities. Though the term *indigenization* or *indigenous* still represents the Africanizing of the Gospel of Christ in some quarters, it too has become questionable. Bediako, for example, describes the indigenization crusade of Idowu as a "false start" for African theology.[38]

The term that has gained currency in recent years, being embraced by both Catholics and Protestants alike, is the term *inculturation*.[39] Aylward Shorter defines inculturation as "the on-going dialogue between faith and culture or cultures." The subject matter of inculturation is Jesus Christ. As such, inculturation is essentially to do with the on-going creative and dynamic relationship between Jesus Christ and culture in such a way that this experience finds expression through elements relevant to the culture but also transforms it into a new creation. *Inculturation* is the term favored by this study and the one that it will employ.

LIMITATIONS

The research is limited to the way Christ is encountered and experienced from within the Akan AICs in Ghana. There are Akan groups outside

34. Shorter, *African Christian Theology*, 150.

35. Ukpong, *African Theologies*, 27.

36. Shorter, *African Christian Theology*, 79–80.

37. Idowu, *Towards An Indigenous Church*.

38. Bediako, *Christianity in Africa*, 116.

39. For a detailed discussion on the history and usage of the term *inculturation*, consult the following texts: Shorter, *Toward a Theology*; Crollius, "What Is so New," 721–38; Ott, *African Theology*, 21–71; Schineller, *A Handbook*.

Ghana in countries such as Togo and Ivory Coast which do not form a part of this investigation. The language groups within the Akan in Ghana that had a majority representation were the Ashanti and Fanti. Although both the qualitative and the quantitative research had a scope that covered the ten administrative regions of the country, the regions of Greater Accra, Central and Eastern had a greater representation. The research is principally concerned with the Christology within the Akan AICs and did not attempt to be comparative with mission related churches, though the Christological comparisons with African churches of western missionary origin would have provided added insight and information. I would, however, point out that issues such as healing, use of scripture, this role and function of Christological titles, prophylactics and benefits, as well as other issues highlighted in this research, are matters of importance to the churches in Ghana generally and therefore to the extent the research speaks beyond the Akan AICs. A further limitation to the research is the focus on the oral Christology and not the oral theology as a whole, although there are obvious areas of convergence.

In spite of these limitations it is hoped that the findings of this research will be relevant for other AICs across Africa, as well as churches of all shades seeking a deeper meaning to the question "who do you [Africans] say that I am?"[40]

DEFINITION OF KEY TERMS

The target population of this research is the adherents and leaders of the Akan AICs of Ghana. Although Akan AICs are by no means a monolithic group, but rather comprised of diverse "single congregation churches" and denominations, they share the same cultural and traditional experience and outlook.[41] It is on the basis of these shared cultural, linguistical, and socio-historical commonalities that the term Akan AICs is used. Though these churches and denominations are continually adapting, growing, and changing in ways that are symptomatic of AICs across the continent, this research found no significant differences in the way they express their faith in Christ.

---

40. This is taken from the question that Jesus asked his disciples in Matthew 16:13, "Who do men say that I am?"

41. Ackan, *Akan Ethics*, 25.

My usage of the term "Akan AICs" is therefore primarily reflective of the cultural and socio-historical backdrop of the Akans, who worship in African indigenous churches in Ghana.[42] It also recognizes the common strands that these churches share in their theology and spirituality, which have been influenced by a shared history and traditional culture.[43] Both qualitative and quantitative methodologies were employed in order to ascertain a clear picture of the source and function Akan AIC Christology.

Important terms integral to this study will be defined at the appropriate place; however, there are a few other key terms and concepts that warrant definition and/or explanation at this juncture. I define the term *Christology* as the "study of the doctrine of Christ and his person and nature." John Pobee maintains that Christology (*Christo* and *logos*) is the word or teaching about Christ.[44] The Greek word *logos,* as Pobee rightly points out, means *word* or *teaching*; however, it could also be extended to mean *conversation* or *talk*. In this work the term *Christology* will not primarily be used as a propositional study of Christ through doctrine or through the formalities of western pedagogy, but through conversations and talk—through the lived experience of Christians who encounter Christ in everyday life. Akan AIC Christology, by which is meant Christ as encountered and experienced by Akan AIC Christians, will also frequently be used.

The term *African Traditional Religion* will be used to mean the original religion of African peoples. The issue concerning the homogeneity or multiplicity of African indigenous belief is a long-standing one. African theologians and teachers of African religious studies are divided as to whether Africa has one traditional religion with a common thread running throughout, expressed through its diversity of manifestations throughout the different cultures and customs within Africa, or rather that Africa has a plurality of religions.[45] The term *African Traditional*

42. The historical background of the Akan is outlined in chapter 2.

43. The categorization of AICs on the basis of cultural, linguistical, and socio-historical commonalities is also not without precedent, but is evident in Daneel's treatment of the Southern Shona independent Churches and in Anders Fogelqvist's study of Swazi independent Churches. See Daneel, *Old and New*; Fogelqvist, *The Red-Dress*.

44. Pobee, "In Search of Christology," 9.

45. An example of this is represented by the views of John Mbiti and E. Bolaji Idowu. Mbiti believes Africa to possess many religions but one religious philosophy. See Mbiti, *African Religions*. The viewpoint of Idowu is that Africa has one religion with one God, though there are other minor deities. See Idowu, *African Traditional Religion*. This view is also represented by the earlier work of E.W. Smith who wrote: "In spite of cultural di-

Religion or *African Religion* is the one favored by this author and is the one that will be employed for this study. Following John V. Taylor, who asserts that "African Traditional Religion is *fundamentally* [emphasis mine] the same everywhere,"[46] and Laurenti Magesa who argues that the differences within African Religion must not lead one to conclude that there is no internal, essential unity within African Religion, I believe African Religion possesses a unity in its diversity of expressions and therefore has a generic whole.[47]

The abbreviation AIC will be used to represent African Indigenous Churches. The massive proliferation of these churches, aptly described by David Barrett as a phenomenon unprecedented in history,[48] makes any attempt to define them as a whole a very risky venture. Nonetheless, Makhubu defines AICs as "black controlled denominations with no link in membership or administrative control with any non-African Church."[49] Kofi Appiah Kubi describes them as "autonomous groups with an all-African membership and leadership."[50] Turner regards them as churches that have been founded in Africa, by Africans, for Africans.[51] Since the increase of an academic interest in these churches, an appropriate term which represents them has been sought.

Initially the term *African Independent Churches* was thought to capture what these churches were and stood for. The word *independent*, however, was later deemed to be something of a misnomer because there are also white churches that had broken away from mainline bodies, and these are not independent in the same sense as AICs. For some this term was also thought to be a condescending one because it suggests that there was some more important reference point outside of these churches.[52] The term *indigenous* appears to be more appropriate because it demonstrates that the churches originate from the African people themselves and not

---

versities there is, I believe, sufficient identity to warrant our speaking of African religion." Quoted Parrinder, *West African Psychology*, 4.

46. Taylor, *Primal Vision*, 19. Italics mine.
47. Magesa, *African Religion*, 17.
48. Barrett, *Schism and Renewal*, 34.
49. Makhubu, *Who Are*, 7.
50. Appiah-Kubi, *African Theology*, 117.
51. Turner, *African Independent Churches*, 6.
52. Appiah-Kubi, *African Theology*, 117.

from Europeans or Americans or other outsiders.[53] With the growing influence of (and interest in) churches and worship styles from Europe and North America, the term *indigenous* carried the connotation of syncretism and the reformulation of old traditions. Terms such as *African-initiated* and *African-instituted* have gained currency in recent years.[54] The term that is adopted in this study is *African Indigenous Churches*. The reason for its preference is, as Jehu-Appiah rightly points out, that it denotes and connotes originality and self-authenticity. It also emphasizes the character of these churches as being unashamedly African while at the same time Christian.[55]

---

53. Idowu, *African Traditional Religion*, 46.

54. For a fuller discussion on the issue of appropriate terminology, see Anderson, *African Reformation*, 10–11; see also Jehu-Appiah, "African Indigenous Churches," 3–11.

55. Jehu-Appiah, "African Indigenous Churches," 11.

2

The Historical and Cultural Routes
of Akan AIC Christology

HISTORICAL BACKGROUND OF THE AKAN

THE SOCIAL-RELIGIOUS HISTORY OF the Akan people is significant to my study of Akan AIC Christology. This section is not intended to be a detailed study of Akan history and culture; such an effort would go beyond the focus of the study.[1] However tracing the cultural and traditional genesis of the Akan is necessary for "earthing" the way Akan AIC Christians express their faith. The present day researcher is more fortunate than his predecessors in having at his disposal the results of historical and cultural research conducted on the Akan as far back as 1887, particularly with the groundbreaking works of Sir A. B. Ellis.[2]

The term "Akan," for all the Twi and allied dialect-speaking people of Ghana, is a recent one; in the past three centuries it has been used in various senses. In the sixteenth century, the word *Akani* or *Akanisten*, according to Eva Meyerowitz, meant a "specialist in gold trading" who came from the hinterland of the Gold Coast, especially from Assin, Adansi, and Akin areas.[3] Before that it was used only of those who had emigrated into the Gold Coast from the Kumbu kingdom, or one of the vassal states at the end of the fifteenth century who regarded themselves as Akan.[4] By the end of the nineteenth and up to the middle of the twentieth century, the

---

1. See Ackah, *Akan Ethics*; Williamson, *Akan Religion*; Meyerowitz, *Akan of Ghana*; Meyerowitz, *Sacred State*; Rattray, *Ashanti Law*; Rattray, *Ashanti Proverbs*; Rattray, *Religion and Art*; Rattray, *Ashanti*; Yankah, *Speaking for the Chief*; Yankah, *The Proverb*.

2. Ellis, *Tshi Speaking People*.

3. Meyerowitz, *Sacred State*, 21.

4. Ibid., 21.

term *Akan*, as a collective term for a group of related languages (comprising those from the south-eastern part of Ivory Coast to the eastern side of the middle Volta), was adopted. These included Nzema, Aowin, Sefwi, the Guan languages, as well as the Asante, Fanti, and related dialects, all spoken in Ghana.[5]

Oral tradition has it that the ancestors of the Akan came down from the north of Ghana.[6] It is generally accepted that the Akans were militarily forced south, but exactly who comprised the military force is unclear, though a number of possibilities have been postulated.[7] There is evidence to suggest that the Akan represent the section of people who in the latter part of the eleventh century refused to accept Islam, choosing to migrate south, rather than accept a position of subordination in a country that they considered their own.[8] This view, though hotly contested,[9] seems to be the most historically plausible.

The Akan are by no means a homogenous group but rather comprised of people from heterogeneous states. Even though they are descended from a common ancestry, they were fragmented by constantly warring against each other. By the end of the fifteenth century the traces of any bond that held them together had disappeared, giving way to various political and linguistic differentiation. There is, however, residual evidence which links various Akan communities together into a common origin, such as the similarity of their political, social, cultural, military, and religious practices, as well as in their linguistic expression.[10]

From a linguistic point of view, the Akan of Ghana fall into two main divisions: Fanti and Twi. The Akan people are principally composed of Agona, Ahanta, Akuapem, Akwamu, Asante, Brong, Denkyira, Fanti, Sefwi, and Wassa.[11] Today it is common to describe all these ethnic groups as

5. Greenberg, "Languages of Africa," 8.

6. Ward, *History of Ghana*, 43; see also Meyerowitz, *Akan of Ghana*, 17.

7. Claridge, *History of the Gold Coast*, 4–7. Claridge suggests that the Fulani drove the Akan into the southern forest; Migeod posits the view that it was the Bantu who invaded the Akan and drove them south, maintaining that this is evident because the Akan languages show traces of Bantu influence. Migeod, *Languages of West Africa*, 300–307.

8. Meyerowitz, *Akan of Ghana*, 120.

9. Ward, *History of Ghana*, 45–50.

10. Bannerman, *Practice of Witchcraft*.

11. Dolphyne, "Volta-Comoe Language," 53; Meyerowitz, *Akan of Ghana*, 17–18; A detailed discussion is also conducted on the Akan languages in Ward, *History of Ghana*, 37; and Ellis, *Tshi-Speaking People*, 306–24.

Akan, but to distinguish different groups linguistically (Twi, Asanti, Fanti, Brong, Wassa, etc). Geographically the Akan area constitutes one half of the 238,533 sq. km. (92000 sq. miles) of the surface area of Ghana.[12] The population of the Akan people was numbered at 5,490,815 out of a total population of 12,296,081 in 1995, which was approximately 46 percent of the population of Ghana. The Ghana Statistical Service projected, based on the same census, that by the year 2000 the total population of Ghana would be approximately 20,102,275.[13] Based on the same 46 percent Akan population, their population would be approximately 9,000,000. Akan is also the mother tongue of nearly half the population of Ghana, and spoken as a second language by 70 percent of the remainder.[14]

Although the Akan have many cultural traits in common with the other ethnic groups in Ghana and Africa in general, they still maintain certain distinctive cultural traits and institutions that are unique.[15] The most significant of these institutions is the identical exogamous matrilineal clan system, which can be found in all Akan groups. Each Akan can identify with one of eight principal matrilineal clans. These are *Ekɔɔna, ɔyoko, Asona, Aseneɛ, Agona, Brɛtuo, Asakyiri,* and *Aduana.* Members of the same clan consider themselves as brothers and sisters, regardless of where they hail from. According to Boahen, "clan membership affiliations and loyalties cut across tribal and political boundaries."[16]

Of the different ethnic groups that make up the Akans, the Ashanti were by far the strongest and the most influential.[17] One of the reasons for this was due to the leadership of the Ashanti King Osei Tutu who united the Ashanti chieftaincies under one common stool in 1701.[18] The next largest group is the Fanti who continue to occupy the coastal areas.

12. Twum-Baah and Kumekpor, *Analysis,* 8.

13. Ibid., 58.

14. Ibid., 55.

15. Boahen in his article, "Origins of the Akan," lists the distinctions of the Akan (3–10).

16. Ibid., 4.

17. A monumental research carried on the Ashanti people was conducted by Robert S. Rattray. See Rattray, *Ashanti.*

18. Ward, *History of Ghana,* 119.

ASPECTS OF AKAN COSMOLOGY
IN AKAN AIC CHRISTOLOGY

In my exploration of Akan AIC Christology, it is important to have a grasp of the Akan traditional religion as this constitutes the cultural backdrop that undergirds the cultural and philosophical thinking of these churches. Christian Baëta was correct in suggesting that what "spiritual" churches have done, is in effect, bring the traditional worldview that underpinned the old religion into their allegiance to the Christian faith: the basic ideas regarding the character of the universe, of its forces, their possibilities, and the modes of their operation have been preserved intact.[19] This research among the Akan AICs in Ghana has revealed that their Christology is the outworking of a dynamic discourse between the Akan tradition and the Christ. Kwame Bediako, commenting on the impact of what he calls "primal religions" on Christianity in Africa, remarks:

> The primal religions of the continent have thus been a significant factor in the immense Christian presence in Africa. While this cannot be taken to mean that there has not been any "paradigm shift" in African religious consciousness, it does confirm that the African apprehension of the Christian faith has substantial roots in the continent's primal tradition at the specific level of religious experience.[20]

Akan traditional religion is nonetheless a vast research area by itself and there are numerous scholars that have dedicated themselves to its enunciation.[21] My intention here is not to rehearse these arguments or to contribute significant insights to the subject matter, but rather to highlight the areas within Akan traditional religion that this research demonstrates impacts crucial areas in the shaping the Akan AIC's understanding and experience of Christ. The areas that will be considered for this reason will be limited to the Akan traditional understanding of *Onyame* (God), *Sunsum* (Spirit), *Abosom* (lower spirits), *Nananom* (Ancestors), and symbolic power. All these have significant influence on the Akan appropriation of Christ within the Akan socio-cultural context.

---

19. Baëta, *Prophetism in Ghana*, 135.

20. Bediako, *Christianity in Africa*, 192.

21. A thorough and thoughtful presentation is conducted by Williamson, *Akan Religion*, 85–111.

As well as highlighting the above areas of Akan traditional religion, I will also emphasize the importance of their function in the everyday life of the Akan. The importance of AIC experience of Jesus on the level of everyday living was deemed by this research to be a very significant aspect of AIC Christology. This functionality of belief in the everyday arena of the Akan is an extension of the functionality of belief within the Akan traditional religious philosophy.

Onyame (Supreme Being)[22]

The Akan have no word or vocabulary for "religion."[23] Through "serving" (*som*) the Supreme Being (*Onyame*), for them religion is not a body of ideas but an act, namely serving God (*Onyamesom*). The Akan likewise speak of serving the gods (*abosom*), an activity termed *abonsonsom*. This aspect of the religiosity of the Akan is seen in the character of names they give to their churches such as Healing Church, Deliverance International Ministry, or Fountain Gate Church of Light. These are very functional, highly symbolic terms which emphasize the activity of their religious faith in *Onyame*. The notion of a Supreme God, for the Akan, is an indisputable reality,[24] a reality that is not built upon propositional truth claims, but rather one experienced and expressed through prayers, folktales, songs, myths, folksongs, proverbs, and riddles.[25] This constitutes a very important aspect of AIC Christology, namely its oral character, which as we shall see in later chapters, plays a crucial part in the way their faith in Christ is expressed and apprehended. An Akan proverb which enunciates the unquestionable nature of the belief in *Onyame* states: *Obi nkyerɛ akwadaa Nyame* (nobody needs to show God to a child), which is simply an indication that the Akan consider the knowledge of God to be an innate quality of humankind.

The Akan commonly use a number of names for God; nevertheless the main term used is *Onyame*, often shortened to *Nyame*.[26] The mean-

---

22. For detailed discussion on *Onyame*, see the following: Danquah, *Akan Doctrine of God*, 31–42; Rattray, *Ashanti*, 139–44, and Meyerowitz, *Akan of Ghana*, 69–83.

23. Williamson, *Akan Religion and the Christian Faith*, 86.

24. This notion was, however, questioned by Ellis in his book *Tshi Speaking People of the Gold Coast*. Ellis argues that the idea of a Supreme Being was borrowed from the missionaries which they encountered; see p. 28ff.

25. Fisher, *West African*, 28.

26. For a detailed discussion of the Akan understanding of God, see Danquah, *Akan Doctrine of God*.

ing of *Nyame* has been the subject of much debate;[27] however, the meaning broadly speaking is "the Shining One."[28] Kwame Gyekye, a Ghanaian philosopher, describes *Onyame* as the "Absolute reality, the origin of all things, the absolute ground and source of life, the sole and whole explanation of the universe, and the source for all existence."[29] Early anthropologists maintained that the meaning of *Onyame* was the "Sky God."[30] This view however has been strongly contested by John Danquah who argues that this is a ploy on the part of western anthropologists to undermine the Akan conception of a supreme being in comparison with so-called higher western notions of God. He argues:

> For one reason or other, it has become the fashion to designate the high-god of "native" races as "sky" God, and one's admiration cannot but be stirred by the studied insistence to dissociate the Akan Onyame from "heaven," keeping him pinned, as far as bearable, to the rather funny idea of "sky."[31]

This notion of *Onyame* as a Sky God was also popularized by an Akan myth that recounted the fact that *Onyame* had retreated to the sky away from human affairs.[32] The point made by Danquah is an important one because such a view of *Onyame* as a Sky God depersonalizes and presents him as completely detached from human affairs.[33] Conversely, the findings of this inquiry support the view that in the life of the worshipping community of Akan AICs, *Onyame* was very active and present in the lives of the people.

Onyame, the Supreme God of the Akan, is known in various forms that are also employed within the worship context and the personal devotions of the Akan AICs. Although *Onyame* is understood in these transcendent terms, his ubiquitous presence is ever near and his name is daily on the lips of Akan people. According to Mbiti, the transcendence of God

27. These debates are outlined in the books cited in the discussions on the meaning of *Onyame* above.

28. Meyerowitz, *Sacred State*, 70.

29. Gyekye, *An Essay*, 70.

30. Rattray, *Ashanti*, 141.

31. Danquah, *Akan Doctrine of God*, 30.

32. The Akan myth maintains that a woman was pounding fufu but kept on hitting *Onyame* (God) on his head with the pestle. This continued in spite of *Onyame*'s irritation; however, and when the woman would not desist, *Onyame* retreated to the sky.

33. Danquah, *Akan Doctrine of God*, 32.

must be balanced with his immanence, since the two are paradoxically complementary. Mbiti posits the idea that God is so "far" (transcendent) that people cannot reach him; yet, he is so "near" (immanent) that he comes close to people.[34]

The issue of the immanence and transcendence of God has been a bone of contention between early anthropologists, who argued that God was associated with the sky and therefore was distant from people, and African theologians who disputed the notion that God was removed from the daily affairs of humankind.[35] Although there is much evidence to support the idea of God as one who has withdrawn from the world,[36] there is equally compelling evidence to support the idea of the immanence of God, experienced in the many acts of worship, sacrifice prayers, offerings, and invocations. God is also associated with many natural objects and phenomena, indicating the traditional belief that God is involved in his creation.[37]

The awareness of *Onyame*, upon which the life of the Akan is contingent, permeates every aspect of the Akan life. Below are some of the short prayers and constant references and invocations made daily to *Onyame* by Akan people, which I recorded:

1. At the start of any undertaking the Akan would say, *Onyame boa me* (God, help me).

2. The expression *sε Onyame pε a* (If it is the will of *Onyame*) is constantly on people's lips at the start or during the course of a pursuit.

3. *Gye Nyame* (Except God) is a popular expression captured in symbolic depiction.

4. If one enquires about another's health, the latter would invariably say, *Onyame adom me ho yε"* (By the grace of *Onyame* I am alright).

---

34. Mbiti, *African Religions and Philosophy*, 32.

35. Danquah, *Akan Doctrine of God*, 5–8; Rattray, *Ashanti*, 139–44.

36. Mbiti lists a number of the different African myths illustrating different reasons why God has withdrawn from the world. See *African Religions and Philosophy*, 33.

37. Mbiti points out that it is important not to see this as pantheism because Africans do not believe that God is nature and that nature is God, but are rather theistic in their theology. They do however believe that God works through his created order. See Mbiti, *African Religions and Philosophy*, 33.

5. Salutations and words of farewell are couched in the form of a prayer to *Onyame*, for instance, *wo ne "Nyame nkɔ*, (I leave you in the hands of *Onyame*).

6. If one narrowly escapes a disaster one would say, *se Onyame ampata a*, (If *Onyame* had not intervened . . .) or *Onyame nko ara* (Onyame alone).

Such sayings are not mere clichés, in the sense that someone in England might say "Jesus Christ!" or "Oh God!" when suddenly alarmed or startled. They are genuine religious expressions and prayers used by those who have confidence in the ultimate power of *Onyame*. These spontaneous religious references or invocations are made only to *Onyame* and never to deities that are direct objects of worship in Akan traditional religion.[38] Within the context of Akan AICs these traditional expressions, which are normally used in reference to *Onyame*, are also extended to Christ. So instead of using the name *Onyame*, Akan AIC adherents used *Yesu Kristo*. For example, they often say *Yesu Kristo boa me* (Jesus Christ, help me) or *wo ne Yesu Kristo nkɔ* (I leave you in the hands of Jesus Christ).

Sunsum (Spirit) [39]

The Akan universe, which is essentially spiritual, is endowed or charged with varying degrees of forces or powers. Busia writes, "To the Ashanti the universe is full of spirits."[40] This force or power is *Sunsum*, usually translated as *spirit*.[41] In this metaphysic, all created things (that is, natural objects) have or contain *Sunsum*. This *Sunsum* is ultimately from *Onyame* who, as the Supreme Being, is the Highest Spirit or Highest power. *Sunsum* then, according to Gyekye, is a generic concept; it appears to be a universal spirit, manifesting itself differently in the various beings and objects in the natural world.[42] *Sunsum* is used in two different but related ways.

Firstly, it is used to relate to self-conscious subjects, whose activities are initiated self-consciously. In this sense, *Onyame*, the deity, and ances-

38. Gyekye, *An Essay*, 72.

39. An interesting discussion on the Akan concept of the *Sunsum*, which is a very controversial term, is conducted by Gyekye, *An Essay*, 88–98.

40. Busia (ed.), "Ashanti of the Gold Coast," 191.

41. Gyekye, *An Essay*, 72.

42. Ibid., 73.

tors are said to be *Sunsum*, (spirit beings with intelligence and will). The second usage is in relation to the mystical powers believed to exist in the world. These powers constitute the inner essence or intrinsic properties of natural objects. *Sunsum* is therefore used in a general sense to refer to all beings and powers, and in a specific sense, to refer to the essence of natural objects including man and woman. Gyekye observes:

> The mystical powers in the world and natural objects are categori-
> cally related to deities, although they are derived ultimately from
> *Onyame.* These deities reside in natural objects such as trees,
> plants, rocks, mountains and hills, rivers and brooks.[43]

Notwithstanding the relatedness of the two uses of *Sunsum*, some schol-ars make a distinction between spirits (which, they argue, include the Supreme Spirit, the deities, and the ancestors) and what they call super-natural powers or forces.[44]

For the traditional Akan, *Sunsum* is an inescapable reality of Akan daily life. Everything he or she sees and observes in the natural environ-ment has a deeper reality. The fact that all created things are held to con-tain *Sunsum* does not mean that the Akan worldview is pantheistic, for the Akan do not maintain that *Onyame* is identifiable with the sum of all things. The creator is not identified with the creature, the author with his work, but *Onyame* is seen as transcending *Sunsum* as well as tran-scending all things created. In maintaining that natural objects contain *Sunsum* or power, Akans attribute to them an intrinsic property, namely, the property of activity—or as Gyekye calls it, the "activating principle."[45] A more appropriate description of the Akan system, according to Gyekye is "panpsychism," which he maintains means everything is/or contains *Sunsum.*[46] The Akan therefore reject by implication the view held by the Cartesians and others in western philosophy that matter is essentially passive or inert, which must be activated. According to Akan thinking, therefore, it is the essence of natural objects to be active and to possess power. This understanding of *Sunsum* governs a very central aspect of

43. Ibid.

44. Rattray for example distinguishes between the magical powers and the deities, regarding the former as among the lowest grades of supernatural power hierarchy; see *Ashanti*, 86.

45. Gyekye, *An Essay*, 75

46 Ibid.

Akan AIC Christology, cosmology, and the use of symbols taken from the natural environment.[47]

Abosom (Lesser Spirits) [48]

Within Akan traditional religion the lesser gods are known as *abosom*. The derivation of the word seems to indicate that the meaning is *to serve a rock*, ɔ*bo* means *rock* and *som* means *to serve*. This definition seems to be inadequate, however, because trees and rivers and other objects can also be *abosom*.[49] The lesser gods are seen as God's representatives on earth who may work for one's good or ill.[50] For the Akan AICs *abosom* are identified with the gods worshipped by Akan traditional religious observers and are usually referred to as false traditional gods or idols. These gods represent the myriad of spirits that permeate the Akan spiritual universe that must be brought under the power and authority of Jesus Christ.

For the Akan the world is one of action, a notion which has developed into what Gyekye calls a "metaphysics of potency."[51] This idea of the world being active is derived from an Akan understanding of the world as being primarily spiritual. Thus, what exists is spirit, and the world teems with spirits or spiritual beings, both malevolent and benevolent powers that cause change in the world. Nothing of significance happens without causal reference being made to powers or spirits.[52] For the Akan, then, everything has a cause, as the Akan proverb states: "Whenever a palm tree tilts, it is because of what the earth has told it." Causal factors and meaning are associated with everyday and banal events, such as a visit from a friend

47. This issue will be explored in more detail in chapter 8.

48. According to Rattray the *abosoms* are emanations of *Onyame* and therefore derive their power from Him; they are sometimes called children of *Onyame*. There is a popular myth in Ashanti, which recounts how *Onyame* had various sons; of whom, one in particular was *a bayeyere* (favourite son). *Onyame* decided to send these children down to the earth in order that they might receive benefits, as well as to be of benefit to humankind. All the sons bore the names of what are now famous rivers and lakes or the names given to rivers and bodies of water in general—for example *Tano* (the great river of that name), *Bosomtwe* (the great lake of the name), *Bea* (a river), and *Opo* (the sea). For a more detailed discussion about *abosom*, see Rattray, *Ashanti*, 145–50.

49. Williamson, *Akan Religion*, 89.

50. Sarpong, *Ghana in Retrospect*, 15–17; Dickson, *Theology in Africa*, 55–56.

51. Gyekye, *Philosophical Thought*, 79.

52. For a very interesting discussion on being and causality with the Akan conceptual scheme, see Gyekye *Philosophical Thought*, 76–84.

not seen for a while, or having one's hand hit by the pestle while pounding fufu.[53] Akan acknowledgement of the pervasiveness of spirit beings in all of life should not be understood as paranoia of the spiritual, but rather a heightened sense of awareness that even in the banal the "spirits" could be at work. The notion of causality is particularly reflected in the Akan AIC understanding of healing and wholeness. For them sickness is not purely a physical phenomenon but has a very important spiritual dimension.[54]

Nananom Nsamanfo (Ancestors) [55]

A very important aspect of the Akan tradition is the role of the ancestors, who are known as *nananom nsamanfo* in Twi.[56] These ancestors are generally assumed to be venerated and not worshipped.[57] The idea of ancestorship within Akan tradition is in harmony with the Akan worldview. In the same way as matter and spirit can happily co-exist without contradiction, as in the case of *Sunsum*, likewise the living and the dead also co-exist. The maintenance of "harmony" between the living and the "living-dead," to use Mbiti's term,[58] is achieved through ritual and symbolism. The ancestors who were the guardians of tradition while alive are expected to continue to protect and guard the living with their increased power and authority. The ancestors live on within the Akan community through the

53. Fufu is made from pounded yam and plantain, which is eaten with soup. It is a popular Ghanaian dish especially for Ashantis.

54. This issue is discussed in chapters 7 and 8 of this work.

55. In order to understand the role of the ancestor in Akan tradition, one needs to know something about the structure of Ghanaian society. Every tribe in Ghana, as in other African countries, is divided into groups technically called clans. Clan members are held to be related to one another and bound together by a common tie. The tie is the belief that all members of the clan descend from one ancestor. The ancestors are people who were formerly respected elders or leaders within the community who have died honourably. No leader or elder who died as a result of an accident or an unclean disease would be elevated to the realm of the ancestors. Such deaths are considered to be "suspect" and possibly caused because of some hidden sin that that individual had done.

56. Fisher, *West African Religious Traditions*, 95.

57. The debate on whether ancestors are venerated or worshiped has been an ongoing one. For a good outline of the arguments, in support of the view of ancestor veneration, see Idowu, *African Traditional Religion*, 178–89, and also Mbiti, *African Religions and Philosophy*, 25–27. In support of the view "ancestor worship," see Spencer, *Principles of Sociology*, 411. See also Sundkler, *Bantu Prophets*, 21–23, in which he argues that the real vital religion of the Zulus is their ancestor worship.

58. Mbiti, *African Religions and Philosophy*, 83.

constant reminder of their glorious deeds recounted through the means of a powerful oral tradition often enacted through libation prayers.

Prominent in Akan cosmology, as well as in other cosmological systems in Africa, ancestorship exerts much influence on Christology in Africa.[59] One of the ways in which this is evident within the context of Akan AICs, which is significant for this study, is the believers" readiness to present their real or felt needs to Christ that pertain to everyday life in very much the same way that traditional observers would consult their ancestors.[60]

Symbolism

Akan and much of West African traditional society view the world in which they live in symbolic rather than scientific terms.[61] Symbolism plays such a central part in Akan life (and African life generally) that it has become a vast research area.[62] The importance of the place and function of symbolism in Akan AIC Christology is one of the major findings of this study.[63]

The Concept of Time in Africa

John Mbiti has argued convincingly that the African concept of time is different from the way time is perceived in the western world:

---

59. Below we discuss the Akan ancestor Christology of Bediako, Pobee, and Akrong.

60. Baëta, *Prophetism*, 135.

61. Sarpong, *Ghana in Retrospect*, 109.

62. This is the case especially in magical rites, which abound everywhere in Akan land, the understanding of which is impossible if its symbolic aspects are overlooked. One area of symbolism that is relevant for this study is the way words function symbolically. Among the Akans AICs, as with Akans generally, words have very serious symbolic representation and this is drawn from the significance which they are understood to have in Akan tradition as a whole. The Ashanti for example consider the number "five" to be an unlucky number simply because it sounds (in Ashanti Twi) like "regret" (five = *num*; to regret = *nu*). Consequently to give someone something in fives (i.e., five apples) is to bequeath bad luck upon them. It is better to give four or three or a number other than *num*. Conversely the number seven (*nson*) is supposed to be the ideal number because of its association in sound with "to be sufficient" (*so*). For a detailed study of symbolism in an Akan context, see Meyerowitz, *The Sacred State*, 91–114 and Sarpong, *Ghana in Retrospect*, 105–15.

63. Symbolism as it relates to Akan AICs Christology is discussed in detail in chapter 8.

> The linear concept of Time, with a Past, Present and Future,
> stretching from infinity to infinity, is foreign to Africa thinking,
> in which the dominant factor is a virtual absence of the future.
> By our definition Time is a composition of events, and since the
> Future events have not occurred, the Future as a necessary linear
> component of Time is virtually absent.[64]

Mbiti's notion that the essence of Time in Africa is what is present and
what is past, raises serious questions as to whether a future heaven, paradise, redemption or salvation in another world is meaningful to Africa.[65]
A logical place to begin exploring this is to examine to what extent "death"
and the "after life" feature in African traditional religion generally and to
Akan traditional religion specifically.

Of course, as with many other aspects of traditional belief, traditions
vary from place to place. However, there are some very interesting points
of convergence in the area of death and the afterlife. One of the universal
beliefs is that death is not the end of life, but only the inauguration of
life in another form.[66] It is also widely accepted that the "hereafter" is an
earthly location.[67] This is particularly the case in West African traditional
belief where people are not excessively reticent about eschatology; de-
scriptions of the afterlife generally include a journey by land to a different
location, which often includes crossing a river. The majority of Africans
do not anticipate any kind of judgement or punishment.[68] The majority
of Africans also perceive life in the "hereafter" to be a continuation of life
more or less as it is in human form. This means his or her personality,
social class, gender, and economical status remain unchanged. Although
the person's "soul" is separated from the body it is believed to retain the

64. Mbiti, "Eschatology," 159. See also *African Religion and Philosophy*, 15–28.

65. Mbiti's idea that Africans have no concept of a future has been sharply challenged
by Kwame Gyekye, who argues that his concept of time was based upon his analysis of
the verb tenses of East African language. See *African Religions and Philosophy*, 15–28. The
structure of these East African languages does not generate a concept of an infinite future.
He argues that this two-dimensional notion of time (present and past) is not indicative of
all African languages; the Akan language, for example, has a three dimensional concept
of time, which includes a distant or infinite future. For a detailed outline of Gyekye's
arguments, see *An Essay*, 169–77.

66. Wiredu, "Death and the Afterlife," 137; see also Sarpong, *Ghana in Retrospect*, 72;
Mbiti, *African Religions and Philosophy*, 149–65; Fisher, *West African Religious Traditions*,
90–102.

67. Wiredu, "Death and the Afterlife," 140.

68. Ibid.

physical/social characteristics of its human life.[69] According to Akan tradition, those who live a full and meaningful life are elevated at death to the position of an ancestor; the life of the ancestors is pictured as one of dignity and serenity rather than bliss; for the rest of the living–dead (as Mbiti calls them) life continues in very much the same way. Death then is regarded as the departure of the soul, itself a kind of body, from the physical place to another plane of existence, namely, the astral. The African land of the living-dead, then, is not heaven in the Christian sense.

Kwasi Wiredu's essay, entitled "Death and the Afterlife in African Culture," lends valuable insight to this issue. He argues that for many African peoples, such as the Akans, the land of the dead is an earthly geographical location similar to "this worldly existence," with a population that is rather like us. He maintains that the ontological make-up of those who have departed from this life is such that they are exempted from the restrictions of material make-up. Consequently they are able to appear and disappear from places without regard to speed or time; they are capable of action from a distance; they cannot be seen or heard except on rare occasions when they elect to be by a particular person or persons.

Wiredu argues, however, that to view the ontological make-up of a departed person in purely spiritual terms would be an over-simplification. He explicates:

> The West African conception should make it clear that it would be a substantial oversimplification to describe it as spiritual in the sense of this word, which implies total immateriality. There is in the conception under discussion only a reduced materiality, and the reduction affects not its imagery, but dynamics.[70]

African traditional religion does not have a final day of reckoning or "Day of Judgment" as in the Christian tradition.[71] The only hope that is offered is that life in the "hereafter" will be pretty much the same as it was while they were in the land of the living. Mbiti states:

> The majority of African peoples do not expect any form of judgment or reward in the hereafter. For the majority of African

69. Mbiti, *African Religions and Philosophy*, 161.

70. Wiredu, "Death and the Afterlife," 140

71. Some African people appear to envisage some kind of Judgment after death. However, this does not have the cataclysmic Cosmic connotation of the Christian Day of Judgment; see Mbiti, *African Religion and Philosophy*, 161.

peoples, the hereafter is only a continuation of life more or less as it is in its human form. This means that personalities are retained, social and political statuses are maintained, sex distinction is continued, human activities are reproduced in the hereafter, and in many ways the hereafter is a carbon copy of the present life.[72]

For those who maintain the tradition of "ancestorship," if they have lived their lives in an exemplary fashion they will be elevated to the esteemed position of ancestor. Yet becoming an ancestor only enables one to help the living to realize human purposes. To a typical Akan, for example, a life that has meaning is one that makes reasonable achievements in the direction of personal, family, and communal welfare. A life of that sort would be a meaningful one even if there were no belief in the afterlife. In point of fact, one's life after death does not figure in one's destiny. Human destiny begins and ends in this world.[73]

The idea of life after death or the continuation of life beyond the "here and now" is perhaps a universal belief held among Africans. In some parts of Africa, a selective few will have the opportunity to become ancestors but for the vast majority there is no hope of salvation or a better life in the world to come. It is perhaps this lack of a better future beyond the "now" that is the basis for prominence of a realized eschatology in the African traditional religions, which has also impacted the AICs" obsession with salvation in the here and now. Although the particularities of Mbiti's thesis on the African concept of time may be brought into question, the main thrust of his argument—namely that time in Africa is a two dimensional phenomenon, with a long past and a present and virtually no future—provides a compelling explanation for the African quest for a salvation that is this worldly orientated. The lack of a promise of a better future in the "after-world" for the African, whose life is often beset with misery and poverty, has perhaps also provided a psychological disincentive to a future orientation.

---

72. Mbiti, *African Religions and Philosophy*, 160.
73. Wiredu, "Death and the Afterlife," 143.

THE WESTERN MISSIONARY MOVEMENT IN GHANA AND ITS IMPLICIT COLONIAL CHRISTOLOGY

The Expansion of the Church Among the Akan

In the previous section I explored the traditional backdrop that constitutes the cultural context out of which the Christology of Akan AIC has emerged. In this section I shall explore the impact and influence of missionary Christianity in Ghana, which also formed part of the socioreligious matrix of Akan AICs that contributed to their Christology.

The nineteenth century saw the Church established among the Akan people in four main denominations. The first among them to arrive was the Basel Mission Society in 1831, who were invited by the Dutch Governor of Christiansborg. In 1835 the Wesleyan Mission landed at Cape Coast. The Wesleyan Mission was predominantly among the Fanti people of the coastal areas. The Basel Mission on the other hand moved from the coastal areas because of the deadly coastal climate and the scourge of malaria which had claimed many of the missionaries" lives, to the higher ground inland, to Akrupong on the Akuapem ridge.[74] The Roman Catholic Mission restarted its work in Ghana in 1880. In 1901 the local Catholic Church was raised to a vicariate Apostolic, and in 1950 it became an Ecclesiastical Province with an archepiscopal see at Cape Coast.[75] The Church of England, in that it enjoyed a monopoly of fort chaplaincies, can claim to have been present in the Gold Coast since the early days of the British occupancy. However, from the point of view of definite missionary activity, it re-established itself in the western parts of the old colony under the title of The English Church Mission.[76]

Western Missionary Christology

Throughout the growth and expansion of the Church among the Akan of Ghana, certain factors inherent in the total situation must be noticed. Foremost of these was the fact that the Church promulgated a Christ who identified with white western colonizers and who was, by and large,

---

74. Williamson, *Akan Religion*, 4.

75. Ibid.

76. For a detailed treatment of the growth and expansion of the church among the Akan of Ghana during these early times, see Williamson, *Akan Religion*, 3–17.

a stranger to the Akan tradition and culture.[77] The church was planted in the first instance, and its growth supervised, by Europeans; indeed the Christian faith according to S. G. Williamson was commonly referred to as the "white man's religion" and not a "universal faith" for all hearers.[78] For many Akans there was a clear link between the faith the European professed and all that they were and stood for.

Therefore the Christ of the missionaries did not address the fundamental needs of the African. This foreignness of missionary Christianity that confronted the Akan people of Ghana has been well expressed by J. V. Taylor who states:

> Christ has been presented as the answer to the questions a white man would ask, the solution to the need a westerner would feel, the Saviour of a world of a European worldview, and the object of the adoration and prayer of historic Christendom.[79]

The missionary impact on the church in Ghana has been the subject matter of volumes of books;[80] it is therefore not necessary for it to be rehearsed here. The Christological pedagogy of missionary thinking which contributed to the development of a Christology more suited to the African outlook is however necessary for this study.[81]

The Missionary Worldview and the Akan

One of the crucial areas that put the early missionaries on the wrong footing from the very outset of their missionary enterprise was their failure to grasp the fact that the Akan operated in a frame of reference that was alien to the western rationalistic worldview.[82] Theirs was a cerebral and discursive way of looking at the world that was reflected in their cerebral religion, which poured scorn upon the Akan perception of a world

77. Debrunner observes that the missionaries often held the preconceived idea that it was Satan and his angels who are worshipped by the Akan people and not the God of Jesus Christ; see Debrunner, *History of Christianity*, 141.

78. Williamson, *Akan Religion*, 19.

79. Taylor, *Primal Vision*, 24.

80. A thorough and insightful overview on this issue has been provided by Hastings, *Church in Africa*.

81. A good general study on African cosmological outlook is provided in a collection of essays edited by Forde, entitled *African Worlds*.

82. Their approach was by and large one that viewed the world from the standpoint of reason and western logic. See Odamtten, *Missionary Factor*, 30–65.

teeming with spirits and beleaguered with powers.[83] According to Ogbu Kalu the AICs confronted the muted pneumatic elements in missionary theology.[84]

The proliferation of western education in the schools, which was for the most part the domain of the Church, further exacerbated this notion of missionary Christianity being, in Taylor's words, a "classroom religion."[85] The gospel of Christ was presented through a discourse that was therefore instructional and not intuitive, by sermon and not by symbols, in a way that appealed to reason and not to the intuition, and often through literary means and not orality.[86] By confining Christ within the protective walls of the rational and within the matrix of the western worldview, Christ could not inhabit the spiritual universe of the Akan consciousness except as a complete stranger.[87] This meant that although the missionaries had a lot of converts, ostensibly, many came for the free education and remained unredeemed in the depth of their subliminal African personality that longed for peace from the ubiquitous spirits of the invisible world.

Western Christology and the Akan: A Case of Misappropriation

In the first in-depth study of the impact of the Christian mission upon the life of the Akan people of Ghana, S. G. Williamson, in *Akan Religion and the Christian Faith*, argues that the missionary methods employed by the early missionaries to the Akan people were at variance with the New Testament approach. Williamson observed:

> It is conceivable that as pure faith, Christianity might have spoken to the Akan in his apprehension of reality. The Apostles and missionaries of the New Testament period seem to have approached their listeners on the basis of what they did believe, at least to the

83. Williamson observes that the primary task of the missionary among the Akan was, as he saw it, the destruction of the traditional and superstition and the implantation of the Christian faith. See Williamson, *Akan Religion*, 54.

84. Kalu, *African Pentecostalism*, 67.

85. Taylor, *Primal Vision*, 24.

86. I will be returning to the theme of orality later on in this work.

87. Bediako maintains that it is difficult not to link our missionary connection with the problem of identity, which came to weigh so heavily on the Christian conscience of so many Africans; he states, "Must we become other than African in order to be truly Christian?" The story of the AICs, he argues, is the answer to this kind of question to the extent that these churches take seriously matters relating to the African religious worldview and the questions it poses. See Bediako, "Biblical Christologies," 114.

extent that they proclaimed Christ as the Saviour of men within a milieu which allowed the existence of "gods many and lords many." The missionary enterprise among the Akan did not take this line, but being western in outlook and emphasis, felt bound to deny the Akan worldview, not only on the basis of what was essentially Christian belief, but on the ground of what was, in effect, a European worldview.[88]

Failure to take seriously the worldview of the Akan people was for Williamson a missed opportunity for effective witness on the part of the western missionaries to the Akan. As a result of the western missiological approach, the missionary was perceived as the purveyor of a new way of life, (economic and social as well as religious and moral), instead of God's revelation in Christ. The Church was seen to spread Enlightenment ideology as well as western understanding of what constitutes a civilized society as Christianity. The Christian faith was therefore favourably received as the "white man's religion," and associated in the Akan mind with the "white man's power and prestige."[89]

The Christological implication of this misappropriation of the Christian faith was far reaching. As a consequence of this missionary approach, the implanted Christian faith failed to meet the Akan in his personally experienced religious need. The Akan became a Christian by cleaving to the new order introduced by the missionaries rather than working out his salvation within the traditional religious milieu and social context. The Christ of the missionary was European by association and a stranger to the Akan spirit-world.[90] It is by and large on the back of this Christological vacuum that the Akan AICs would rise to prominence promulgating a Christ who was actually in their own image and one who was not a stranger to the African worldview.

THE ROAD TO INDEPENDENCE: LIBERATION AND TRANSFORMATION

This wrestling with the western packaging of Jesus Christ has led a process that has now become known as "African Christian Theology." Nevertheless, African Christian Theology must not be seen to exist in a vacuum but

---

88. Williamson, *Akan Religion*, 138.

89. Ibid., 166.

90. Bediako, "Biblical Christologies," 87.

must be seen as an expression of a much wider phenomenon, namely, Africa's rediscovery of identity and selfhood against the background of colonial rule and imperialist domination. The partition of Africa between the European powers of France, Britain, Portugal, Spain, Germany, and Belgium at the Berlin conference of 1884-85 had a devastating and long lasting effect on Africa. It did much more than project the internal politics of Europe onto Africa but, as Emmanuel Marty rightly observes, it drained African societies of their very existence, trampled African culture underfoot, confiscated its lands, smashed its religions, destroyed its magnificent artistic creations, and wiped out extraordinary possibilities.[91]

The transition of African countries from colonial status to nationhood was to a large extent the beginning of the process of re-Africanization.[92] This had implications for African politics, economics, and religion; it also added impetus to the call for a gospel, indeed a Christ, which addressed the real contextual African situations, and for a Christology in which Christ was at home in an African context. Kofi Appiah-Kubi aptly states the new theological task that African Christians had been faced with: "our theological task must be one that enables us to answer the critical question of our Lord 'who do you (African Christians) say that I am?'"[93]

Although the leaders and members of the AICs have not been traditionally invited to sit at the theological table of the African Christological quest, their originality and boldness in their efforts in appropriating Christ from within their culture has placed them centre stage for analysis. AICs have been described as the "raw material" of African theology.[94] The developments and refinements of AIC's theology and practice today suggest that they have gone beyond the description of "raw material," but rather constitute a vibrant and genuine African response to biblical Christianity. Fashole-Luke maintains that a careful and critical study should be made

---

91. Martey, *African Theology*, 8.

92. Re-Africanization was essentially a political term used by many post-independent African countries who were attempting to restore African culture and values back into society. As a term for *inculturation* it was considered broad, sweeping, and overly politicized and has been replaced by other terms outlined in the introduction of this work. See Ela, *My Faith*, 144–48.

93. Appiah-Kubi and Torres (eds.), *African Theology En Route*, 116.

94. Fashole-Luke, "Quest for African Christian Theologies," 159.

of AICs to assess their value for the development of African theology.[95] Kwame Bediako suggests that AICs pointed toward the direction in which broad sections of African Christianity were moving.[96] Burgess Carr says that African theology "comes to life" in the music, prayers, liturgy, church structures, and community life of AICs.[97] It is here I believe some of the most creative and innovative Christological developments are taking place. AICs are showing the way for an authentic African Christology that arises out of an African context and is responsible to African people.

AFRICAN CONTEXTUAL CHRISTOLOGIES

Inculturation and Liberation Christologies in Africa

In responding to the Christological question, African theologians have mostly adopted two different approaches to theological reflection about Jesus Christ: the inculturationalist approach, which uses mainly the African traditional worldview, and the liberationalist approach, which has a socio-political ethos.[98] This latter approach is generally found in South Africa as "Black theology" and is centred primarily on liberation from racial oppression.[99] This approach is linked to North American Black theology and is also influenced by Latin American theology of liberation. A second kind of liberationalist approach, simply called African liberation theology, is found especially in independent sub-Saharan Africa.[100] The theological base upon which this approach rests is broader than South African Black theology, for it attempts to integrate the theme of liberation with the rest of the African socio-cultural background and is more affiliated to Latin American liberation theology. This model is also preferred by African women who are critical of the cultural Christological approach,

95. Ibid., 159–75.

96. Bediako, *Christianity in Africa*, 66.

97. Carr, *The Relation*, 160–61.

98. For a clear and concise enumeration of these two positions, see Nyamiti "Contemporary African Christologies," 62–76.

99. Young, *Black and African Theologies*, 62ff; Mofokeng, *The Crucified*; Moore (ed.), *Black Theology*; Boesak, *Farewell to Innocence*; Becken, *Relevant Theology*; Buthelezi, "Violence and the Cross," 51–55; Muzorewa, *The Origins*, 101–13; Salvodi and Sesana, *Africa*.

100. Magesa, "Christ the Liberator," 79–92; Maimela, "Jesus Christ," 31–42; Waliggo, "African Christology," 93–111.

maintaining that for them African traditional cultures are included in the contemporary structures of oppression.[101]

The inculturationalist or religio-cultural approach takes seriously the African pre-Christian religious experience and knowledge and is the approach that is more related to this study because of my focus upon the Akan AICs in Ghana. In this model it is the traditional African worldview that serves as a point of departure. According to this view, Jesus' presence in Africa today cannot be acknowledged without also acknowledging Africa's past religious knowledge and experience. Justin S. Ukpong maintains that there are five different inculturationalist approaches that characterize the meaning of Jesus in an African context: the "incarnational approach," the "logos Spermatikos (Seeds of the Word) approach," the "functional analogy approach," the "paschal mystery approach," and the "biblical approach."[102]

The basis of the incarnational approach is outlined in my discussion in chapter 1, where I discuss incarnation *per se* as a model for inculturation of Christianity in Africa. The logic of this approach, I maintained, is that just as Jesus was incarnated into human nature and human context, so too must the gospel of Christ be incarnated into African culture taking on the expression and values of African people. The critique of this approach is the same as they are for the idea of incarnation as a general model for inculturation.[103] The "Logos Spermatikos (Seeds of the Word) approach" is held by Efoé-Julien Pénoukou in his book *Églises d'Afrique: Propositions pour l'Avenir*. The basis of Pénoukou's thesis is that Christ as the eternal *Logos* (Word) pervades all cultures even if he is not recognized or known. Cultures then need to be opened to the gospel and converted to Christ, and the gospel likewise needs to be opened to African cultures through which it is expressed and finds meaning.[104] The functional analogy approach, out of which many thematic Christological contributions have come to us, has contributed some very insightful images of Christ

---

101. For African Women on Christology, see Edet and Ekeya, "Church Women of Africa," 4; Nasimiyu-Wasike, "Christology and African Women's," 123–35; Souga, "Christ Event," 29; Oduyoye, "Women and Christology," 4.

102. Ukpong, "Christology and Inculturation," 40–43.

103. Shorter, *African Christian Theology*, 79–80.

104. Pénoukou, *Églises d'Afrique*; Pénoukou's approach is an application of the *Logos Spermatikos* theology of Justin Martyr and Clement of Alexandria to the modern problem of inculturation.

in Africa.[105] Christologies of liberation in Africa are another approach which seeks to address the Christological question in Africa.

Aylward Shorter in his book *Towards a Theology of Inculturation* demonstrates the fourth approach, which is the "paschal mystery approach." According to Shorter, Jesus in his earthly existence was limited in his contact with other cultures. But after the resurrection, he belongs to all cultures and can identify with them through the proclamation of the Good News. He emphasizes the causal link between the resurrection and inculturation.[106] The final approach is the "biblical approach." This approach is based upon the notion that Jesus is one with the Father (John 10:30). It purports that since Jesus is one with the Father and Africans do worship God, Jesus has actually been worshipped in African religion. It therefore seeks the hidden Christ in African religion who has been present even before the dawn of Christianity.[107]

Akan Ancestor-Christologies

Although this study is concerned primarily with the Christologies of Akan AICs and is therefore in essence a grassroots investigation, the Akan Ancestor Christologies will be introduced because they are perhaps the most developed Christological approach in recent years.[108] A further reason why the Ancestor Christologies will be singled out from the other Christological approaches is because, by contrast to their popularity as a theological construct, they were of little significance at the grassroots level, which raises interesting questions that will be explored in the later

---

105. Thematic approaches include the following: Santon, "Jesus, Master of Initiation," 85–102; Kabasélé, "Christ as Chief," 103–27. Sawyerr also maintains that Christ is to be seen as Elder Brother; see *Creative Evangelism*, 72; Kolié, "Jesus as Healer," 128–50; Wachege, *Jesus Christ Our Mūthamaki*; Nyamiti, *Christ as our Ancestor*; Shorter, "Christ as Nganga," 133; Schoffeleers, "Christ in African Folk Christology," 73–88; Ukpong, "Immanuel Christology," 55–64.

106. Shorter, *Towards a Theology*, 84–87.

107. This view is represented by Mbiti; see Mbiti "Is Jesus Christ in African Religion?" 21–29 and Bahemuka, "Hidden Christ," 1–14.

108. Nyamiti, although not an Akan, has been one of the main supporters of this view and has influenced Akan Ancestor-Christology; see *Christ as Our Ancestor*, "Ancestral Kinship in the Trinity"; "The Mass as Divine and Ancestral Encounter," 28–48; "Uganda Martyrs," 41–66; "African Tradition and the Christian God,"; Bediako, *Jesus in Africa*, 20–33. Pobee suggests that Christ should be seen as the Greatest Ancestor or Nana of the Akan. See his *Towards an African Theology*, 94–98.

chapters of this work. This Ancestor Christological approach is also readily transmittable to an Akan context because of the strength of the ancestral tradition in the Akan traditional religion.

J. B. Danquah was the first to postulate the idea of *Onyame* as *Nana* or Ancestor. Nana, according to Danquah, means *grandfather* or *grandmother* and was later applied to an elected chief, *Opanyin*, who was deified at death because of his integrity, honesty, and impartiality in the dispensation of justice.[109] Following Danquah, a number of theologians have postulated a Christology based upon the Akan understanding of ancestor. The Ancestor Christologies of Kwame Bediako, John S. Pobee, and Abraham Akrong are outlined below as contributing significant insights to the Akan quest for an inculturated Christ.

KWAME BEDIAKO—JESUS CHRIST THE SUPREME ANCESTOR

In his book *Christianity in Africa* Kwame Bediako commends AICs for "self-consciously seeking to be African more than the churches of missionary origin."[110] Being Christian and maintaining one's integrity is the recurring theme that permeates Bediako's theology, which comes into sharp focus in his Christology. For Bediako the historical significance of the death and resurrection of Jesus of Nazareth in Palestine in the first century AD is the revelation that unlocks all other signs of God's presence in this world:

> The consistent New Testament pattern of affirmation about Jesus Christ, therefore, is to work from the actual historical achievement in the life, ministry, death and resurrection of Jesus Christ, to the theological elaboration of the universal significance and application of that achievement.[111]

Only by interpreting the particularity of the incarnation of Jesus of Nazareth in its universal and cosmic dimensions and significance do we fully capture the enormity of God's self-disclosure in Christ.

According to Bediako, therefore, accepting Jesus as "our Saviour" involves making him at home in our spiritual universe and in terms of our religious needs and longing.[112] For Bediako it is essential that Christ be

109. Danquah, *Akan Doctrine of God*, 30–42.
110. Bediako, *Christianity in Africa*, 63.
111. Bediako, "How is Jesus Christ Lord?" 38.
112. Bediako, *Jesus in African Culture*, 5–10.

proclaimed in a way that is relevant and that brings continuity to Africa's pre-Christian past, answering Africans" religious quest and fulfilling their deepest needs.[113] Christ not only brings salvation to the African but also liberates him/her from the fears that are resulting from the traditional view and experience of reality.[114] If Jesus is proclaimed in terms of the worldview of the European missionary, he does not make sense to the African.[115]

Bediako therefore applies the Saviour power of Christ to the Akan traditional worldview and maintains that in this context Christ should be proclaimed as supreme Ancestor. Only by giving Jesus this title and by developing an Ancestor-Christology can Jesus be the answer to the needs and fears that Africans traditionally brought to their clan-ancestors.[116] The attraction of the AICs for Bediako lies in their readiness to employ traditional resources in order to proclaim the Christian faith meaningfully, thereby allowing Jesus Christ to remove the fears that Africans traditionally have towards their clan-ancestors. Bediako believes that the AICs inculturation approach to Christianity in Africa is a prerequisite to an Akan Ancestor-Christology and that, in this regard, AICs point toward the direction in which the Christian faith may be made meaningful to the African personality.[117]

JOHN POBEE—JESUS THE GREAT AND GREATEST ANCESTOR

The link between Akan Ancestor-Christology and AICs comes to bear even stronger in the Ancestor Christology of John Pobee.[118] Like Bediako, Pobee asserts that Jesus Christ must be meaningful to the African context, which for him is the Akan context. In "Toward Christology in an African Theology" outlined in his book *Toward an African Theology,* he places emphasis on the humanity and the deity of Christ as the starting

---

113. Van den Toren points out that, although Bediako frequently refers to the continuity between Africa's pre-Christian past and the gospel, he never points out the discontinuities between Africa's pre-Christian past and the gospel. See van den Toren, "Kwame Bediako's Christology," 218–31.

114. Bediako, "Biblical Christologies," 114.

115. Bediako, *Theology and Identity,* 7.

116. Bediako, *Christianity in Africa,* 217; see also Bediako, *Jesus in African Culture,* 16, 28.

117. Bediako, *Christianity in Africa,* 66.

118. For an interesting discussion on AICs and Ancestor Christology, see "Confessing Christ," 145–51.

point for an Akan Ancestor-Christology. With reference to Jesus' humanity he asserts, "the humanity of Jesus is one aspect of New Testament Christology which the attempt to construct a Christology in an Africa theology cannot skirt."[119] Through the credo *Christ is true God and true man,* Pobee expresses Christ's divinity and humanity according to the Akan understanding. Christ's kinship, circumcision, and baptism are rites of incorporation into a group.[120] He further purports that Akan humanity expressed through fear of death and finitude in knowledge is found in Christ's humanity,[121] ancestorship in his divinity. He states:

> In Akan society the Supreme Being and the ancestors provide the sanctions for the good life and punish evil. And the ancestor holds that authority as minister of the Supreme Being. Our approach would be to look on Jesus as the Great and Greatest Ancestor—in Akan language *Nana* . . . As *Nana* he has authority over not only the world of men but also of all spirit being, namely the cosmic powers and the ancestors.[122]

Both Pobee and Bediako recognize the potential for conflict in adopting the Ancestor-Christology model but stress that such a model has enormous potential for inculturating Christ in an African context.[123] In Pobee's exploration of Christology in the context of AICs, which he based upon "The Church of Christ on Earth through the Prophet Simon Kimbangu," he articulates the view that the Ancestor-Christology is a corollary of the African notion of chieftaincy, which is a symbolism adopted by the church of Simon Kimbangu as well as in the ministry of other AICs such as MDCC. The Akan Ancestor-Christology of Pobee, which is based upon the ancestorship of Akan traditional religion—but which could be drawn from traditional religion elsewhere in Africa, therefore has an affinity with the AICs because of its close attention to culture in presenting Jesus to African people.

119. Pobee, *African Theology*, 84.
120. Ibid., 89.
121. Ibid., 90.
122. Ibid., 94.
123. Bediako, *Jesus in African Culture*, 41.

ABRAHAM AKRONG – JESUS THE AKAN PARENT ANCESTOR

Abraham Akrong posits another type of Akan Ancestor-Christology. Along with Bediako and Pobee he also establishes a link with AICs.[124] He grounds his idea of Akan Ancestor-Christology upon the idea of family and is concerned about the universalizing of the ancestor relationship beyond that of the particular ethnic or clan grouping. For Akrong, God is the Ancestor of all the human race and Jesus Christ is to be seen as the Elder Brother of all peoples. He asserts:

> Our ancestor can now be viewed from the position of Jesus Christ, the Ideal Ancestor of the human race. The relationship between the ancestor and the living is founded on the family line that binds the ancestors and the living into children-parent relationship. Jesus, the Ideal Ancestor of the human race, has broadened the scope of the family to include all human beings in order to remind us of the reality of God's family that embraces all human beings.[125]

Since Jesus Christ is our pre-eminent ancestor by virtue of his status he can receive all the titles that are usually bestowed upon chiefs and ancestors. As the great warrior of the human family who dies to rescue human beings from the bondage of evil forces, Jesus Christ the God-man becomes the visible presence of God.[126] The appellations that are bestowed upon Jesus according to Akrong are indicative of the songs that are sung and the worship genre of the AICs.[127] For Akrong, as with Bediako and Pobee, the worship contexts of Akan AICs provide a fruitful environment in which an Akan Ancestral-Christology discourse may develop.

The issue of Ancestor-Christology will be explored later in this study particularly with reference to the questionnaire survey and interviews which were conducted with Akan AICs adherents. The study will explore whether the notion of an Akan Christology as enumerated by the above Ghanaian theologians reflects the experience and insights of AICs at the grassroots level.

---

124. For the full text of the Ancestor-Christology of Akrong, see Akrong, "Christology from an African Perspective," 119–30.

125. Ibid., 125–26.

126. Akrong, "Christology from an African Perspective," 123.

127. Ibid., 124.

3

Factors Influencing the Origins and Development of Indigenous Churches in Ghana

INTRODUCTION

THE EMERGENCE OF AICs on the continent of Africa has been a phenomenon so rapid and widespread that it has forced its way onto the academic agenda of the study of religious movements in Africa. Since the first academic research on these religious phenomena, writers have pondered the cause (or causes) of the growth of this new religious movement.[1] Each AIC has its peculiar and unique set of reasons that has contributed to its emergence and development within its own national and local setting; and in spite of similarities, causes must not be universalized.[2] As a whole, however, this movement can be located in the wider context of the rapid spread of Christianity in Africa during the late nineteenth and twentieth centuries.[3]

Issues surrounding causation are rather complex.[4] Allan Anderson rightly points out that in discussing the question of causation we must distinguish between factors that account for the *origins* of AICs from those that should rightly be considered as contributing to its subsequent *growth* and *development*.[5] In addition to this, one has to carefully evaluate what should be considered as "background causes" or secondary causes from those which are to be considered "primary causes."[6] Nevertheless

---

1. An early study is Sundkler, *Bantu Prophets*.
2. Anderson, *African Reformation*, 23.
3. Hastings, *Church in Africa*, 493.
4. See Daneel's assessment of the literature in *Quest for Belonging*, 68–101.
5. Anderson, *Reformation*, 23.
6. Daneel, *Quest*, 68.

42

there are some significant events and personalities that appear to figure quite prominently in the causal and developmental factors of indigenous churches in Ghana.

RELIGIOUS FACTORS

Among the various theories posited to account for the emergence of AICs, the "religious factors" feature prominently.[7] Although it is difficult (if not impossible) to make arbitrary distinctions between religious, socio-political and economical factors, the general position of those who advocate religious causative factors consider AICs primarily as a new religious movement responding to religious needs. Harold Turner, who conducted extensive research on Aladura churches, stresses the religious nature of these churches, arguing that they provided security, fellowship, and spiritual guidance in the midst of crumbling traditional structures and the influx of foreign religious groups.[8] Religious factors are usually based upon the traditional critique of western mission in Africa as one failing to meet the cultural and religious needs of Africans.

In my earlier assessment of "The Western Missionary Movement in Ghana and its implicit Colonial Christology,"[9] I argued that the western mission church in Ghana promulgated a Christ who identified with white western colonizers and who was, by and large, a stranger to Akan traditional culture. The inability (or unwillingness) of western missions to appropriate Christ particularly and Christianity generally into a Ghanaian context in a way that was meaningful and affirmative of Ghanaians constituted a major reason why western Christianity was resisted.[10] David Barrett, who believes that reaction to European mission was the common cause for the emergence of AICs across the continent, maintains that western missions had exhibited a "failure in love" in their attitude toward African people.[11] It was not just their insensitivity to Ghanaian culture that caused this apparent reaction to their message, however, but also the

7. A good example of the religious causative approach is seen Turner, *History of an African*.

8. Turner, *History of an African*, 371–2.

9. See chapter 2.

10. There were some attempts on the part of the missionaries to grapple with Ghanaian culture in order to appropriate mission more effectively. One such publication was Beecham, *Ashantee*.

11. Barrett, *Schism and Renewal*, 154, 184.

inadequacy of the message and its efficacy for an African cosmological outlook.[12]

An example of this was the church's attitude toward witchcraft and evil spirits, which was usually dismissive as opposed to recognizing that, for the African, they constituted a real and immanent threat, against which, one needed to be protected.[13] Robert Wyllie in his study of prophet-healing churches in southern Ghana maintains that the emergence of the MDCC in Winneba reflected a sense of disenchantment with orthodox mission Christianity, which seemed incapable of offering practical solutions to the kinds of problems that ordinary people could expect to face at anytime.[14] David Bosch—speaking out of a South African context, but which also reflects the Ghanaian situation—further argued that the white missionaries often proclaimed a superficial and impoverished gospel. The preaching of the word and the catechist, he maintained, did not touch on many facets of life or struggle of the African.[15]

The inability of western mission churches to grasp the salvatory needs of the Ghanaian was most clearly expressed in the area of *illness*. The missionaries by and large condemned traditional healing practices, and the provision of western medicine through hospitals and clinics was in short supply to meet the needs of the expanding Christian community throughout the country.[16] Here the church simply had no message and provided inadequate alternatives, which therefore left a vacuum aptly filled by a proliferation of faith healing Prophets.

In addition to the frustration and disenchantment with missionary Christianity experienced by Africans, there was also a reluctance to continue to accept the patronizing attitudes and racialist inequalities meted out by white colonial church officials. Adrian Hastings, in discussing the causes and motivations of independency and Prophetism, writes:

> . . . it was, still more, the racialism within the church, the impression—in most cases very well grounded—that even able and experienced African ministers remained second-class members of the church, always inferior to even the most junior missionary recently arrived from Britain. This was a matter of authority exer-

12. I have discussed the Akan cosmological outlook above.

13. Makhudu, *Who Are the Independent Churches?*, 26.

14. Wyllie, *Spiritism in Ghana*, 21.

15. Bosch, "God in Africa."

16. Beckmann, *Eden Revival*, 24.

cised, of salary, of details of human behaviour such as the sharing of meals. The missionary churches were so integrated into racialist society that their membership was profoundly alienating for black people.[17]

In a West African context the collapse of Bishop Crowther's Niger Episcopate at the hands of CMS missionaries, determined to assert their position of power, was a case in point and which some would argue set the stage for the proliferation of indigenous Christianity across West Africa.[18]

The Quest for Self-expression and Freedom from Western Missionary Tutelage

The unfavourable reaction to missionary Christianity and their racial attitudes toward Africans, in part, precipitated a number of secessions from western mission churches in Ghana. These churches to varying degrees were characterized by a desire for African self-expression and freedom from missionary control. In Ghana they included the National Baptist Church, the African Methodist Episcopal Zion Church, and the Nigritian Church.

Dr. Mark Hayford founded the National Baptist Church in 1898 and it is purported to be the first established African Church in Ghana.[19] The significance of this church movement was that Hayford forged effective links with other separatist movements across West Africa in an effort to consolidate churches seceding from western missions. In the same year he officially organized a fellowship of independent Baptist Churches from Sierra Leone to Cameroon. This was a new era of independence.

Another church that emerged in this climate of secession was the African Methodist Episcopal Zion Church (A.M.E. Zion).[20] This church originated in America within the Methodist Church as a black protest movement for self-expression and determination in 1796.[21] It was established in Ghana under the direction of Bishop Small and placed under

---

17. Hastings, *African Church*, 529.

18. Ibid., 493.

19. The issue of the first established African church in Ghana is a matter of dispute. The Twelve Apostle Church, which was started by William Wade Harris, also lays claim to this status. See Opoku, "A Brief History of the Independent Church Movement," 17.

20. Yates, "History of the African Methodist." See also Sackey, "Brief History of the A.M.E."

21. Opuku, "*Brief History*," 14–15.

the leadership of Reverends Egyir Asaam and T.B. Freeman, who started a branch in Keta in 1898. At a time when the hegemony of western missionary Christianity stifled the African personality and undermined their cultural expressions and selfhood, their message of native effort, self-reliance, independence, and self-respect rung loud in the ear of Ghanaians.

The formation of the Nigritian church is an example of secession triggered by a desire for self-expression against restrictive church policies. Rev. J. B. Anaman, a former Methodist minister, founded the Nigritian Church in 1907.[22] He led a group of forty dissident members of Anomabu Methodist Church who had been expelled from the church for flouting the church's ruling concerning singing bands. The rigorous vernacular singing and music, which drew upon traditional African rhythms, were seen by church authorities to desecrate the church, as well as belonging to annals of their traditional fetish past. The Nigritian church's usage of the vernacular and singing bands was in accordance with the growing national aspiration for African self-expression and a longing to worship freely and independently of foreign interference. Such secessions and the formation of indigenous church organizations were confidence-boosters for Ghanaians, who were previously considered too inept to be at the helm of church leadership.

Translation of the Bible into Ghanaian Languages

The translation of the Bible into Ghanaian vernaculars was also a key religious factor in the emergence of indigenous churches in Ghana. In 1871 the first Twi Bible was translated and published by the Basel Mission. By 1874 the Bible was further translated into Ga and Ewe. J.G. Christaller's widely acclaimed Twi grammar dictionary and collection of proverbs were also completed and published by 1881.[23] David Barrett contends that scriptural translation is a significant contributing factor toward the development of African indigenous churches. He states: ". . . an event of fundamental importance in the life of the tribe took place: the Holy Scriptures were translated and published in the tribe's own language."[24] Kwame Bediako is of the view that "[t]here is probably no more important single explanation for the massive presence of Christianity on the

22. Ibid.
23. Debrunner, *History*, 143.
24. Barrett, *Schism*, 127.

African continent than the availability of the Scriptures in many African languages."[25]

The most important function that vernacular Scripture played was enabling the African Christians to distinguish between what was taught by the missionaries and what was taught in Scripture. The Scripture translated into the vernacular became an independent standard of reference, and it soon became apparent that much of what was taught by missionaries was more a reflection of their own cultural baggage than from the Bible.[26] The Old Testament was of particular interest because it resonated with much of what was important within an African outlook on life: the importance of fertility and sexuality, the place of ancestors, polygamous practice, the importance of land and a host of other cultural and religious similarities.[27]

It was above all surprising to see the practice of polygamy in the Bible, which the missionaries fought hard to eradicate by imposing strict prohibitions for members.[28] Particularly striking was the agreement between the African worldview and that of the Old Testament. Although the missionaries (as good Protestants) believed in the centrality of the Bible they were not accustomed to making the connections or seeing the continuity between the Biblical context and the contemporary one that the Africans were discovering.[29]

The translation of the Bible into the vernacular was also a factor in a new process of growing self-awareness. A people whose culture had been hitherto undermined was nevertheless important enough to have the Bible—the Word of God—in their own mother tongue. The impact of the Bible was so significant that many of the indigenous church leaders modelled their leadership style and imagery on Old Testament Prophet figures, which were probably familiar figures in Africa before Christianity arrived.[30]

Although the above, primarily religious factors, contributed significantly toward the origins and developments of AICs in Ghana, the strength

---

25. Bediako, *Christianity in Africa*, 62.

26. The issue of vernacularization is considered in some detail in ch. 6.

27. See Daneel, *Quest*, 84–5.

28. Barrett, *Schism*, 117.

29. Hasting, *Church in Africa*, 527.

30. Beckmann, *Eden Revival*, 24.

of the general movement toward independence was in the combination of socio-political factors that overlapped with the religious factors.

SOCIAL AND POLITICAL FACTORS

During the latter part of the nineteenth and the first two decades of the twentieth century, certain changes in Ghanaian society had a significant bearing on the growth and development of African indigenous churches. To a large extent economic development was the main mediating force whereby the individualistic, competitive, acquisitive attitude and values of the West were introduced into Ghanaian society. Although before the nineteenth century new means of wealth and power were introduced through the sale of guns and gunpowder, this brought little disturbance to social order and scarcely affected the more loosely knit societies of the hinterlands.[31] The social and political changes during this period, however, were more wide spread and deeply felt by even those at the margins of society.

Indigenous Churches and African Nationalism

The researchers on AICs that base their emergence upon socio-political factors understand indigenous churches to be political protest movements against a background of colonial paternalism and the rise of black nationalism. Beckmann for example believes the independent church movement in Ghana to be the religious counterpart of political nationalism.[32] The training for leadership given to African ministers, and their growing self-confidence in working alongside Europeans, may be regarded as positive stimuli to the development of the nationalist movement.[33] Though church organizations did not take a definite part in nationalist agitation, prominent members were often outspoken on political issues. The nationalist voices of men like Edward Wilmot Blyden, who was highly critical of missionary Christianity and advocated the establishment of an independent West African Church,[34] and J. E. Casely Hayford a Methodist, became

31. Kimble, *A Political History*, 128–29.

32. Beckmann, *Eden's Revival*, 123.

33. Kimble, *A Political History*, 161.

34. See Blyden, *Christianity, Islam, and the Negro Race*, 15. For information on the life and works of Blyden see Lynch, *Edward Blyden*.

more and more prominent.[35] In the growth of self-governing institutions the churches were usually ahead of the government, and they provided some African leaders with a forum and an unaccustomed freedom of expression, both in the pulpit and the press.

In his book *Ethiopia Unbound,* Casely Hayford, a distinguished politician and layman, accused the missionaries of haughtiness in their relationship with Africans and caricatured the type of Christians bred by mission churches:

> At the head of the choir was the school-master whose attire certainly invited attention. In his elegantly cut-away black morning coat and beautifully glazed cuffs and collar, not to speak of patent leather shoes, which he kept spotlessly bright by occasionally dusting them with his pocket-handkerchief, tucked away in his shirt sleeves, he certainly looked a veritable swell, but he also did look a veritable fool—and this is the sum total of half a century of missionary zeal.[36]

Such voices of dissent contributed greatly to this new African cultural assertiveness which decried the imposition of western religiosity upon Ghanaians.

The Gold Coast Aborigines Right Protection Society (ARPS), particularly through their newspaper, the *Gold Coast Aborigines,* and the National Congress of West Africa, also played a pivotal role in advancing the cause of African nationalism.[37] The interesting and complicated story of the rise of nationalism in the Gold Coast has already been told in great detail and does not need be rehearsed here.[38] What needs to be recognized, however, is that this movement added significantly to the momentum that would eventually lead to the emergence of African indigenous churches in Ghana.

The language and sentiments of African nationalism, much of which came via the African American movement in the USA, coincided with a

---

35. The Wesleyans, for example, besides introducing a printing work-shop, as part of their educational programme, were responsible for some of the earliest Gold Coast newspapers. *The Christian Messenger and Examiner* was produced in Cape Coast by the Rev. T. Freeman and the Rev. H. Wharton as early as 1859; this was succeeded by *The Christian Reporter.* See Kimble, *Political History,* 162.

36. Casely, *Ethiopia Unbound,* 101–3.

37. For an account of the Gold Coast A.R.P.S., see Kimble, *Political History,* 374–403.

38. Kimble, *Political History,* 161–67.

growing feeling of frustration that emanated from Africans in western mission churches and those that had seceded and formed indigenous churches. This nationalist influence was seen most notably in the establishment of A.M.E. Zion mentioned above, which appealed to awakening color-consciousness. At the inaugural meeting held in Cape Coast in 1898, T. B. Freeman Jr. (one of its leaders) is reported as stating the ethos of the church as follows:

> This church composed of Africans and entirely governed and worked by Africans was indeed "bone of our bone and flesh of our flesh," which would naturally take a much greater interest in their missions in the motherland than can be possible with missionary boards and missionaries of an alien race who are not above the color question.[39]

Although the church did not rally the mass of support that they expected—possibly to do with foreign origin and rhetoric—it laid nonetheless another brick on the road toward the Africanization of Ghanaian Christianity.[40] The forty dissident members of the Nigritian Church who were expelled from the Methodist Church for singing in the vernacular and playing their traditional drumbeats also (mentioned above) were no doubt also greatly encouraged by the wave of nationalist consciousness that was indicative of the time.

Social Change

The development of African indigenous churches in Ghana has been also closely identified with rapid social change that created a climate of anomy and uncertainty during the indirect rule of the colonial rulers between 1880-1920.[41] To start with, the super-imposition of external authority of colonial rulers seriously weakened the powers of the Chiefs, and the sanctions at their disposal.[42] The prevention of inter-tribal warfare, for example, deprived them of their main means of gaining new prestige, territory, and wealth. Traditional gods also proved no match against the might of Europeans who encroached upon traditional land, desecrated shrines, and declared worshipping traditional gods tantamount to wor-

---

39. *Gold Coast Aborigine.*

40. Opoku, *A Brief History*, 14.

41. Annorbah-Sarpei, "Rise of Prophetism," 27–33.

42. These sanctions included chaining, mutilation, and enslavement of prisoners.

shipping Satan and his angels.[43] This sometimes led to harsh conflicts between Christianity and the traditional religion. Such conflict more often led to the defeat and humiliation of Chiefs and other such guardians of the traditional religion.[44] The religious authority of the Chiefs and their ability to invoke supernatural sanctions was therefore undermined by the introduction of Christianity, which offered not only the prestige of association with the ruling colonial government but also the utilitarian advantage of education, which in turn led to wider economic opportunities.[45] These events paved the way for the message of indigenous prophets such as Harris and Oppong, for whom the disenfranchised traditional observers constituted an *evangelica preparatio*.

The period was also marked by social and economic uncertainties. The cocoa boom instigated an economic and social revolution in Ghana.[46] Thousands of people up-rooted from their villages, leaving behind many of the local traditional and ancestral gods, found new villages in the cocoa growing areas. Economic boom and newfound wealth created a feeling of hedonism that found expression in the so-called "dances" of *Asiko* and *Sibisaba*. These were new forms of socializing which involved young people—particularly young women—dancing provocatively and singing to brass band music.[47] When the value of cocoa (which brought great wealth to farmers) began to fall, this brought about much insecurity and resulted in an increase in witchcraft beliefs, which in turn led to an increase in anti-witchcraft cults.[48] Although the explanations of the rise of the witchcraft cults vary, the prevailing social disorientation and uncertainties played

---

43. Debrunner, *A History*, 141.

44. The most famous of these conflicts was the one over *Nananom* or *Brafo*, the tutelary spirit of the Fanti, established at Mankessim, spiritual capital of that nation. Methodist Christians made farms in the sacred grove of *Nananom* and approached it with a levity and irreverence. This was highly disrespectful and displeasing to those who considered him a distinguished ancestor. The conflict that ensued led to the elders of the village being publicly whipped in the market place at Cape Coast amidst the universal applause of the people. See Cruikshank, *18 Years*, 141.

45. For a detailed discussion on the impact of Christianity upon traditional religion, see Kimble, *Political History*, 151–61.

46. See Ward, *History of Ghana*, 396–411, for a detailed discussion on the social impact of the cocoa trade upon Ghana.

47. Burnett, "Charisma and Community," 69.

48. See Debrunner, *Witchcraft in Ghana*, 61–75, for a discussion on the cocoa trade and witchcraft. See also Burnett, "Charisma and Community," 67–70.

a key role in their proliferation.[49] The influenza epidemic, which had a previous outbreak in 1891 and had caused a number of deaths, resurfaced killing thousands and added to this climate of uncertainty and anomy.[50]

Traditional religion in its old form, now discredited by Christianity and to which many who had migrated to unfamiliar areas were not sufficiently engaged, no longer brought protection and meaning. It was within the new indigenous churches that many sought protection from witches and a "place to feel at home."

Kwame Nkrumah as Osagyefo (Redeemer)

The 1950s saw acceleration in the movement advancing the national self-consciousness of Ghanaian people. The prevailing political climate at the time in Ghana was summarized by the popular maxim "*man be thy self.*" This was indeed the rallying cry for many nationalist politicians and for those who were struggling for the national independence of Ghana from Britain. Although the period witnessed a rise in the number of indigenous churches and an increase of Africans in positions of leadership in mission churches, the vast majority of the mission churches still had expatriate leadership.[51] This state of affairs made the church a scapegoat for politicians, many of whom argued that the continued presence of expatriates as heads of churches served to confirm the impression of the church as another front of the European onslaught on Africa.[52] This foreign aspect of the church stood in opposition to what Nkrumah stood for, namely national and cultural self-consciousness. This brought conflict between Nkrumah and the mission churches. Nkrumah believed western mission Christianity to be the instrument of social oppression; in his words, he maintained "religion is the instrument of bourgeois social reaction."[53]

Nkrumah's message resonated with the African indigenous churches, who were themselves in effect a protest movement against the historic churches and their western leadership. The attitude of the indigenous

49. The most popular view in regard to the rise of the anti-witchcraft cults was that they were a new creation that arose out of social uncertainties and disorientation. Some maintain that they were a resurgence of a pre-colonial cult. See McCaskie, "Anti-Witchcraft Cults," 125–54.

50. Patterson, "Influenza Epidemic."

51. Pobee, *Kwame Nkrumah*, 54.

52. Ibid., 55.

53. Nkrumah, *Consciencism*, 13.

churches to Nkrumah, at least in the earlier years of his rule, was very positive. The former Head Prophet of the MDCC, Jehu-Appiah, is widely reported as even being a great friend of Kwame Nkrumah.[54] The sympathetic ear given to Nkrumah's message on the part of the indigenous churches was further increased when Nkrumah narrowed the gap between his political nationalism and indigenous church prophetism by adapting the traditional role of the *omanhene* to the contemporary situation.

In the first place Nkrumah took to himself certain titles, which outraged the historic churches. The two most provocative ones were *Osagyefo* (Redeemer),[55] which literally means "one who saves the battle" or "deliverer." The second was the title *Asomdwehene* that literally means "Prince of Peace." Christians specifically used this title of Jesus Christ. Nkrumah promised an early "paradise" on earth (Ghana) in 10 years; in 1950 the creed of the CPP was based upon the Apostolic Creed and Christian hymns were adapted and regularly used at CPP rallies.

Indeed, *The Evening News* newspaper compared Nkrumah to Jesus; it read:

"Angels were singing 'the Messiah is coming' when in 1909 at Nkroful a woman was labouring to bring forth the Apostle of Freedom." It also stated, "Nkrumah is alright," "Nkrumah is our Messiah," "Nkrumah never dies," and "If you follow him he will make you fishers of men."[56]

David Burnett in his assessment of Nkrumah's usage of religious symbolism remarks:

> The use of clear Christian symbolism illustrates the widespread influence of Christian ideas among the people of the Gold Coast, and Nkrumah, as an astute politician, realised the value of biblical imitation for slogans in his political campaigns. The biblical imagery provided ready-made metaphors to communicate his message to people who had at least heard the preaching of a Christian evangelists even if only a minority were Christians.[57]

Nkrumah was perhaps the first Ghanaian prophet of liberation, political as well as cultural.

---

54. See Burnett, "Charisma and Community."

55. This title was first used of Osei Tutu I (1697–1731) of Asante when he delivered from the domination of Denkyira.

56. Cited in Bartels, *Roots of Ghanaian Methodism*, 13.

57. Burnett, "Charisma and Community," 187.

It was not so much that Nkrumah was deified as Christ, but was being seen as a prophet of liberation and change; and admirers were perfectly at ease in communicating this through symbols and means that were Christian and overtly African. I want to propose here that Nkrumah's usage of symbolism, both African and Christian, added to the legitimization and popularization of an African expression of Christianity in Ghana.[58] Also, his boldness in accepting a comparison with Christ, ostensibly linking Christ to the struggles of an African people, was further adding to a liberative interpretation of how Jesus could be understood and how one could be both Christian and African.

Before national independence in 1957, indigenous churches had already begun to spring up in large numbers. However, according to David Barrett, by 1967 this movement had mushroomed enormously to at least two hundred distinct bodies with two hundred thousand adherents.[59] Although Nkrumah could not be credited with this massive increase, which for the most part was the culmination of a combination of factors, he clearly played a significant role.

AFRICAN PROPHETS

Although the religious and socio-political factors outlined above contributed greatly to the conception and emergence of indigenous churches which mirrored the African (Ghanaian) cultural outlook, the *character* of African indigenous churches in Ghana owed a great debt to two African prophets: William Wade Harris and Samson Oppong. These two preachers have been singled out because of the mass conversions that ensued as a result of their preaching. They also provided a model through which the best of African traditional culture and Christianity could be exemplified. Their ministries were both timely and pertinent because criticism of Christianity as a European brand (which begun in a modest form in the publications of Edward Blyden in the 1880s[60]) became much stronger at the beginning of the twentieth century.[61] Members of the African intelli-

---

58. For more on Nkrumah and religion, see Pobee, *Kwame Nkrumah*, 39–46.

59. Barrett, *Schism*, 19.

60. See Blyden, *Christianity, Islam, and the Negro Race*, 15.

61. Debrunner, *History*, 240.

gentsia were particularly vociferous criticizing Christianity itself and not only the missionaries.[62]

It was during this period, according to Haliburton, that Prophet Harris "like a meteor, flashed across parts of the West African landscape, rushing through the waste places of the sky."[63] The ministry of the Prophet came as a breath of fresh air to many who were torn between their Christian faith—clothed in European garb—and their African identity. This feeling was captured by J. E. Casely-Hayford,[64] a brother of Dr. E. Hayford and the Revd. Dr. Mark Hayford.

In a daily journal published in 1915, he wrote the following as he observed Harris at work:

> He says of the Christ that he took the form of a babe in order that by his helplessness he might indicate the true nature of humility. He reminds you that the Kroo man is the scavenger of the world … Mammon has used the Kroo man all these years. And now God has need of him … God is using him now in person of William Waddy Harris.[65]

The impact of Prophet Harris" ministry was far reaching, particularly for its significance in the development of African Christian expression.

In Prophet Harris we see the embryo for the development of an African indigenous spirituality and an Akan Christology in Ghana. The power of the Prophet's ministry was best demonstrated in his ability to appropriate the Christian evangel into what was in Ghana an Akan traditional context. His use of water, a calabash, a tall rod or cane, would have been symbols that Akan traditional observers would have been familiar with. Even the use of a cross and a Bible as symbols of power would have reverberated with the Akan worldview that maintained that natural objects have a life force in and of themselves.

The efficacy of the Prophet's message and ministry, however, was demonstrated poignantly in his ability to strike at the heart of the African deepest "soul-need,"[66] which was for protection and deliverance from fear

---

62. Ibid.

63. Haliburton, *Prophet Harris*, 1.

64. Brother of Dr. Mark Christian Hayford the founder of the National Baptist Society mentioned above.

65. Haliburton, *Prophet Harris*, 78.

66. I am using this phrase to mean the deepest and most fundamental fears of the African personality to which salvation in Jesus Christ can be most meaningful. Éla la, in

of oppressive and evil spirits. Through the Prophet's public triumph over witches and workers of juju[67] and magic, he demonstrated the supremacy of the power of Christ over all these powers, thus bringing peace to the African heart. It is here, therefore, where we begin to see an inkling of an African Christ who enters the Akan worldview and is victorious over its malevolent powers, which are ubiquitous within it.[68]

In a very similar fashion to the Prophet Harris, Samson Oppong preached against the use of fetishes and charms, threatening to call down fire if the villages did not burn them.[69] With his background and experience in the practice of witchcraft, Oppong was able to make his message appropriate in such a way that spoke meaningfully the needs of the people that formerly came to him for protection and revenge. The Methodist Church in Kumasi collaborated with Oppong, as they had also collaborated with Harris, and several thousand were won for their church through his ministry.

As a result of these and other such ministries, hundreds of thousands of people came to faith in Christ in Ghana and across West Africa. One of the key features of this new appropriation of the Christian message was its emphasis on the power of the Holy Spirit, particularly in confronting issues of illness and witchcraft. This had struck a strong chord within the "souls" of African people, for whom traditional religion remained the strongest element of their culture. It was the ability to appropriate the Christian message into this worldview that led to the rapid expansion of African indigenous churches during the period 1922 to the 1970s.

The first African indigenous churches to be established in Ghana were the Musama Disco Christo Church, the Saviours Church (also known as Memena Gyidifo), the Church of the Twelve Apostles, and the African Faith Tabernacle Church.[70] The evangelistic type ministries of Harris and Oppong had entered a new era of African independence

---

his book *My Faith*, 33–54, explores this whole issue of translating the Christian message into the language and symbols of African culture.

67. *Juju* is a West African term for witchcraft.

68. This Christological theme is discussed in later chapters.

69. For a full account of the life and ministry of Samson Oppong, see Debrunner, *Story of Samson Oppong*; Bediako, "Relationship Between"; Haliburton, "Calling of a Prophet," 84–96.

70. These churches are discussed in Baëta, *Prophetism in Ghana*, 9–68.

through the birth of African indigenous churches, churches that were led, financed, and organized by Africans for Africans.

These movements were not purely secessions and reactions to western mission Christianity but a part of a wider receptiveness and responsiveness to the Christian message in Ghana and across Africa. Independency was also a part of the primary movement of mass conversion, of which, mission Christianity enjoyed enormous numerical success, so much so that after 1910 many of them were grossly under-staffed and simply overwhelmed by the enormity of the African harvest. Hastily trained evangelists and catechists had to be trusted to teach the masses of converts who wanted to be baptised.[71] Many of the indigenous church prophets and founders did not set out to establish churches or to head mass movements but were essentially taking on the missionary's task because it seemed so important.[72] Harris for example encouraged his converts to wait for missionaries and to attend their churches; Oppong on the other hand was a great asset to the Methodist Church, which he encouraged thousands of his converts to join. The main motivation was rather a deep conviction that God had called them as prophets to turn people to Jesus Christ.

AFRICAN INDIGENOUS CHURCH CHRISTOLOGY AND THE MAINLINE DENOMINATIONS

The rise of indigenous churches in Ghana by and large has been a spontaneous movement. For the most part, it has been a movement that has continued within the western Protestant theological tradition of the churches from which they seceded. Many have argued that, in their effort to inculturate Christianity within an African setting, some have (by virtue of certain practices and unorthodox theological viewpoints) positioned themselves outside the mainstream Protestant theological position.[73] Some even questioned the validity of them being described as "Christian Churches" and described them as an aberration of Christianity.[74] The initial impression of these churches was that they were syncretistic sects quite apart from orthodox Christianity. Many Methodists, for example,

71. Beckmann, *Eden,* 24.

72. Hastings, *The Church,* 531.

73. Oosthuizen's early study of indigenous churches by and large took this position. See *Post-Christianity in Africa.*

74. Ibid., xiv.

described Prophet Appiah (Akaboha I) and his followers as "false prophets" as foretold in the Bible and denounced them as heretics.[75]

Turner summarizes the hostile reports of the Methodist and Presbyterian churches toward indigenous churches in Ghana in the 1950s:
"These reports are usually hostile, and refer to the "cheap Christian sects"
which "infest the district" with their "dark influence" "like a spiritual can-
cer eating steadily into the Church.""[76] The basis of these criticisms was
primarily due to the perceived unorthodox practices that were observed
being carried out by indigenous church adherents. The practice of polygamy is an example of this, which has brought heavy criticism from
both black and white leaders within mainline mission churches.[77]

Christology

One of the areas in which they have invited strong criticism from western
mission churches is in their understanding of the person and the work
of Christ, or their Christology. It has been argued that because of their
overemphasis on the Holy Spirit they had a weak Christology. Much of
the academic debate surrounding the position of Christ has been in as-
sessing the movement in southern Africa, particularly in the light of messianic attributes of Christ seemingly being transferred to group leaders.[78]
This issue of them having a "weak Christology" was also evident in the
churches in West Africa.

Turner, for example, in his assessment of the Church of the Lord
(Aladura), raises grave concerns regarding the actual degree to which

75. Burnett, "Charisma and Community," 130.

76. Turner, *African Independent Churches*, 191.

77. The MDCC—who state in clause 18 of their declaration of faith: "We believe that
(as an African Church) polygamy is not a moral sin"—particularly came under "fire" for
this practice. See Turner, *African Independent Churches*, 58–60, for a discussion of their
position on polygamy.

78. Perhaps the most damning viewpoint of all regarding African Zionism and messianism came from Beyerhaus, who maintained that the Black Messiah indulges in self glorification and deification among his followers and in the process became a beguiling threat
to Christians from the traditional churches. Beyerhaus found little in either Zionism or
messianism that had anything to do with what he called "authentic Christianity." Christ
became purely a pseudonym for the messianic leader. He writes, "This complete substitu-
tion is especially notorious in the messianic movement. The entire Christian concept of
God is unrecognized; Christ is ousted; the Holy Spirit is usurped by the traditional spirit
manifestation, and God the Father is equated with the traditional deity. See Beyerhaus,
"Begenungen mit messianischen," referenced in Daneel's *Quest for Belonging*, 182.

the Christological pronouncements—evident within the hymnal and the liturgies, the catechism, and the occasional publications—were integral to the faith of the church.[79] In the first instance he detected relative confusion between the persons and functions of the members of the Trinity, which was in stark contrast to the impeccable declaration of a Trinitarian faith documented in the 1939 constitution, in the catechism, in the shortened creed, and in the hymns.[80] Expressions cited include: "Ye sons of Christ," "cleansing power of God" or "cleansing power of the Holy Ghost," "Jesus our everlasting God," "Father cleanse us with your blood," and so forth. The shift in emphasis toward an Old Testament kerygma, wherein Christ played no part in the cosmic renewal and salvation, he maintained, also gave rise to a reduced Christology. Here belief had become dissociated from Jesus Christ and become simply "trust in God." In the pronouncements and later writings of Oshitelo, "Jesus Christ" is increasingly sidelined to the periphery of his message.[81]

In an article entitled "Pagan Features in West African Independent Churches," Turner discusses some of the excesses of indigenous churches in relation to the sacraments.[82] The sacrament of Baptism, he states, is transferred into the realm of magic and "pagan purification rites," where it is regarded as efficacious for particular human needs and detached from all Christian significance. Baptism, he adds, is also used as a rite of admission into a particular independent group, rather than as a sign and means of incorporation into the body of Christ. The Lord's Supper is also usually neglected among these churches and some have discarded it altogether. Baëta asserts that "spiritual churches in actual fact function as if our relationship is only with God the Father and it is only he that is prepared to meet all our needs."[83] Turner also states that "[i]t is not so much that he (Jesus Christ) is ignored, as that his divinity is taken for granted, and his humanity overlooked, so that he is readily absorbed in the term God, whose present manifestation in the Spirit is of more importance than his historical work in the flesh."[84]

79. Turner, *History of an African*, 344.

80. Ibid.

81. Ibid.

82. Turner, "Pagan Features," 165–72.

83. Baëta, *Prophetism*, 146.

84. Turner, *History of an African*, 344.

The offering of sacrifice in the holy places has also invited criticisms on the basis that Christ is the last and final sacrifice. This issue was (and still is) so contentious that apart from inviting criticism from mainline churches it was also a reason for schisms.[85] Turner argues that this practice makes plain the complete failure to understand the vicarious nature of the sacrifice of Christ, and the tendency toward an earnest spirituality that amounts to salvations by works.[86] Another area that has invited criticisms is prayers said to venerated dead leaders to intercede on behalf of the supplicant. At Mozano, the "holy city" of the MDCC, a mausoleum has been erected at the burial place of the church's founder, his successors, and their wives to which supplicants come to pray for their needs. Written requests are also placed on the graves in hope that answers would come as the leaders are now close to the Lord.[87] The activity and power of the Holy Spirit in the life of the individual and the church is clearly an area in which the older churches can learn something from indigenous churches. This however often led to a Trinitarian imbalance in which direct revelation from God through the "spirit" is divorced from the Christ of the Scriptures. This type of direct access to the "spirit," argues Turner, outside of a balanced Trinitarian outlook, puts the church in a dangerous position, especially among their illiterate members who might allow its manifestation to assume primal forms.[88]

INDIGENOUS CHURCH RESPONSE TO MAINLINE CHURCH CRITICISM

From the outset, African indigenous churches have considered themselves to be "Christian churches" that were in a continuous line of succession with those biblical characters who too had experienced the power of the Holy Spirit. Attempts therefore to isolate them from the wider Christian community were taken very seriously. The Bible played a key role in the legitimizing of their practices and teachings, which for the most part were interpreted literally. Church teachings and declarations of faith were therefore often accompanied with an array of scriptural support. The theological inadequacy of AICs leaders in comparison to their African mission

85. Ibid., 350.
86. Ibid., 352.
87. Asamoah-Gyadu, "Renewal Within," 96.
88. Turner, *Religious Innovation*, 169.

church counterparts who often comprised the educational elite (many of whom had studied overseas) was nonetheless clearly evident. Added to this was the prestige and financial backing that the mission churches enjoyed due to the ability to access western support and partnership.

Theological Training

Indigenous churches were rather ambivalent toward formal education, which usually meant westernization at the same time. Their religiosity was more African in orientation and therefore less congruent to education. It was also dependent on the charisma of the leader rather than the trained professional, and on divine power rather than human wisdom and skill. The perceived benefits received by black mission church leaders, however, prompted a number of different indigenous churches to seek support from overseas missions to set up Bible colleges and theological institutions to train their leaders.[89] The prestige and economic benefit gained from such contacts was evident within the mission churches that they sought to emulate.

The Mennonite Mission Board, for example, was approached in 1957 by a Ghanaian pastor of several dissident indigenous church congregations, for whom they worked but with few resources.[90] In 1969 Reverend Weaver set up Bible classes for indigenous church leaders and in the same year the Lutheran Church (Missouri Synod) also began work in Ghana with indigenous churches in the area of theological training. The works of both the Mennonites and the Lutherans helped to form the Good News Theological Training Institute (now Good News Theological College and Seminary), which trains leaders from within indigenous churches.[91]

The continuous exposure to what was by and large western evangelical theology—that was and still is the most popular theological position in Ghana today—curbed some of the more excessive practices and unbiblical theologies of these churches. The majority of their leaders, especially the younger ones, adopted the evangelical theological position. Bible studies, such as the ones conducted by Edwin Weaver that included both indigenous churches as well as mission related churches, also helped to

89. The possible motives behind the indigenous churches desire to establish their own schools is discussed by Turner (ibid., 324–26).

90. Beckmann, *Eden Revival,* 40–41.

91. Ibid.

conform indigenous churches to an evangelical position, though in many areas certain idiosyncratic practices and beliefs were maintained.[92]

Ecumenical Co-operation

Another means by which indigenous churches have sought to respond to the criticism and "snubbing" of mission churches has been through the formation of various ecumenical organizations and co-operation.[93] As early as 1898 Dr. Mark Hayford founded the National Baptist Church and attempted to forge links with indigenous churches across West Africa. In 1962 several of the more prominent indigenous church leaders formed the Pentecostal Association of Ghana. This was modelled after the Christian Council of Ghana, to which they were not welcomed.[94] It was intended to encourage indigenous churches to learn from each other and to thrash out issues of mutual concern. In 1968 another group of smaller indigenous church leaders organized the Ghana Council for Liberal Churches and managed to get government recognition.[95] Through such organizations and co-operation a deeper engagement with Scripture and tradition was gained as well as a shared solidarity.

As indigenous churches began to grow so did the curiosity of the mainline denominations. There was a growing realization that the indigenous churches were creatively producing new, indigenized usages which were in many respects more acceptable theologically than was first thought. The study committee of the Bawku presbytery of the Presbyterian Church, who initiated contact with indigenous churches, both to learn and to teach, was a good example of this growing curiosity.[96] A year later the Presbyterian Church of Ghana synod assigned persons to study indigenous church methods of prayer, Bible studies, and worship styles in more depth.

These types of formal and informal co-operations with older mission churches reinforced the existing tendency to model themselves on the older churches and to gain wider acceptance. To this end areas that

92. Weaver, *Kuku*, 123–27.

93. For some historical details of the ecumenical progress of the indigenous church movement across the continent, see Daneel, *Quest,* 109–13.

94. Turner, *Innovations*, 174.

95. Beckmann, *Eden*, 43–4.

96. Weaver, *Kuku*, 52.

were perceived to be offensive or erroneous theologically were discontinued or conducted away from the gaze of non-members.

Re-thinking Christology

The effects of these ecumenical and other contacts, as well as formal theological training on indigenous churches are mixed. The benefits of recognition by the world Christian community, with wider experience and broader outlook, nonetheless were obvious. Even so, there areas in which indigenous churches have sought to replicate mission church theology and practice without allowing the meaning to penetrate to the grassroots level. These areas include the sacraments of Baptism and Holy Communion, whose Christological symbolism is often wrongly associated and meaning misunderstood.[97] There have also been practices that have undergone modification on the basis of modernization and progress.

One such Christological practice that has been modified is the prohibition of using western medicine.[98] The Prophet Jehu-Appiah of the MDCC was always interested in divine healing, but in 1925 during a seven-day fast he was told by God to take divine healing seriously. Soon after he prohibited the use of *edur*, which means *charm, herbal medicine*, or *western medicine*. The reason given for this was that Jesus and his disciples did not use any of these methods in their healing practice. Over the years this is one of the areas in which their Christology has been modified.

During one of my visits to Muzano I was taken to see a number of long-term sick people kept in small huts. I asked if they were allowed to use western medicine. I was told:

> They are allowed to use western medicine and we do sometimes give them when we have it. Formerly this was not so and even today some of the old people don"t take it. But because of education we have changed that because we now know that Christ can choose to heal anyway he likes, by medicine or divinely; after all, in everything it is his power working, even in the medicine.[99]

There has thus been a genuine effort to respond to the criticisms and challenges that have confronted indigenous churches, and in various ways they have been able to adjust while maintaining their distinctiveness. The

97. This issues is explored in more detail in later chapters

98. Baëta, *Prophetism in Ghana*, 54.

99. Visit to Mazano on 4th July, 1998.

coming of a new Pentecostal wave that would take the country by storm would prove to be the greatest challenge that would confront of them all.

THE CHALLENGE OF PENTECOSTALISM TO THE DEVELOPMENT OF AKAN AIC'S CHRISTOLOGY

The rise of Pentecostalism in Ghana is another stage in the development of African indigenous churches and has contributed toward the formation and shape of their Christology. Pentecostalism in Ghana has been the subject matter of some interesting research in recent years that has recognized it as a continual development of African indigenous Christianity.[100]

Various missions from the United States and Great Britain, most of which have been derived from revivalist Protestantism, most notably Pentecostal in spirituality, have proved popular in Ghana.[101] Many maintained much of the zeal and theological fervour of the missionaries who came to Ghana in the early nineteenth century, but some also reflected the influence of the African-American Pentecostalism, which has its roots in the 1906 Azusa Street revival.[102]

According to the Ghana Evangelism Committee's national survey updated in 1993, the growth of Ghanaian Christianity occurred in two main areas.[103] The first was in those churches belonging to the Pentecostal Council, which had among their members denominations such as the Assemblies of God, the Church of Pentecost, The Apostolic Church, and the Christ Apostolic Church. The second group was of churches categorized as "mission-related," where the most successful were the Churches of Christ, and the New Apostolic Church. These Pentecostal and revivalist churches, which began to take hold in the mid-twentieth century, did not insist on the African ceasing to operate in the spiritual worldview of the traditional religion, but maintained that Christ was even greater than the powers of the spirits or ancestors.

These churches were places where spiritual healing and exorcism were a part of the "spiritual landscape." They were places where the

---

100. For more on this see Larby, *Pentecostalism*. See also Asamoah-Gyadu, "Renewal Within," 90–124. For a continent wide discussion of Africa Pentecostalism, see Kalu, *African Pentecostalism* and Anderson, *Introduction to Pentecostalism*, chapter 7.

101. Beckmann, *Eden*, 116.

102. For more on this, see Hollenweger, *The Pentecostals*, 21–6.

103. Ghana Evangelism Committee, *National Survey*.

African could come for miracle healing and deliverance from curses. This Pentecostal wave brought an appropriation of the gospel message where it was now possible to experience the power of Christ within the realm of the African worldview generally, and the Akan one specifically.

The character of this Pentecostal spirituality played a crucial role in accelerating the pace of indigenous expressions of Christianity in Ghana. Pentecostalism championed certain key areas of Christian expression, which struck a chord with the frustrated masses of Ghanaians who had grown wary of the cerebral spirituality of western missionary Christianity. These were traditional ways of worship, divine healing and deliverance, speaking in tongues, special emphasis on the baptism of the Holy Ghost, charismatic preaching, dreams and visions, and all that characterizes Pentecostal experience.

Pentecostal spirituality also helped to redefine a very important aspect of Christianity; this was the area of Christology. The Christ of Pentecost was in stark contrast to the Christ preached by the early missionaries. This Christ of "Pentecost" healed the sick, cast out demons, raised the dead, and gave food to the poor and needy. The Christ of "Pentecost" was "at home" within the Akan primal worldview and triumphed over all its spiritual entities. The *crucis glorae* of western mission Christianity was exchanged for the *Christus Victor* of Pentecostal triumphalism.

The explosion of Pentecostalism upon the Ghanaian church scene, which gave rise to new Charismatic churches, also had an adverse impact on indigenous churches that were, by the 1980s, experiencing rapid decline.[104] The harsh criticisms of the new Pentecostal churches, which castigated indigenous churches as syncretistic traditional worshippers and even devil worshippers, also forced leaders to change their approach on seeing the members exodus the churches for the new pasture of the young and upwardly mobile charismatic ministries. The "African culture" that these churches championed in the 1950s and 60s was no longer so much an issue.[105] Many indigenous churches therefore metamorphosized into charismatic churches in order to survive.[106] The notion of healing,

104. For more on the cause of the decline of indigenous church in Ghana, see Gifford, *African Christianity*, 95–6; see also Asamoah-Gyadu, "Renewal within," 90–124.

105. Gifford, *African Christianity*, 95.

106. Asamoah-Gyadu argues that the drift of members into charismatic ministries was not the only reason for the decline of the indigenous churches, which he maintained attracted different clientele. See "Renewal Within," 90–124.

already present within indigenous churches, was extended to health and prosperity in many cases, particularly among the younger AIC leaders who sought to model themselves on charismatic leaders such as Duncan Williams and Mensah Otibil.[107]

The prosperity Christology espoused by the plethora of Charismatic ministries also found its way into indigenous churches. This Christology extended beyond the cosmic powers of Christ to bring healing and wholeness and added a social and financial element of health and wealth that could also be accessed through the domain of spiritual breakthroughs. Indigenous church leaders have sought to adjust their approach to the changing religious climate. However, their inability to allow changes to permeate their structures and pastoral approach in line with the educated and enterprising youth who have not been accommodated by their power structures could mean, in Glifford's view, that as a movement AICs will continue to decline.[108]

CONCLUSION

So far the wider issues surrounding the development of Akan AIC Christology have been examined. These issues in their various ways have contributed toward defining the Christological approach of Akan AICs. In the next chapter I will focus the discussion more specifically upon the Christological apprehension of Akan AIC adherents, examining the means by which they define their Christology.

---

107. Gifford, *African Christianity*, 95.
108. Ibid.

4

The Source of Akan AIC Christology

INTRODUCTION

THE THEOLOGICAL REFLECTION ON what it meant to be both "Christian" and "African" without contradiction led to theologians like John Mbiti, as early as 1967, to turn to the African Indigenous Churches for insight and innovation:

> One of the reasons for these sects established and run by Africans is a search for freedom of expressing the Faith in a manner suitable to African conditions and background, which has not always been achieved in denominations under the control of missionaries from Europe and America.[1]

Although Mbiti's paper was based upon Harold Turner's investigation of the sermons preached by Aladura rather than his own field research, he did recognize that AICs were an invaluable source for understanding Christology in Africa.

The AIC contribution to the Christological quest in Africa has been overshadowed by the pneumatological over-emphasis given by researchers as well as the *messianic* tendencies exhibited by a small minority of AICs, particularly in southern Africa.[2] Earlier notable studies of AICs in Ghana tended to take a collective approach in examining the history and theology of different AICs or of one particular AIC in Ghana.[3] This was

---

1. Mbiti, "Some African Concepts," 51.

2. Daneel maintained that two grave dangers that beset AICs are the enormous emphasis on the works of the Holy Spirit in the prophetic group, which could result in an impoverished Christology and the tendency to underrate the cross or to see it as a stumbling block. See Daneel, *Quest for Belonging*, 258.

3. See for example Wyllie, *Spiritism in Ghana*; Baëta, *Prophetism in Ghana*; Beckmann,

necessary due to the relative ignorance of researchers on the AICs as a movement at the time of these researches. This research will break from this trend, however, and focus on reflecting a grassroots Christological perspective that is present within Akan AICs in Ghana.

The Akan contextual Christologies put forward by Bediako, Pobee, and Akrong discussed in chapter 2 have for the most part critiqued the western Christologies that have been introduced to the missionary movement in Africa. An important question to be asked is to what extent are these Christological propositions a true reflection of the people at the grassroots of the Church's life and community? Or, to put it in another way, to what extent are these Christologies the reflections of "professional theologians," or to what extent are these reflections indicative of a "local theology"[4] arising out of the faith of the local community? I concur with Robert Schreiter in maintaining that theology is intended for a community and is not meant to remain the property of a theologian class.[5] It was this concern that led me to support my ethnographical research with a nation-wide survey questionnaire of the Christological views of Akan AIC leaders and members, to whom we now turn. In the consideration of Akan AIC Christology the distinctive characteristics and common features that they share with each other as category will be highlighted.

SOURCE OF AKAN AIC CHRISTOLOGY

The Christian faith hinges upon faith in Jesus Christ; thus, the resources that we draw upon to construct our Christology are of crucial importance. This section explores the sources of Akan AIC Christology. The questions that were posed to the various individuals within the AICs in the questionnaire were designed to ascertain the primary influences responsible for shaping their Christology.

One of the questions put to respondents was *How do you best experience the presence of Christ? Tick the three which you find most important.* The number of responses and percentage break down are as follows:

Eden Revival; and Weaver and Weaver, *From Kuku Hill.*

4. I am using this term in the way defined by Schreiter, namely as the dynamic interaction among gospel, church, and culture. See Schreiter, *Constructing Local Theologies*, 16–17.

5. Ibid., 17.

Reading the Bible	1918 (77%)
Sermons Preached at Church	1440 (58%)
Prayer	824 (33%)
Visiting the Sick and Needy	604 (24.1%)
Participating in the Lord Supper	593 (24%)
Worshipping and Praising God in Church	1766 (71%)
Working for Justice in Society	304 (12.2%)
Other	44 (2%)

Reading the Bible

These figures clearly indicate that the Bible has been an important source for Akan AIC Christology.[6] The survey showed that 77% of respondents indicated that their own personal Bible reading was an important means of experiencing the presence of Jesus. The percentage of males is slightly higher: 51.2% compared with 48% of females, and there was no significant correlation between this source of Christology and a particular age range. There were also slight differences in the responses from MDCC (79%), the Church of Eli (65%), and the Church of the Lord Brotherhood (74%)—which are the older and more traditionally inclined AICs, and the more charismatically inclined AICs[7] such as the New Covenant Church (43%), Pentecostal Healing Church (52%) and the Living Church of God (50%). This seems to imply that the traditionally inclined AICs churches hold a higher view of the bible as a means of spiritual formation.

The Bible has been long established as a powerful symbol for AIC leaders as seen in the cases of the Prophet Harris and Appong. Both Harris and Appong use the Bible in their healing and preaching.[8] The figures, however, seem to indicate that the Bible has a devotional function for Akan AICs as well as a symbolic one. This concurs with Beckmann's research of Eden Revival that shows the Bible was seen as the ultimate

---

6. This point is endorsed by Anderson, who argued that the Bible is the measuring rod by which most AIC theology is conceived and continuously modified, and for this reason churches bear witness to Christ. See *African Reformation*, 232.

7. The phrase "Traditionally inclined" is used to describe AICs that liberally draw upon Akan culture, and "charismatically inclined" are those churches that draw more upon charismatic churches.

8. Haliburton, *Prophet Harris*, 74; see also Hastings, *Church in Africa*, 533.

authority and the source for moral guidance.[9] Christian Baëta, in his research of the MDCC, also draws attention to the fact that the two testaments of the Bible were regarded as having equal authority by the church. Additionally, it was reported, he maintains, that the founder of the church, Joseph William Egyanka Appiah,[10] repeatedly declared that God had said to him, "Why do some believe in the New but not the Old Testament? I am the same God who speaks in the Old Testament as in the New."[11]

Although the emphasis on the equality of the Old and the New Testaments could have been a justification for the incorporation of Old Testament tradition,[12] it does however indicate that the Bible is normative for the founder of the MDCC. The Bible, then, stands out as the principal source of Christology for the Akan AICs, much as it is for many of the other AICs in Ghana and elsewhere. This underlines the massive importance of the text of the Bible in contemporary African Christianity.

Worshipping and Praising God in Church

According to Kenneth Ross, singing and worshipping God is one of the central expressions of the Christian faith in Africa.[13] *Worshiping and Praising God in Church* was the next popular option. The survey showed that 1766 (71%) of respondents maintained that they experience the presence of Christ through worshipping and praising God in Church. During my visits to MDCC in Accra New Town and the Ossa-Madih Church in Chappes Conga, Winnaba, it was very evident that during the singing, dancing, and worshipping, the adherents became overwhelmed with the presence of Christ, spoke in tongues and prophesied. Often while the believers were "slain in the Spirit," they uttered "Jesus! Jesus! Jesus! Hallelujah! Thank you Jesus!" This appeared to be an indication that something more than just experiencing the outpouring of the Holy Spirit

9. Beckmann, *Eden Revival,* 59–60. Daneel in his research on Shona AICs also noted that scripture is focal and is accepted as the final authority. See Daneel, *Quest for Belonging,* 250; West, *Bishops and Prophets,* 174; Jules-Rosette, *African Apostles,* 89; Anderson, *African Reformation,* 32.

10. Also known as Jemisemiham Jehu-Appiah, *Akaboha I.*

11. Baëta, *Prophetism in Ghana,* 43.

12 An issue that frequently emerges from sermons is the distinction between the Old and the New Testament. The Old Testament is sometimes used to sanction legalism and polygamy; see Daneel, *Quest for Belonging,* 252.

13. Ross, "Current Christological Trends," 163.

was taking place. In addition, an intimate engagement with the person of Christ was occurring.

During a meeting with some members of the MDCC in Accra New Town, I asked what they liked most of all about coming to church—worshipping Christ was a clear choice for the vast majority of the group. On pressing them further by asking what it was about worship that they liked, Mother Beatrice, a senior member of the church and renowned healer, stated in Fanti:

> When I come to church and worship I forget that I don"t have money. I find release and strength to overcome all my problems and struggles. I just take them all to Jesus and I feel happy and I can dance and sing because He gives me strength to overcome my problems.[14]

With emphasis usually placed just on the Holy Spirit, the Christological dimension of worshiping and praising God in church is very often overlooked by researchers of AICs. Among Akan AICs, however, worshipping and praising God in corporate ecclesia is a means of drawing closer to Christ mediated through the power of the Holy Spirit. Jesus is clearly the object of worship. Through songs and prayers, worshippers are able to pour out all of their sorrows and wants before Christ, who is very close to them during the act of worship. Through the exuberant singing, clapping of the hands, drumming and dancing, they are elevated beyond their often debilitated lives of struggle and poverty.

Sermons Preached in Church

Experiencing Christ through the Sermons Preached in Church was another category that received a high percentage response. Of the 2500 respondents, 1440 (57.8%) maintained that listening to sermons preached in church was a means of experiencing Christ. These figures were marginally higher among churches that were located in the rural areas compared to those churches situated in city locations. Some examples of city based churches are Victory Voice of Christ (50%), Christian Hope Ministries (43%), and Christ Mission Church (53%); examples of rural based churches are Church of Eli (76%) and the Grace Universal Mission Church (68%). Christ's position in preaching is probably one of the su-

14. Recorded group discussion Sunday, July 4, 1999.

preme criteria when evaluating the Christian nature and uncorrupted character of the proclamation of the word of God.[15]

There is a relationship between this option and the "reading the Bible" option, which is possibly due to the sermons within the Akan AICs being very biblically based.[16] During my visits to Akan AICs throughout the different regions, I observed that the homiletical preference was expository preaching.[17] Sermons were usually concrete and narrative based as opposed to being abstract and philosophical. The sermons were also very rich in metaphor and moral instruction. Each metaphor suggests a specific form of conduct for members.[18] The dialogical nature of the sermon allows a high degree of interaction between the preached word and the congregation. It is through this process of dialogue between the preached word of God or the sermon and the response of the congregation that the written word becomes the living word.

It is therefore through the congregational response to the sermon that the presence of Christ is encountered and experienced. The dialogical nature of preaching is also further evidenced by the "spontaneous interruptions" of songs that result in what Jules-Rosette calls "intensification and acceleration of the message."[19] Although not prescheduled, the songs pick up and elaborate the theme of the sermon. The interjection of songs serves a number of functions. Firstly, it fills the gaps and pauses,[20] thus reinforcing the oral nature of Akan AICs spirituality, which is expressed in a continual flow of sound. Secondly, it reinforces the "call and response motif," which is a very important tradition for the Akans.[21] Thirdly, it informs the preacher that his/her message is being heard and understood;

15. Daneel, *Quest for Belonging*, 250.

16. Rosette maintained that the sermons are brief and based upon Apostolic doctrine, which gives guidance for moral behavior. See *African Apostles*, 105.

17. During the sermon a reader would often read the text and the preacher would comment on each verse. See also Jules-Rosette, *African Apostles* 105.

18. During my visits to different AICs, I observed that preaching was motivated toward good moral and upright behavior.

19. Rosette, *African Apostles,* 106.

20. Ibid., 106.

21. This "call and response motif" is evident in traditional libation prayers and also in traditional Akan songs and choruses.

and fourthly, it allows members to contribute to and be a part of the message that is being preached.[22]

Prayer

Prayer was the next highest option with 824 (33%) of respondents, indicating that it was a means of experiencing the presence of Christ. Prayers with family and friends—which invariably include Bible reading as a central feature—normally take place during "out-dooring" ceremonies,[23] prayer meetings, thanksgiving,[24] wake keepings,[25] weddings and engagements ceremonies. Praying with family and friends also reinforces the community ethos for which African societies are well known.

Visiting the Sick and Needy

Visiting the Sick and Needy and *Participating in the Lord's Supper* both received 24%. The option *Visiting the Sick and Needy* was designed to ascertain the degree to which altruism formed part of their spiritual enrichment in Christ. The relatively low percentage given to this option may reflect the fact that, for the Akan AICs, "drawing closer" to Christ is associated with spiritual practices such as praying, worshipping, and reading the Bible. Visiting the sick and needy is not a luxury for spiritual piety but a part of everyday life, which is one often fraught with need and plagued with sickness. Within an Akan traditional context, sickness and need are often understood as having a deeper causal factor, one usually associated with the deities and other spiritual entities.[26]

For the Akan AICs, sickness is also viewed as having a deeper meaning (either of curses or spiritual retribution) for something that the person has done and must seek to put right.[27] The focus therefore is not usually on *what* has happened—which would no doubt trigger feelings of

22. I will explore this issue further in chapter 8.

23. This is done on the eighth day of the birth of a child, during which family and friends gather and special prayers are said for the child who is also officially named; prayers are also said among family and friends when members are ill.

24. This is when a member of the family has something to be particularly thankful about, such as healing after a long-term sickness.

25. This is the gathering of family and friends and well-wishers after the death of a loved one during the days before the actual funeral.

26. See Gyekye, *An Essay*, 77.

27. Ibid., 78.

compassion and empathy, which in turn could be understood as spiritual piety—but rather *why* it happened. Hence, one's visit to the home of a sick person is often embroiled with solving conflicts and bringing reconciliation. Though prayers will be said before departure, the emphasis will be upon restoring the imbalance that has led to the sickness. When a church leader or a healer visits a sick person, there is emphasis on confession and repentance, followed by prayers for healing.

Working for Justice in Society

Closely related to visiting the sick and needy is the option of *Working for Justice in Society*, which was the least selected option with 304 (12%). This, however, is not indicative of the lack of interest that Akan AICs have in socio-political affairs or social action projects, which is demonstrated by the phenomenal contribution of churches like Kristo Asafo.[28] The neat compartmentalisation of personal spiritual piety and social action is not easily demarcated here, because the world is not understood in strictly socio-economic and scientific terms. Whatever takes place in the natural world is indicative of a deeper spiritual reality. Working for justice purely as a human endeavour is therefore of no lasting benefit because it is a means of dealing with the symptoms and not the cause.

The issue that face AICs is one of empowerment and not lack of interest or concern. The establishment of the ecumenical AIC movement "Organisation of African Instituted Churches" (OAIC) is a good example of the willingness of AICs to take socio-economical issues seriously. Through this ecumenical organisation AICs feel they are increasingly empowered and encouraged to deal with educational and economical development issues.

For instance, during my many visits to *Muzano* it was evident that all farming and irrigation activities were surrounded and supported by Christian ritual. Schools and industrial activities were also drawn into the daily Bible reading and prayer sessions of the holy cities. The Akan AICs" social liberation programmes are therefore often integral to their healing ministries, which make any assessment of their contribution in this area a complicated affair. The issue of social action within the Akan AICs is

---

28. Kristo Asafo is an Akan AIC church which has projects for homeless people, providing housing and employment. They also contribute thousands of pounds every year to government projects directed towards helping those who are poor and marginalized.

clearly an area which warrants further investigation; what seems clear, however, is that the notion that Akan AICs are too "spiritually minded to be of any earthly good" is a simplistic and inaccurate assumption.

Holy Communion

The last option within this category was *Participating in the Lord's Supper*, which was selected by 593 (24.0%) of respondents. Although the figures for the Lord's Supper as a means of "experiencing the presence of Christ" may appear to be very low in comparison to the rest—particularly in the light of the question addressed, namely *how best do you experience the presence of Christ?*—a number of factors that came to light during the focus group discussion must be taken into account. Communion within the Akan AICs is conducted less frequently than in the other mainline churches. For many of the Akan AICs, communion is a very special and sacred celebration to be preserved for special occasions.[29]

There is also a sense of ambivalence, and in some cases even trepidation, that accompanies the celebration of this sacrament for many Akan AICs. The idea of being cursed if one takes it unworthily is a strong deterrent in itself, but is compounded by the language of blood sacrifice, which has a deep significance for Akans. However, even with the infrequent nature of the celebration of Communion, still one quarter of the respondents selected this practice as one that brings them closer to Christ. A number of the pastors maintained that they officially had it once or twice a month; yet, when pressed on the actual times in the last two years, it was usually two or three times a year.

Among Akan AICs preparation for Communion is of vital importance. This begins with fasting and prayers with a lot of emphasis placed on confession. In the weeks prior to Communion, sermons are focused upon moral purity and ritual cleansing.[30] The fear that many of the Akan AIC adherents have regarding "being cursed" if the Holy Communion is taken unworthily is a very real one and a major deterrent for the regularity of this sacrament.

---

29. Daneel suggests that confining communion to special occasions when the principal leader is present accentuates the rare, exclusive, even mystical significance of the sacrament. See Daneel, *Quest For Belonging*, 227.

30. Myles, *Reflections*, 6.

The sacrament of Holy Communion does form part and parcel of Akan AICs church practice and its adherents take the teaching behind it seriously. It might even be said that the seriousness with which this practice is taken is, ironically, the very reason why it is not practiced as much as perhaps their leaders would like, or even with the regularity of the other church traditions in Ghana. Stressing the importance of this sacrament without driving adherents away from the "Lord's table" because of fear of being cursed is another challenge that faces Akan AIC leaders in appropriating the gospel within their traditional context.

Baptism

The sacrament of Baptism was not included in the questionnaire but it was incorporated into our focus discussions on Communion. The entire group acknowledged that baptism was an integral part of their teaching and practice. As with the Communion, there is great emphasis upon cleansing and purity. In Akan tradition, water is a very powerful symbol; there is a strong tradition of water-deities or spirits, which could even possess candidates while they are in the water.[31] This concern is very evident in the Akan AICs" approach to the sacrament of water baptism.[32] Before the actual baptism takes place prayers are offered in order to cleanse the water lest the baptismal candidate be exposed to malevolent spirits. For Akan AICs baptism is a means of initiating the new believer into the kingdom of God.[33] Anderson comments that "[i]n baptism, believers die to the old life, and are washed from their sins because of the sacrificial death of Christ. They rise from their burial under water in newness of life, as Christ too was resurrected from the tomb."[34]

The widespread use of water rituals in Akan and other African religions for spiritual purification,[35] and the Christian interpretation of baptism as an effective symbol of cleansing from sin, provide a strong

31. Turner suggests that this idea of "water-deities" accounts for the reduced emphasis on the Holy Spirit during the baptism ceremony.

32. All major bodies of water are given names of the Sons of Nyame—the Supreme Being—and are understood as having spiritual powers. For a detailed discussion on this issue, see Rattray, *Ashanti*, 145–46.

33. Botchway, "OSSA-Madih Church," 11.

34. Anderson, *African Reformation*, 231.

35. See Rattray, *Ashanti*, 146; Turner, *History of an African*, 195; Sundkler, *Bantu Prophets*, 201–11.

contextual link for Akan AICs. I was privileged to attend a number of Akan AICs baptismal services, which provided very informative insight for this research. It was particularly striking to me the degree to which the water itself was a focus of much attention. To begin with, as I have mentioned, much prayer is offered to purify and exorcise spirits from the water.

SOURCES DRAWN FROM AKAN RELIGION

The categories just discussed were designed to assess the degree to which Akan AICs draw upon their church and community experience in shaping their Christology. In order to attain the degree to which more traditional practices contributed to their Christological apprehension, they were asked: *Do members of your church practice any of the following?* Below are the responses:

Sacrifice	102 (4.0%)
Reverence to Ancestors	10 (0.4%)
Offering prayers to dead leaders	155 (6.2%)
Visiting the Juju Priest	2 (0.1)
Pour Libation	3 (0.1%)

Sacrifice

Of the 2500 respondents surveyed, 102 (4.0%) indicated that their members offered sacrifice. Of the 102 responses, 62 came from respondents who were members of MDCC; 18 from members of the Gate of Heaven Church; 20 from Healing Hand of God Church; 1 from Christ Redemption Church, and 1 from Saviour's Church of Ghana. The single individual affirmative respondents from Christ Redemption Church and the Saviour's Church of Ghana were at odds with the rest of the members who answered "no" to this question. This may indicate that the question was misunderstood or respondents answered "yes" by mistake, or indeed that they intended to answer as they did; either way the figures were too small a variable to be significant. Of the other three churches, Christ Redemption Church, MDCC, and the Saviour's Church of Ghana, the MDCC had the most developed and articulated view on animal sacrifice, and in some cases are notoriously known for this practice.

The issue of animal sacrifice is seen as being very controversial for many churches, even among those who are Akan AICs. There are two main areas of controversy: firstly, sacrifices are strongly identified with Akan traditional religion and practice and, secondly, it appears to represent a blatant acknowledgement that the death of Christ is not entirely efficacious.

The controversial nature of this practice by MDCC led them to address this matter in some detail in one of their booklets:

> The issue of animal sacrifice and offerings in Christian worship has become a subject of misunderstanding among many Christians. They say because Jesus has died animal sacrifices are no longer necessary, quoting Heb 10:1–6. But such persons are not putting bible in perspective. They put all the sacrifices of the Old Testament together as if they were all for the same purpose. But sacrifices never began in the Old Testament to save men from their sins. Otherwise Adam and Eve and later Cain would have performed it and returned to the Garden of Eden. Some important Old Testament sacrifices and offerings include that of Cain and Abel (Gen 4:4, 5; Heb 11:4; [see also] Noah [in] Gen 8:20–22; [and] Abraham [in Gen] 22:12), when one studies these sacrifices carefully, one notices that no reference is made in these to sacrifice for sin. They were gifts in thanks to God; this is different from sacrifice for the atonement of sin. They were gifts in thanks to God and this is different from sacrifice.[36]

During one focus group discussion on this issue, the rest of the group were unanimous in their condemnation of this practice. The argument posited by the MDCC that the nature of the sacrifice was not toward forgiveness of sin but thanksgiving was also not accepted. The consensus of the group was that all sacrifices in the Old Testament had been perfected in Christ; thanksgiving offerings are also now replaced with prayers and not literal sacrifices. The firm stance for what could be described as a more orthodox interpretation of animal sacrifice by the rest of the focus group, along with the relatively small number (4.0%) that practice animal sacrifice, suggests that the practice is a marginal one within Akan AICs.

---

36. Musama Evangelical Committee, *Some Common Elements*, 36.

Offering Prayers to Dead Leaders

The other significant option chosen by respondents in this category was *Offering Prayers to Supreme Leaders who Have Died*, asking them to intercede to God on their behalf. Of the 2500 respondents surveyed, 155 (6.2%) maintained that this was practiced in their churches. Of that number, 50 (32%) were from MDCC; 44 (28%) from Church of the Lord Brotherhood; 44 (28%) from Bible Life Evangelical Church, and 17 (12%) from Christ Redemption Church. Based upon these figures it would appear that this practice is a marginal one. The practice of "praying to a supreme leader to intercede on one's behalf," however, strikes at the heart of any AIC claim to being a "Christian Church," and therefore any such assumption must not be taken lightly.

During focus group discussions the idea of *Okyeame* as a paradigm for the Akan leader was mentioned a number of times. It was clear that for some in the group this idea was new. However, it was a model that they felt reflected their position in relation to Christ and the people they are called to serve. It was said that just as the king's linguist had a position of authority among the people, he himself was aware that he was a servant of the king. The practice of using speech intermediaries in royal discourse may be a useful paradigm for understanding the mediatoral role of Akan AIC's leadership.

In most parts of Ghana the word *Okyeame* (Twi for linguist) connotes rhetorical competence *par excellence*.[37] The *Okyeame* is a social mediator of speech; their role is to speak on behalf of the chief or king. The element of acting on another's behalf is an integral part of the *Okyeame's* meta-communicative duties. Within an Akan context therefore it is the role of the mediator to introduce or bring someone into the presence of a superior being, which ostensibly means the mediator cannot be equated or granted equal status with the one he/she represents.

Other Options Selected

The other options in this category: reverence of ancestors, visiting the juju priest, pouring libation, were all selected by a very insignificant number of the respondents to draw any significant conclusion.

---

37. Yankah, *Speaking for the Chief*, 18.

CONCLUSION

The finding of the research is very revealing as it pertains to the foundation of Akan AIC Christology. Although there are many areas in which traditional idioms and culture have an important role, the Bible remain the main source in the formation of their Christology. The low response pertaining to the practice of "praying to supreme leaders" document that such practice is rarely carried out among Akan AICs. It is Christ who is at the center of their spirituality, albeit mediate through traditional idioms and culture.

5

The Function of Akan AIC Christology

IN THE PRECEDING SECTION we examined the source of Akan AIC Christology from the qualitative and quantitative data gathered from the Akan AICs in Ghana. From this initial assessment it appears that Akan traditional thought structure is actually more important than the translating of traditional religious practices into Christian ones. The Akan thought structure, which is expressed through orality, is evident in the importance they attach to preaching, worship, singing, and reading (hearing) Bible. The significance attached to symbolism—such as water and blood, and their priority of community expressed through the importance of activities in church and with family and friends—also demonstrates this. Practices that were overtly taken from traditional religion such as sacrifices, consulting dead leaders (in ways that ancestors are consulted), and pouring libation were by and large ignored as practices adopted into their Christian appropriation of Christ.

In this section the function of Akan AIC Christology will be considered on the basis of the qualitative and quantitative data gathered. The section is divided into three areas of discussion: namely, 1) predominant Christological titles, 2) predominant Christological benefits, and 3) predominant Christological prophylactic.

PREDOMINANT CHRISTOLOGICAL TITLES

The Christological titles presented to the respondents in the questionnaire were based upon the recording of titles used in relation to Christ during services visited in preparation for this survey. *Conqueror, Chief, Brother,* and *Ancestor* were titles seldom used during this period but were included because of their popularity among African theologians as a Christological model for appropriating Christ in an African context. By presenting these options to the adherents, it was hoped that the validity of such models would be tested. The 2500 respondents were asked, *which* three *of the following titles best describe Jesus to you?*

The answers were as follows:

Saviour	1867 (74.6%)
Messiah	1551 (62%)
Lord	1444 (57.7)
Healer	1382 (55.2%)
God	724 (28.9%)
Conqueror	334 (13.3%)
Chief	76 (3%)
Brother	61 (2.4%)
Ancestor	60 (2.4%)

Saviour

It is evident from these figures that by far the most commonly chosen categories are the biblical "umbrella" terms *Saviour* and *Messiah*, which demonstrates the powerful influence of the Bible in the lives of the Akan AICs. A total of 1867 (74.7%) respondents opted for the functional biblical category of Jesus as *Saviour*.[1] In traditional Akan life, the name or title *Saviour* is rarely used whether in connection with God or men, although God's acts of saving people from calamity, danger or death are commonly acknowledged.[2]

The term *Saviour* in Twi vernacular is often rendered *Osagyefo*, which literally means *one who saves the battle*, and was used as an honorific title for chiefs.[3] To become a Christian therefore is to commit oneself to the saving power of God and implicitly to Jesus Christ. Within an Akan traditional context, it is not enough for Christ to be the perfect manifestation of splendor or the focus of adoration and worship, but he must also be the one with the "power to save." As *Osagyefo*, Jesus is the one who

---

1. Sundkler, in his assessment of the title "Saviour" in the context of Bantu prophets in South Africa, maintained that the term "Saviour" in certain settings was not biblical but belonged more to the veneration of Isaiah Shembe. See *Bantu Prophets,* 197.

2. Mbiti, "Our Saviour," 399.

3. Ibid.

saves from the enemies of life, which include sickness, witchcraft, sorcery, magic, barrenness, failure, troublesome spirits, danger, misfortune, calamity, and death as far as the individual is concerned. As *Osagyefo* he saves from drought, war, oppression, foreign domination, slavery, locust invasion, epidemics, floods, and so on, as far as the wider community is concerned.

In an article that explores the meaning of "Jesus our Saviour" from an AIC perspective, Mbiti contended that, for "our Saviour" to be meaningful, he (whether God the Father or Jesus Christ) must be able to deliver from and keep away practical enemies of the life of the individual and the community. He states, "Unless the Christian faith comes to assist in this battle, it does not bring them the type of salvation they want and appreciate. That which attacks, destroys, bridles, and protects against these enemies of life, is clearly salvatory."[4]

Mbiti's notion that Jesus is our "Saviour" because He is almighty and not because of his redemptive atonement and resurrection as Christ was not borne out by the focus group's assessment. Within the focus group discussion on the major Christological titles, the views were very much in line with the survey findings, with functional biblical categories receiving strong support. Unlike Mbiti, however, Jesus as "our Saviour" was strongly associated with his death and resurrection and not just because he is almighty. The fundamental value of Christ as *Saviour (Osagyefo)* is that it helps Akan AIC Christians to reconceptualize the transforming power of Christ in familiar categories and symbols that they can trust and accept. In this way, when Christ is addressed with traditional salvation and empowering titles, he invokes feeling of security and well-being associated with the ancestors. When Akan AICs members address Jesus Christ as *Osagyefo*, they are reconceptualizing the salvation work of Christ in traditional roles that still have validation in Akan society. This is a type of validation that has been denied them through slavery and colonisation and one that they are once again discovering through Jesus Christ as *Osagyefo*.

Messiah

Messiah and *Lord* were the next Christological titles, selected by 1551 (62%) and 1444 (57.8%) respectively. According to Mbiti, "'Messiah' does

4. Ibid., 406.

not fit into the thought-forms of African peoples, and it has no real influence on their understanding of Jesus. This does not mean that the title is rejected but is simply dormant like a bud in winter."[5]

Although the term is unknown in the Akan religious context, Mbiti's suggestion that *Messiah* does not fit into African thought-forms does not take into account the dynamic nature of African religion. This research found that, although the concept of *Messiah* mediated through the Bible was a new one, it was readily adopted and adapted by Akan AICs.[6] The fact that over two thirds of the questionnaire sample opted for *Messiah* as the title that best describes Jesus to them is evidence of the resilience and dynamism of African thought-forms.

When it appeared that the category *Messiah* was one of the highly preferred options for describing who Jesus is among the Akan AICs, I explored further the meaning attached to it as well as how it was being used in the context of Akan AICs. This was explored in three main forums: 1) the focus group of AIC pastors; 2) during teaching sessions of my third year Missiology class, taught at the Good News Theological College and Seminary; and 3) within a Theological Education by Extension class of AIC pastors and leaders from different churches in Cape Coast.

The initial question posed to each of these groups was *what do we mean when we say "Jesus is the Messiah"*? The answers were very biblically based. All the above-mentioned groups posited ideas of Jesus as the Jewish Messiah, the anointed one of God, Jesus as the chosen one, and the Lamb of God. In an effort to probe further they were asked *what images do you have of Christ as Messiah?* With slight variations in terminology, all the forums consistently stated: *Paramount Chief* in the traditional sense as a warrior, *Saviour, Anointed One, Conqueror, Warrior, King,* and *Deliverer.* What seemed to be emerging from the ensuing discussions was that the term *Messiah* was used as an umbrella-term in which many of the more traditional images of Christ were located.

---

5. Mbiti argues that *Christ, Son of David,* and *Son of Man* also have no special relevance to traditional African concepts. See "African Concepts," 58.

6. The concept of a "Black Messiah" has, however, been associated with AICs in a South African context. This probably owes more to western theological projection onto the African religious landscape as opposed to indigenous appropriation. See Sundkler, *Bantu,* 278–94; Daneel, *Quest for Belonging,* 180–84; Anderson, *African Reformation,* 230–32; see also Martin, *The Biblical Concepts.*

On the whole, the predominant Christological categories are clearly the biblical ones, which, as I have shown, reinforce the idea that the Bible is normative in shaping Akan AICs Christology. Although the other categories—*chief*, for instance, which received 76 (3%) or *ancestor*, which receive 60 (2.4%)—are less likely to be selected as a Christological title (because they feature less prominently in scripture) their images and purpose are appropriated into the functional biblical category of *Messiah*. There seems to be considerable diversity and experimentation with the usage of *Messiah* as a Christological title among Akan AICs as opposed to it lying dormant, as Mbiti has suggested.

God (Onyame)

The two commonly used names for the *Supreme Being* in Akan are *Onyame* (the shining one) and *Onyankopɔn* (the only great one). It may appear rather peculiar that the term *God* was only opted for by 724 (29.0%) of the respondents, and yet this is the term most often on the lips of the Akan AICs when referring to the *Supreme Being*. One of the reasons for this is possibly the fact that Akan AICs think about the *Supreme Being* more in terms of "functionality" as opposed to ontology. On being asked to choose a category that best describes Jesus to them, what Jesus "does" (for instance, *saves* and *delivers*) is more important than who he is (his ontological make-up), though the two are inextricably linked. The preference for the categories *Messiah*, *Lord*, and *Saviour* over the category *God* could also be indicative of a biblical portrayal of Christ in a context in which the Bible has normative value in the formation of Christology.

Lord (Awurade)

The title *Lord*, which in an Akan AIC context speaks of the magnificence and splendour of Christ, was selected by 1444 (57.8%) of the respondents. *Lord*, (Awurade) in Twi, is a term used very often by Akan AICs to express adoration and worship to God and is therefore often used in a context of worship. *Awurade* also speaks of the authority and divinity of Christ. Kwame Bediako reflecting on the use of the term in an Akan context notes:

> The Lordship of Christ in relation to the natural "spirit-father" or ancestors finds its concrete focus in the way in which Christ's Lordship may be related to the significance of kingship in the

society. This close connection between the place and function of ancestors and the meaning of kingship, on the one hand, and Christology, on the other, is due to the fact that the reigning chief (or king) occupies the stool (or throne) of the ancestors.[7]

Although the Lordship of Christ finds parallels with the Akan understanding of kingship and royalty, as Bediako as suggested, one must not underestimate the more recent impact that biblical thought-forms have upon their understanding of Jesus as Lord. For Akan AICs the Lordship of Christ goes beyond the ancestral paradigm and the royal protocol of Akan religion to one that has universal significance and impact.

For the Akan AICs, worship is the ultimate response to the supreme sovereignty of Jesus as the Lord. For them worship involves the whole person: body, mind, and spirit and is expressed most powerfully in community; it is therefore very vibrant, expressive, and emotional. Akan AIC worship is divided into two sections: *praise* and *worship*. During the *praise*, worshippers dance and wave handkerchiefs to God to a very up-tempo drum beat played upon a traditional drum (*atupan*). The *worship*, distinct from *praise*, is much slower and more expressive; often adherents fall prostrate on the floor, eyes red with tears; others fall to their knees with hands raised and voice effusive with song. *Awurade* is the preferred expression used for *Onyame* within Twi worship songs such as: "He has risen from the dead and he is Lord, he is Lord/ Every Knee shall bow and every tongue confess/ That Jesus Christ, He is Lord, He is Lord."[8]

Although Akan AICs prefer to describe who God is through functional terminology, this however by no means detracts in any way from the awe and splendour that is attached to God. One of the ways this reverence and "dread" is expressed is through the use of appellations or honorifics of respect and endearment reserved for kings or chiefs. They include such terms as *Nana* (Elder or Chief), *Otumfo* (the All-powerful), *Osagyefo* (Saviour), and *Odeefoo* or *Daasebre* (The Magnanimous One), to name just a few.[9]

7. Bediako, "Biblical Christologies," 149–50.

8. Author unknown.

9. See Kuma, *Jesus of the Deep Forest*, 47–48, for an extensive range of appellations and honorifics.

Healer

Christ as *Healer* was opted for by 1382 (55.3%) of respondents. It is the fourth most popular category after *Saviour, Messiah,* and *Lord,* which are all biblical titles. There was some variation to the *Christ as Healer* option between churches which were "traditionally inclined" and rurally based, and churches which were "charismatically inclined" and situated in the major cities. Gethsemane Grace Healing Church and the Lamp of God Mission which are both "traditionally inclined" rurally based churches which opted for "Christ as healer" 79% and 84% respectively and Latter Days Church (49%) and Jesus Never Fails Church (59%) which are "charismatically inclined" city based churches is are examples of this disparity.

The *Healer* option is very significant because it is the only "non-biblical umbrella category" that has received such a high response rate. Christ as healer and the priority of healing in an Akan context is therefore a window into the African's constant quest and struggle for life. For the Akan, the aspiration to life is so primary that the persons called to administer healing hold a place of eminence.[10] In a context in which sickness, poverty, and death are ubiquitous, Africans are obsessed with healing and wholeness. Their quest for healing and wholeness is personified in Jesus Christ who is healer *par excellence.* Salvation is therefore essentially freedom from sickness and affliction of all kinds and the agents that bear them. Allan Anderson puts it well: "They proclaim and celebrate a salvation (or healing) that encompasses all of life's experiences and afflictions. They offer power to provide a sense of dignity and coping mechanism for life."[11] In many ways the Akan AIC healer replaces the traditional Akan healer. The traditional Akan healer has a many-sided role, combining functions that in our modern societies are fulfilled by specialists of very different kinds.

Michael Gelfand, a physician and one who has conducted extensive research into the role and function of the *Nganga* (as they are known in Zimbabwe and elsewhere), describes them as the kingpins of African communities whose scope of activity embraces more or less everything affecting an individual or his/her family. He states:

> European society has no one quite like the *nganga,* an individual to whom people can turn in every kind of difficulty. He is a doctor

10. Kolié, "Jesus as Healer," 132; see also Cox, *Fire From Heaven,* 254–56.

11. Anderson, *African Reformation,* 250.

in sickness, a priest in religious matters, a lawyer in legal issues, a policeman in the detection and prevention of crime, a possessor of magical preparations that can increase crops and instil special skills and talent into his clients. He fills a great need in society; his presence gives assurance to the whole community.[12]

The traditional healer has largely supplied the primary paradigm for an indigenous African Christology, which has been championed by the *Sunsum Osore* or the "Spiritual Churches." Although AICs are not unique in their usage of this Christological paradigm, they have placed the paradigm of Christ as *healer* more centrally than any other church or movement in Africa.

Daneel, in his research of the prophet-healing movement in Zimbabwe, maintains that the prophet-healers see their faith-healing activities as a replacement for and in opposition to the traditional *nganga* practices. He writes,

> As can be seen in the Shona prophetic healer movements, the prophetic healers see their faith-healing activities as a replacement of the traditional *nganga* practices. Nevertheless, their diagnostic and therapeutic work—the focal point of these churches and certainly the most effective recruitment technique—are based largely on the insight and practices of the nganga.[13]

Daneel outlines some of the most obvious similarities as what he calls the *diagnosis* of the factors contributing towards the state of the afflicted. In other words, both the healing prophet and the traditional healer ascribe the causation of disease, misfortune or lack of success, to the spirits (ancestral, vengeful or alien spirits), evil powers, or wizardry. The prophet-healer, however, attributes the source of his powers to the Holy Spirit and not to his benevolent ancestor or with any other means.

Furthermore, unlike the traditional healer, he does not seek to comply or appease the spirit/s, but instead, aims at the introduction of the Christian message of liberation into the deeply rooted conceptual world of the African believer. It is at this existential level—where the prophetic healer seriously considers both the believer's fear of the afflicting spirit and the need for protection—that the confrontation between Christ's "good news" and the traditional worldview takes place. In this direct con-

12. Gelfand, *Witchdoctor*, 47.
13. Daneel, "Communication and Liberation," 77.

frontation, ancestral demands and the symbolic enactment of the reign of Christ in faith-healing procedures are of central significance.

The view often postulated that the AIC prophet-healers have compensated for or filled the vacuum left by the diviner seem very likely.[14] This argument, however, as Anderson has warned, must not be overstated;[15] AICs are an appropriation of the Christian message into an African context and not just a reaction to traditional religious practices. The area in which the Christology of Akan AICs has been very effective is in the prophylactic function that the benevolent ancestor once fulfilled. Christ the healer, whose liberating power is at work through the Holy Spirit, has now superseded this.

The Akan AIC healing practice provides a release of tension through a cathartic ritual and beliefs that heighten the hope of each member. Thus the healing ceremonies of these churches involve a union of patient, his family, the larger group, and the supernatural world, by means of a dramatic, emotionally charged, aesthetically rich ceremony that expresses and reinforces shared beliefs. In addition, the spiritual leaders, or prophet, offer healing and spiritual and supernatural protection to members. They therefore attract converts with such diverse needs as illness, money, education problems, or being bewitched, much as traditional Akan healers do.

Conqueror

The category *conqueror* was a significantly preferred option than the last three options with 13.3%. This ties into the notion that Jesus is seen above all else as *Christus Victor* (Christ supreme over every spiritual ruler and authority).[16] This perception arises from Africans" keen awareness of forces and powers at work in the world that threaten the interest of life and harmony. Jesus is victorious over the spiritual realm, particularly over evil forces, and so meets the need for a powerful protector.[17] The category *conqueror* is also tied into the theme of liberation.[18] The theme

14. Oosthuizen, *Healer*, 33–34.

15. Anderson, *African Reformation*, 235.

16. "Christus Victor" plays a crucial role in the theologies of Milingo, *The World in Between*; see also Mbiti, "Some Concepts of Christology," 54.

17. Bediako, *Jesus in Africa*, 22.

18. For a detailed study of Christ as liberator, see Magesa, "Christ the Liberator," 151–62; also Maimela, "Jesus Christ," 22–31.

of liberation within the Akan AICs is not a socio-political one but rather spiritual, which will ultimately have social-political implications because of the belief in multi-dimensional continuity.

The method for dealing with social ills within Akan AICs is not through social action and protests; such action would locate the heart of the problem in the human realm instead of the realm of spirits. Among Akan AICs, problems are solved through prayer and fasting; once the problem is dealt with spiritually it is just a matter of time before the situation comes good on a human level. The portrait of Jesus as the *Christus Victor*, and in his works of healing, exorcising the possessed, and delivering the captive goes beyond the title *conqueror* but is rather a generic motif that permeates throughout the Akan AIC's perception of who Jesus is. As Lord, Saviour, God, Messiah, or Healer the *conqueror* motif is present within these depictions of Christ.

Chief

Out of the 2500 individuals who were asked which titles best describe Jesus, only 76 (3%) answered *Chief*.[19] The concept of *Chief* can be seen in a similar respect to that of the concept of *conqueror* in that both advance a *Christus Victor* Christological approach. In an Akan context the concept of *Chief* is very powerful and laden with traditional religious meaning and mystique. From a Christian perspective it represents a religious order of African religion out of which believers have come and to some extent a religion of an older unenlightened era. The conflicts that sometime erupt between the church and the traditionalist further exacerbate this polarization of the two faiths.[20] It is difficult to ascertain whether these low figures regarding Jesus being understood as *Chief* is a refusal to use *Chief* per se as a Christological title, or more a case of neglecting the concept of *Chief* because of its associations and connotations with that of Akan religion.

Within the prayers of Akan AICs Jesus is portrayed as the great warrior of the human family who dies to rescue human beings from the

19. For a detailed discussion of the concept of "Christ as Chief," see Kabasélé, "Christ as Chief," 103–13; see also Akrong, "Christology from an African," 119–29; Pobee, *Toward an African*, 81–98.

20. An example of this conflict is the ban on drumming during the month of May by the "Ga" traditional Council. They maintain that noise of this nature disturbs the gods during their season of land fertilisation. This has led to great physical conflict between churches and the traditional supporters.

bondage of evil forces. His decisive defeat of the forces of evil qualifies AICs to put his title in the semantic domain of the warrior-ancestor who is personified in the Chief in his capacity as the defender of his people.

Abraham Akrong, a Ghanaian theologian and a strong promulgator of the analogy of "Christ as Parent-ancestor," articulates this well:

> Jesus is the head or chief of this new community. This qualifies him to be the paramount chief of all the families of God because he is the Son of God and heir to the throne of God. Jesus Christ becomes the link between human beings and God by virtue of his position as the chief of all the families of God. In this capacity he is the pre-eminent agent of God's salvation and the mediator par excellence of God's power of salvation. As the reigning chief of all families of God it is his duty to bring justice, peace and harmony among all the people of God (humanity) and create the spiritual and existential conditions for the fulfilment of our lives as ordained by God.[21]

Although Akrong's Parent-ancestor Christology (discussed in chapter 2) presents a neat theoretical and theological Akan Christological model, it fails to account for the tensions that often exists between Christianity and Akan religion and the impact that this has upon self definition and distinctiveness.

The *Chief* analogy, as with the *Conqueror* analogy, is also considered misleading because it is a *theologia gloriae* lacking a *theologia crucis*.[22] In other words, the *Chief* analogy denotes authority and power derived from other ways than suffering. It appears from the survey questionnaire and discussion within the focus group that the associations and connotations of traditional analogy are actually stumbling blocks to Akan AICs" overt use of them. This refusal to use traditional terminology, however, is not necessarily a rejection of the ideas and images behind the concepts. This was not only evident in the use of *Chief* as a preferred Christological category but also in the use of the concept *ancestor*, to which we now turn.[23]

---

21. Akrong, "Christology from an African," 123.

22. Pobee discusses the "Chief analogy" in the light of its *theologia gloriae* and *theologia crucis*. See *Toward an African*, 97–8; see also Waliggo, "African Christology," 93–109, in which he examines what image of Christ the suffering people of Africa have and what should be the ideal and most relevant image of Christ to the contemporary suffering people of Africa.

23. I discuss ancestral Christology in some detail in ch. 2.

Ancestor

Given the popularity of this concept as a Christological model for a West African context, the extent to which this analogy was ignored as a Christological title was surprising. The survey indicated that only 60 (2.4%) of Akan AICs opted for this as a title that best described Jesus to them. In an effort to distinguish whether the idea of *ancestor* as traditionally understood, or the term *ancestor* as demonized by western missionaries, was being rejected, it was decided to explore the term *ancestor* and its Akan equivalent *Nana*[24] (the Twi vernacular for *ancestor*) within the focus group.

From the discussions that took place it appeared that there was a different level of engagement with the word *Nana* than with its English equivalent *ancestor*. Even though the term *Nana* would be favored over the term *ancestor*, it appears that this is down to language familiarization and not theological appropriation. The term *Nana* in general usage is used of one who is an elder or chief and ultimately an ancestor. When the term is used of Christ, it is therefore subject to clarification and extension beyond its usual application unless it is being used loosely as one who has authority. This is most probably the way it is used by Akan AICs, whom I suspect would be unwilling to extend its usage beyond this basis. I would therefore question John Pobee's notion that Jesus be looked at as the Great and Greatest Ancestor-in Akan Twi *Nana*.[25] The centrality of the Bible within the context of Akan AICs would make it unlikely that such a traditional and non-biblical title be applied to Jesus.

What seems a more feasible approach would be to apply the nature of the ancestral relationship between the Akan and their ancestors to the relationship of Jesus as "Son of God" or "Servant of God," "King of kings," "Lord of lords," "Saviour" and other such terminology that can engage with both the Akan worldview as well as the Bible and indigenous African Christians. Put another way, it is not theological legitimation and proposition of African terminological usage of traditional concepts that gives validation, but scriptural affirmation, and therefore any terminology

---

24. In Akan society *Nana* is used of the illustrious ancestor as well as of the Supreme Being, called *Nana*. This may indicate that the ancestors live in the court of God and exercise some authority under God.

25. Pobee, *African Theology*, 94.

that will be employed by AICs must be one that can mediate between the biblical worldview and that of the African.

Elder Brother

The last option within this section is *Christ as Elder Brother*. The number that opted for *Elder Brother* as a title to describe Jesus was 61 (2.4%). African writers have variously described the concept of Christ as an *Elder Brother* as a Christological paradigm.[26] Within an Akan context the idea of *Elder Brother* is closely tied into the notion of Christ being "one of us," a member of the Akan family who has shared in our African experience in every respect, except our sin. Therefore, through his death and resurrection, Christ takes the place of our natural "spirit-father." Christ thus becomes for us the only mediator between God and ourselves, becoming not only our *Elder Brother* but also our ancestor.[27]

François Kabasélé reflects on these two images of Christ as both *ancestor* and *Elder Brother* and maintains that they function complementarily.[28] Within the context of Akan traditional religion, as in the context of the Akan AICs, the idea of the Elder Brother is also tied into the concept of *Nana*, and therefore takes on the complementary function posited by Kabasélé. Although the concept of *Elder Brother* is not an unusual one within the Akan context, it is far less a title that would be used to describe Christ when compared to the other options. In a universe teeming with spirits Christ must be presented as an imposing figure able to subdue the enemies of life, to which a title like *Elder Brother* does not easily lend itself.

One of the weaknesses in approaching the Christology of Akan AICs by studying Christological titles, is that quite often the meanings of the titles overlaps. In addition, Africans do not approach theology in the systematic way this approach does. As we have illustrated above, the Akan approach is one of functionality, which is seen in the preference for the titles that describe Jesus in functional terms.

---

26. See for example Akrong, "Christology from an African Perspective," 128–29; Bediako, *Jesus in Africa*, 26–27, and Kabasélé, "Christ as Ancestor," 116–26.

27. Bediako, *Jesus in Africa*, 26.

28. Kabasélé, "Christ as Chief," 121.

PREDOMINANT CHRISTOLOGICAL BENEFITS

In order to further derive the function that Jesus Christ is perceived to have in human life respondents were asked: *Of the following benefits promised by Jesus, which* one *do you find most important?* The results were:

Eternal life after death	1670 (67.0%)
Forgiveness of sins	452 (18%)
Daily fellowship with God	123 (5.0%)
Mending broken relationships (reconciliation)	79 (3.0%)
Defeat of evil forces	71 (2.8%)
Power to become a better person	40 (1.6%)
Power to transform society	24 (1.0%)
Healing of the body	27 (1.0%)

Eternal Life after Death

These figures clearly demonstrate that the primary benefits with which the respondents are concerned are the personal and spiritual matters of eternal life after death, forgiveness of sins, and fellowship with God. It is what Jesus offers at the personal rather than the social level that is clearly the most important for Akan AICs. The option *eternal life after death* was by far the most popular category selected (67%). Churches located in the Northern, Upper East, and Upper West regions showed a higher preference for this option than churches in the more southern regions such as Greater Accra and Central regions. The figures showed Northern, Upper East, and Upper west as 82%; 73%; and 97% respectively, and for Greater Accra and Central regions the figures indicated 71% and 54% respectively.

The Akan understanding of death and the afterlife provides valuable insight into why *eternal life after death* is deemed a very important benefit promised by Jesus. In Akan society death is inevitable. Akan sayings and proverbs underscore death's inescapable reality: *Obiara bɛ wu* (every man will die); *Onyimpa ba, obra tware wu* (for man that is born of a woman, life should end in death). There is another traditional saying: *Atwenetwem di nda; dee bɛba mmba da. Owuo bɛba nso wose odeba bɛba, a, ommba da* (the long awaited arrives late, what is most expected to happen is delayed). Death therefore, is the ultimate end and part of being human even though it may even be delayed.

In Akan thought, death is the natural and inevitable lot of every human being, yet it is dreaded. The Akan saying *Owu ye yaw* (it is painful to die) is an expression of this. Another example is *Owuo Kwaaku, abo-abusua-dom ntoro a osi nkete hye dom* (beware, beware, for death is alive, there he is, there he is, he who is a member of *Abusua* [clan] and belongs to *Ntoro* [lineage] and who delights in the wanton destruction of many).[29]

These proverbs and sayings echo the Akan belief about death; however, what actually happens to a person's spirit at death is an area of great uncertainty.[30] There is also uncertainty regarding the ontological make up of the departed[31] as well as their final destination.[32] The promise and assurance of *eternal life* offered by faith in Christ resonates very forcefully within the Akan person who is constantly seeking to appease the gods to ensure a safe passage from this world to the world of the spirit-ancestors. Akan traditional religion, which leaves a question mark over the destiny of the living that face the inevitability of death, is therefore a *preparatio evangelica* for the faith appropriated by the Akan AICs. The issue of death and the after-life is an important one in understanding Akan AIC Christology and one that we will be examining in more detail in our discussion of Eschatology in the context of Akan AIC's soteriology.

Forgiveness of Sin

A total of 452 (18.0%) respondents selected *forgiveness of sins* as the most important benefit offered by Jesus. Their selection of *eternal life* and *for-*

29. Antubam, *Ghana's Heritage*, 65.

30. The spirits are classified in three groups: 1) ɔsaman-pa, the good spirit, who behaved responsibly on earth and reached the full allocation of years therefore promoted to the realm of the spirit-ancestors; 2) ɔtɔfo, one killed in battle or through an accident—he is honoured because his end was not his own fault; then 3) ɔsaman-twɛntwɛn (a hovering about spirit) which remains on earth for a period of time, for reasons not quite clear.

31. Exactly what the ɔsaman (departed-spirit) is cannot be explained; it is not the ɔ kra, generally believed to return to *Onyankopɔn*, nor the person's *sunsum* (spirit) which passes through the male line to his children. The physical body is buried. Thus the spirit of the departed seems to be divested of the elements which made him or her a living being. See Williamson, *Akan Religion*, 92.

32. The world of the *asamanfo* (departed spirits) is not *Onyankopɔn's* place of abode, but a special place under the earth called the *asaman*. At death *Onyankopɔn* decides whether a person shall go directly to the place of the dead, or continue for a while to haunt his earthly habitation (probably because, as in the case of one who dies through an accident, "destiny" has not yet been fulfilled). See Rattray, *Proverb*, 36.

giveness of sins as the two most important benefits offered by Jesus is an indication of the impact and the normative function of the Bible within an Akan AIC context. The faith of the Akan AICs is a biblical one that places great emphasis upon trust in Christ for the forgiveness of sins and the gift of eternal life. This is further evident in the doctrinal statements of many of the Akan AICs. The statement put forward by the MDCC is an example of this:

> Every Christian is aware of the fall of man, which was the result of the sin of disobedience and pride. But we have the assurance that with the death of Jesus, if we feel sorry for our sins, and change our minds and do the right thing, we shall be considered as the true children of God.[33]

It has been argued that African culture is a shame culture and not a guilt culture.[34] Within our focus group this issue of *shame* and *guilt* in regards to sin was discussed. Members of the group saw the idea that private sins outside of the public arena would have no bearing on their Christian conscience as a false assertion. Much emphasis was laid upon the role of the Holy Spirit in convicting the heart of sin.

The abhorrence of disgrace and the safeguard of honour has been the cause of many quarrels, tribal wars of old, as well as suspicions, antagonisms, and rivalries.[35] "Disgrace is worse than death" is a famous saying in Ghana.[36] With such strength of feeling surrounding shame and public disgrace, it is perhaps understandable that one could conclude that the culture is one of shame and not of personal guilt. The issue of Africa comprising of a culture of "guilt or shame" may differ according to different countries and ethnic groups and is one in which this particular finding would not seek to be dogmatic of Africa's position generally. However the centrality of scripture among the Akan AICs, as has been demonstrated in this work, may have possibly served as a corrective in this regard.

---

33. Myles, *Musama Disco*, 25.

34. Taylor, *Primal Vision*, 174–76. See also Welbourn, "Some Problems," 182–94.

35. For a detailed and insightful discussion on the issue of shame within Akan culture, see Sarpong, *Ghana in Retrospect*, 65–66.

36. Ibid., 65.

The Function of Akan AIC Christology

Daily Fellowship with God

The next highest option was *Daily Fellowship with God*, with 123 (5.0%) choosing it. This again reflects Akans" preference for the personal and spiritual benefits offered by Jesus as opposed to social benefits. It also reveals another important aspect of African life: the need to have worship as a way of life. This is very evident within the Akan traditional culture and belief system. Rattray, in his research on the Ashanti, claims that almost every compound had its own *Nyame dua*, or altar to the Supreme God. These altars were in the shape of a forked branch cut from a certain tree.[37] The daily fellowship with God that was certainly an important feature of traditional Akan practice has been incorporated into the religious practice of Akan AICs. The MDCC, drawing unapologetically upon Akan traditional customs in the formation of their Christian tradition, emphasizes this need for constant fellowship with God in their liturgy.

In the little book entitled *Key devotional prayer rituals of Musama Disco Christo Church* they state:

> The Musama Disco Christo Church follows the Christian principle of praying on all occasions, and in the spirit, as enunciated in Ephesians 6:18. Thus the Musama Church, by the Grace of the Holy Spirit, has prepared special prayers with Rituals for the specific occasions in the everyday life of her members.[38]

These prayers and rituals include prayers for bathing and washing, prayers before receiving a stranger or visitor, prayers before meals, prayers before travelling in a vehicle, and prayers for slaughtering an animal. The prayer for bathing reads, "O lamb of God, who takes away the sins of the world, I beseech Thee, bathe every part of my body cleaning me of all stains of sin as Thou bathest Thy Twelve Apostles. Amen."[39] Prayer for travellers in a vehicle follows as such: "I bow before the Eternal Throne and cry unto the Lord God who is the Guide to all travellers to deliver me from any danger of accident as I travel in His name in this vehicle. O Mighty Father, steer this vehicle safely home for Thy Name sake (Lord's Prayer)."[40]

The *Daily Fellowship with God* option, then, gives us insight into the importance of the immanence of Christ for the spirituality of Akan AICs.

37. Rattray, *Ashanti*, 142.
38. Myles, *Key Devotional Prayers*, 1–2.
39. Ibid., 6.
40. Ibid., 11.

It also reflects the deeply religious personality of Akans AICs in particular and Africans generally. Mbiti is correct in his observation that religion permeates all departments of (African) life so fully that it is not easy or possible always to isolate it.[41] This is the reason why Akan Twi and many other African languages do not have a word for religion because religion is not just an ideological construct or a body of belief but daily responding to the Almighty through the various acts of worship and devotion or other activities. Having "daily fellowship with God" in community and not just as individual acts of personal religious piety is very important to Akan, demonstrated in Morning Prayer often convened as early as four or five o'clock every morning.

Other Options Selected

Of the rest of the options in this category *healing of the body* was surprisingly the second to least preferred option, selected by 27 (1.0%) respondents. It is perhaps more predictable that the *power to transform society* was the least preferred option, given that the promises of Christ are seen in more personal and spiritual terms than in social terms.

PREDOMINANT CHRISTOLOGICAL "PROPHYLACTIC"

In another approach to the issue of benefits promised by Christ, respondents were asked: *Of the following evils, which three do you think Jesus helps you to overcome the most?* Below are the results:

The Devil	1770 (70.8%)
Sickness	1408 (56.3%)
Evil spirits	1123 (45.0%)
Sexual immorality	728 (29.1%)
Fear and death	658 (26.3%)
Envy and hatred	593 (23.7%)
Pride	500 (20.%)
Injustice in society	375 (15%)
Witchcraft	344 (13.8%)

41. Mbiti, *African Religions*, 1.

The Devil and Evil Spirits

Among churches which were more "traditionally inclined" the figures were marginally higher. The MDCC for example, as a more traditional Akan AIC denomination showed: Devil (85%); Sickness (78%), and Evil spirits (59%). The Pentecostal Healing Church as a more charismatically inclined AIC denomination showed: Devil (69%), Sickness (67%), and Evil spirits (45%). The three main options selected by respondents (the Devil, sickness, evil spirits) are closely related and represent the greatest threat to life for Akan AICs. Laurenti Magesa calls them "the enemies of life" or "anti-life agents."[42]

It appears that the biblical understanding of evil in terms of the "Devil" is more popular than traditional categories such as witchcraft and evil spirits. Birgit Meyer, in her work *Translating the Devil*, maintains that African perspectives on the Devil were originally derived from missionaries attitudes. Her research (based upon the Ewe people in Ghana) is helpful here in depicting missionary attitudes to African religion, which they branded as *Abosamtɔwe*, "people belonging to the Devil."[43] Much of the missionary preaching was directed toward compelling Africans to turn away from the Devil (African religion) to Christ.[44] This notion of turning away from the Devil to Christ (and not from African witchcraft to Christ) has been adopted by Africans.[45]

The theme of the Devil, however, is not one that has attracted very much attention in the study of AICs or even in the study of African religion. According to Birgit Meyer an analysis of the meaning of the Devil-concept is missing in the study of African Christianity. This is, she maintains, in spite of the fact that this link has existed in European history for centuries.[46] In view of the prominence of the "Devil" discourse highlighted in this study, a thorough research is warranted.

---

42. Magesa, *African Religion*, 178.

43. Meyer, *Translating the Devil*, 83.

44. Ibid.

45. The Prophet Harris and many African prophets thereafter who admonished people to turn to Christ and away from witchcraft are exceptions. In associating the message of Christ to the African worldview they represented a new paradigm in evangelising Africans.

46. Meyer, "If You Are a Devil," 120.

Sickness

The next evil that respondents claimed "Jesus gave them power to overcome" was *sickness*; over half 1408 (56.3%) of the respondents selected this option. The Devil and evil spirits are perceived by Akan AICs as agents of affliction, and sickness is used as their weapon to afflict. Among Akan AICs (as with many African traditional religions) sickness is much more than a physical ailment; it has a much more deep-seated problem, namely the loss of power, which will ultimately lead to death. Sickness therefore drains the life force (known as the *kra* in Twi) from the individual. This is put well by Magesa:

> All illness, but particularly a serious one, means erosion of power, and a sick person is spoken of as "losing" or "gaining power as the illness progresses or recedes. Thus, a person might become so sick that he or she loses the "power" to sit, stand, or even cough or breathe. This power is not merely the energy to perform those human functions, but the decline of one's being itself.[47]

The threat that sickness poses to the life-force (ɔkra) of an individual, necessitates a Christology that reinforces and restores the force of life or "power."

The role of the prophet-healer is therefore pivotal because principally he or she is the channel through which the life force of Christ is mediated.[48] Mediating the life force of Christ, who is the ultimate Life-force as well as the source and giver of ɔkra to all human beings, is crucial. Akan AICs prophets and healers mediate the life force or ɔkra of *Onyame* in several ways, the principal being prayer. Prayer is a form of mediation because the healer or the prophet, by laying hands upon the sick person and interceding on their behalf to God, draws from the ultimate Life-force, which in turn revitalizes the life-force of the sick person thus bringing healing to the body. Healing therefore is not to "physically cure" someone *per se* but to revitalize his or her life-force to the proper equilibrium.

Another means of revitalising the life-force of a sick person is to have him or her make contact with symbols endowed with the life-force of God. It could be the healer, the Bible, holy water, something belonging to a person with a powerful ɔkra, (an item of clothing or a holy place or

47. Ibid., 178.

48. Anderson discusses the importance of the role of the prophets in *African Reformation*, 234.

location that has been the setting of great miracles).[49] Sick people therefore have Bibles placed upon their head,[50] are made to wash in or drink
holy, and wear items of clothing belonging to a spiritual person who is
considered to possess a powerful ɔkra. During the traditional naming ceremony of an eight-day-old child, the grandfather would often spit into the
mouth of the baby to strengthen his or her ɔkra or "life force." A child with
a strong ɔkra is less likely to be susceptible to sickness or misfortune.

Sickness among Akan AICs (as in AICs in other parts of Africa) is
related therefore to the holistic theology of salvation or soteriology. The
AICs holistic understanding of salvation has been well noted elsewhere;
however, I would further emphasize the Christological basis on which
this holistic soteriology is centred.[51] Much is said about the pneumatological basis of the power to overcome sickness; yet, it is Jesus Christ that
the Akan AICs put their faith in as the one who has conquered sickness
and affliction.

Witchcraft

The other category that is related to those above, namely, the Devil, evil
spirits and sickness, is *witchcraft*.[52] This category selected by 344 (13.8%)
respondents is relatively low, but may be explained by the popular notion
that to overcome the Devil assumes power to overcome witchcraft also.
Although there is evidence of blending of images of witches and the Devil
in studies about witchcraft in Africa,[53] very little link is made with the
Devil. In pondering this issue Birgit Meyer asserts,

> The main reason for this neglect of the blending of the Christian
> Devil and the African witch seems to be the relative separation
> of anthropological discourses on African Christianity on the one
> hand, and African witchcraft on the other. Whereas the latter is

49. Ibid., 236.

50. William Wade Harris during his ministry would pray for those who came to
hear him and then place the Bible on their heads; if they had an evil spirits it would be
exorcised.

51. Anderson, *African Reformation*, 233–38.

52. For a detailed discussion on witchcraft in Africa, see Evans- Pritchard, *Witchcraft,
Oracles and Magic*; Haule, *Witchcraft and Christian Morality*, 20–26; Daneel, *Background
and Rise*, 156–58; Onyinah, "Akan Witchcraft."

53. See Debrunner, *Witchcraft in Ghana*, 3.

concerned exclusively with non-Christian concepts of evil, the former does not at all concentrate on evil.[54]

Meyer advocates further studies about the African ideas about the Devil, which she maintains has not received the same level of attention as the African understanding of God. The centrality of God in Christian doctrine cannot be denied; however, in order to reveal the peculiarity of African Christianity, it is fruitful to concentrate on the dark side of the Christian religion.[55]

Among Akan AICs witchcraft is taken very seriously. It is seen as the "enemy of life," and as such imbued with power to even take life. Members found to be involved in any form of witchcraft are immediately expelled.[56] As the "enemy of life" and also the "instrument of the Devil,"[57] witchcraft is the antithesis of the zest for life that is central to religiosity of Akan AICs specifically and African religions generally.[58]

Sexual Immorality

Sexual Immorality figures highly as one of the evils faith in Jesus overcomes. Nearly a third, 728 (29.1%), respondents selected this option. Sexual offences[59] are taken very seriously among Akan (as with many other African ethnic groups).[60] Unlike the West where the impact of sexual conduct is predominantly confined to the private domain, sexual

54. Meyer, "If You are a Devil," 120–21.

55. Ibid., 121.

56. Baëta, *Prophetism*, 44.

57. The phrase "the instrument of the Devil" in reference to witchcraft was one frequently used by members in the focus group during a number of discussions on the issue and the AICs.

58. Tempels and Magesa both argue that African behavior is centered on the pursuit of power, or what they both call "life-force"; more power means greater control. This power is ultimately received from God and used for the benefit of the whole community. The other side of the argument is that witchcraft is the enemy of life because it seeks to violate the principles that maintain harmony within the African cosmology.

59. Fornication, incest, rape, seduction, homosexual relations, sleeping with a forbidden relative or domestic animal, intimacy between relatives, all constitute sexual offences among the Akans.

60. When adultery was discovered in traditional Akan society it was severely dealt with: the guilty person was whipped, stoned to death, made to pay compensation, beheaded, or dismembered. This severe manner of punishing adultery and other sexual offences has been modified or relaxed in modern times, but not altogether abandoned.

offences in Africa are of public concern because improper use of sex has implications for the wider community. Among Akan AICs the traditional taboos concerning sexual conduct are combined with the biblical mandate for sexual purity.[61] Sexual immorality is therefore considered an evil because it constitutes a violation of a taboo[62] as well as a sin against God. The purpose of its prohibition is to maintain harmony in the community. Within Akan thought, the rhythms of the life-force of nature and of humanity are always in interrelated, influencing each other for good or evil. The delicate balance between them must therefore be carefully preserved. By Jesus helping Akan AICs to overcome sexual immorality, he is preserving the divine order and averting chaos.[63] The preservation of balance ultimately depends upon human ethical behaviour, including the observation of taboos and the edict of holy writ.

Other Options Selected

The *fear and death* option selected by 658 (26.3%) is related to that of *eternal life* in the previous category. Most of what has been said about *eternal life* and *death* is applicable here too. Ultimately death is the great enemy. The moment death wickedly severs ties among living relatives is a dramatic and sorrowful one, which occasions rites and rituals.[64]

Envy and Hatred selected by 593 (23.7%) respondents, and *pride* selected by 500 (20%), were options intended to ascertain the degree to which personal spirituality forms part and parcel of their Christology. Overcoming personal sins such as envy, hatred, and pride is clearly not at the top of the agenda of what Akan need Jesus to help them overcome. This is borne out by the previous category selection *power to become a*

---

61. Polygamy was a very heated and controversial topic in the focus group discussions. The group remained split in their opinion as to whether such a practice was endorsed by scripture. With the proliferation of the new charismatic churches that reject this practice, AICs who engaged in it do so inconspicuously. Perhaps the most ardent defender of the practice is the MDCC who have sought to justify it on the basis of scripture and their African tradition.

62. A taboo is something forbidden. The word is derived from the Polynesian term "tabu," which means *forbidden* and can be applied to any sort of prohibition. Sarpong discusses the different kinds of taboo in a Ghanaian context in his book *Ghana in Retrospect*, 51–58.

63. Magesa, *African Religion*, 153.

64. See Sarpong, *Ghana in Retrospect*, 29–31, for a thorough analysis of burial rites among the Akans.

better person, chosen by 40 (1.6%) respondents. On the other hand, just as *power to transform society* 24 (1.0%) was the least commonly chosen benefit, so *injustice in society* was also one of the least chosen evils. The social significance of Christology among the Akan AICs is clearly not seen as important as matters pertaining to personal spirituality and morality, though the 15% who did opt for *injustice in society* and the 24% for *power to transform society*, in the previous category, demonstrate that it is by no means a entirely neglected concern.

CONCLUSION

This chapter sought to assess the function of Akan AIC Christology. The field research has shown that the dominant sources that are instrumental in the construction of Akan AIC's Christology are reading the Bible, worshipping and praising God in Church, and the sermons preached at Church. The Bible (with emphasis placed upon the hearing of it), prayers, sermons and worship, demonstrate the importance of orality in the shaping of their Christological discourse.[65] The research further reinforces the view espoused by other researches that in the Christology and practice of AICs, the Bible is the principal source and measuring rod by which AIC theology (Christology) is conceived and continuously modified.[66] This provides encouraging support to the view that the growth of Akan AICs in Ghana is not a "bridge by which Africans are brought back to heathenism,"[67] but rather that they are a vibrant Christian translation of the message and hope of Christ in an African context.

The functionality of Akan AIC Christology was assessed according to the predominant Christological titles, benefits, and prophylactic that Akan AIC adherents consider to be most important. What seems to be clear is that the biblical umbrella terms—*Saviour, Messiah*, and *Lord*—are by far the dominant Christological titles employed by Akan AICs. This once again reinforces the priority that is given to the place of scripture in the development of AIC Christology.

65. I will also be developing the issues of orality further in ch. 8.

66. Turner, *History*, 95; Jules-Rosette, *African Apostle*, 89; Anderson, *African Reformation*, 232; West, *Bishops and Prophets*, 174–75.

67. This view was posited by Sundkler, in his earlier publication; see *Bantu Prophets*. Sundkler however retracted this view upon further investigation of the movement; see *Zulu Zion*, 190–205.

As was confirmed in focus group discussions, the traditional images are often located within the broader and rather flexible biblical categories. This is particularly true of the terms *Saviour* and *Messiah*, in which traditional images are often drawn upon as a means of appropriating their Christological import. The *healer* paradigm as the only "non-biblical umbrella" title for Christ, the fourth highest category after the biblical terms, demonstrates the degree in which Christian religion is culturally infinitely translatable. Taken broadly (body, spirit, world, etc.) *healing* and the *pursuit of wholeness* is perhaps the essence of Akan AIC Christology. This is evidently an area that warrants further exploration and one that I will return to later in this work.

Finally, the research further indicates that benefits that Akan AICs consider the most important to receive from Christ are those which concern personal and spiritual matters, though social issues are not entirely neglected. The issue of *eternal life* was patently a Christological benefit that was a very high priority for Akan AICs, while conversely, evil personified as *Sasabonsam* is the greatest threat to life, health, and wholeness; against these Christ provides the ultimate protection.

6

Christology and Vernacular Apprehension

IN THE EARLIER DISCUSSION of Akan AIC Christology, it was noted that the Bible emerged as a pivotal reference point in the development of Akan AIC understanding of who Jesus is. The survey indicated that 77% of respondents saw "reading the Bible" as their primary means of experiencing the presence of Christ. The idea that the Bible plays a significant role in the life and spirituality among Akan AICs is also true of AICs in a wider context than that of the Akan.[1] It will be helpful, therefore, to consider the question of the place that the Bible actually occupies in the context of Akan AICs and how this impacts their Christology. It will be also interesting to discover the way the Bible is used and how its usage influences the shaping of Akan Christology.

To the Akan AICs, the Bible occupies centre stage.[2] It is the primary witness of God's revelation and the blueprint for life, ethically, morally, socially, and spiritually. Christologically, the Bible presents a Christ who reigns supremely over the "principalities and powers" of the world of the New Testament, a belief accepted by Akan AICs.[3] As this research has

1. Nthanburi and Waruta, "Biblical Hermeneutics," 40–47; Anderson, *African Reformation*, 220–24; Bediako, *Christianity in Africa*, 63–66; Turner, *African Independent Churches*, 83–84; Baëta, *Prophetism in Ghana*, 43–44; Sundkler, *Bantu Prophets*, 75–78; Peel, *Aladura*, 48–49.

2. Kinoti and Waliggo (eds.) maintain that to the AICs the Bible is central. It is seen as the primary witness of God's revelation. See *The Bible in African Christianity*, 43; Sundkler found that in many of the AICs in South Africa the Bible plays a key role in preaching and teaching, *Bantu Prophets*, 277; Barrett draws a definite link between the translation of Scripture and the founding of AICs. In communities that had a translation of the complete Bible, he detects a higher percentage of the emergence of AICs, *Schism and Renewal*, 109. Anderson also argues that, for the great majority of the AICs, the Bible is central to their beliefs and practices; see, *African Reformation*, 220.

3. Dickson argues that there is a cultural continuity between the world of the New Testament and that of Africa generally and Akan specifically. See *Theology in Africa*, 141–84.

shown, the Christological categories that were most dominant for the Akan AICs were the biblical "umbrella" terms and not the seemingly "traditional" terms such as *ancestor* or *chief*. This is primarily due to the seriousness with which Scripture is taken; it is who the Bible declares Jesus to be that is most important, as opposed to the theological construct of academics.[4] The authority of the Bible is therefore unquestioned among Akan AICs, who use it to justify and give legitimacy to their practices and teachings.

It has been convincingly argued by a number of African theologians and scholars of African religions that the main reason why the Bible has gained such a strong footing among AICs is because of its accessibility and apprehension through the vernacular.[5] During our survey we recorded the languages in which the services were conducted. The results were as follows:

LANGUAGE USED in Church Services

Twi	75
Twi and English	8
Twi and Ga	6
Twi and Ewe	5
Twi and Dagumba	4
Total number of Churches	98 (100%)

The figures in the table above clearly illustrate the degree to which the vernacular is used within the Akan AIC services. Out of the 98 churches that took part in the survey, 75 of them conducted their church services in the Twi language alone. Of those using the Twi with English translation, the number totalled 8 and 6 churches employed the Twi language with

---

4. Schreiter (ed.), *Faces of Jesus*, is an example of the theological constructs put forward by academic theologians.

5. Bediako maintains that there is probably no more important single explanation for the massive presence of Christianity on the African continent than the availability of the Scriptures in many African languages; see *Christianity in Africa*, 62. Nthamburi and Waruta argue that many of the locally founded churches use vernacular Bibles, which play a very significant role. The translation of the Bible into African languages became a medium through which biblical hermeneutics was promulgated by indigenous churches; see "Biblical Hermeneutics," 42.

the Ga. Five churches used Twi and Ewe, while four had their services in Twi and Dagumba.

The dominant language in all these churches was Twi. In the Twi services readings, sermons, songs, etc., were all given in the Twi vernacular. Within the bilingual services, the scriptures were read in both Twi and the other four above-mentioned languages. Sermons were interpreted but most songs were sung in the Twi vernacular. The extent to which the Twi vernacular and other local vernacular languages are used during church services highlights further the importance of the study and the impact of the local vernacular upon Christian apprehension. The ability of the Akan AICs to hear the gospel in their own language, and to express in their own tongue the message presented to them, lies at the heart of the Akan AICs apprehension of *Yesu Kristo*.6 In this regard therefore, language is not merely a social or psychological phenomenon, but a theological one as well. Within the development of Akan initiated Christianity of the post-missionary era, the importance of the vernacular in appropriating Christianity to Akans is playing a crucial role.

The Postmodernist renaissance of the value of the "local" and the postcolonial has brought "vernacular" into the limelight in recent years in the West.[7] Postcolonial vernacular hermeneutics gives priority to local cultures against what Sugirtharajah calls "the stranglehold of Western interpretation and its claim to universality."[8] According to Lamin Sanneh this vernacular standard was the "magnetic field" in which the attempt to transmit Christianity from Europe was primed for indigenous assimilation.

Kwame Bediako, who has consistently called for the vernacularization of Christianity in Africa, believes this to be the means of appropriating the gospel in a way that addresses the "felt needs" of African people:

> The existence of the vernacular Bible not only facilitates access to the particular communities speaking those languages, but also creates the likelihood that the hearers of the word in their languages will make their response to it in their own terms. Probably nowhere else in the history of the expansion of Christianity has this occurred quite as widely as in modern Africa.[9]

6. This expression is used for Jesus Christ in Ghana.
7. Sugirtharajah discusses this issue in "Vernacular Resurrections," 11–16.
8. Ibid., 12.
9. Bediako, *Christianity in Africa*, 220.

In the post-missionary era of the presence of the Christian faith in Africa, the significance and the importance of vernacular apprehension is receiving increasing recognition.

Lamin Sanneh has made a significant contribution to the issue of translation and vernacularization. In his work *Translating the Message*, he argues forcefully that Africa should distance itself from western hermeneutical hegemony: "The idea of the Church rooted in African soil, self-propagating, self-reliant and furthermore, reared on the vernacular Scripture, must sharply diverge from the notion of a local Christian society that is set to receive in drips Western cultural transfusion."[10] Similarly, Kwame Bediako, also a strong advocate of the vernacularization of Christianity in Africa, adds his voice to this vernacular campaign: "The extent to which a church can be said to possess a viable heritage of Christian tradition in its indigenous language is the extent of that church's ability to offer adequate interpretation of reality and a satisfying intellectual framework for African life."[11]

Historically there has been a lot of emphasis placed upon "how" the message of Christ was transmitted by western missionaries onto African soil. However, more recently there has been a shift in focus with emphasis being placed on the way Africans have assimilated the message of the gospel more meaningfully into their base communities. AICs phenomenologically have been acknowledged as successfully appropriating or "Africanizing" the Christian faith; however, very few have actually recognized that their "method of appropriation" is actually a point of departure from the historical methods of indigenizing mission. This point of departure is seen in their refusal to use the western missionary movement as their starting point for translating the gospel but rather their vernacular apprehension of Holy Scripture.

Perhaps a good example of this is seen in the MDCC attitude toward polygamy. In their article of faith and declaration they state: "We believe that (as an African Church) polygamy is not a mortal sin" (Gen 16:23; 2 Sam 12:8; Matt 19:10–11; 22:30; 1 Cor 7:7–9 and 28, 36; Heb 13:14).[12] Although one may question whether these scriptures are grounds upon which to base a defence of polygamy, there is a sense in which the Church

10. Sanneh, *Translating the Message*, 112.

11. Bediako, *Christianity in Africa*, 61.

12. Myles, *Musama Disco*, 9.

is seeking to wrestle with the problem of plural marriages from the perspective of Scripture and not according to the values placed upon them by western missionary Christianity.

I would like to argue that the Akan AICs in Ghana are also representative of this "hermeneutical point of departure" in the area of Christology. Through the vernacular translation of Scripture Christ addresses Akan AICs in their own language. They also conceive that God, who speaks in the Christian Scriptures using their vernacular tongue, is the same God whom their forefathers knew. They can identify with such a God and feel at home with his written and spoken word. The Christ they encounter through Scripture, therefore, does not come to them through the medium of the western missionary, but rather through their vernacular apprehension of the Bible.

Lamin Sanneh perhaps best represents this vernacular paradigm, advocating the "unhinging" of western mission from the narrow colonial context and placing it in the much broader setting of African culture. For Sanneh the importance of the Bible translation and its priority in missionary work are an indication that God was not so disdainful of Africans as to overlook the revelatory viability of their languages. Through the very process of Scripture translation, Christology—a central category of Christian theology—is appropriated into the Akan worldview, suggesting that Christianity had been adequately anticipated. Sanneh asserts:

> Translation assumed that the abstract Word of God would find its true destiny when embodied in concrete local idiom, lending credence to the theological insight that the Word of God had always carried the burden of the incarnation, and that its historical manifestation in Jesus Christ concentrated and made visible a process that is occurring throughout history.[13]

According to Sanneh therefore, the essential categories of the Christian faith are—to use Andrew Walls' expression—"culturally infinitely translatable."[14]

The centrality of Scripture says, then, that the African religions are not to be by-passed for therein will the African find the language and idiom in which his or her faith is to be articulated and experienced. Sanneh further asserts,

13. Sanneh, "The Horizontal," 165–71.
14. Walls, "Gospel as the Prisoner," 39.

The enterprise of Scriptural translation, with its far-reaching assumptions about traditional religious categories and ideas as a valid carriage for the revelation and divine initiative that precedes and anticipates historical mission, concedes the salvific value of local religions.[15]

It is this "foregrounding" of culture through language in the quest for the significance of Christ through vernacular apprehension that makes AICs Christology indigenously appealing.

AKAN AIC BIBLICAL HERMENEUTICS AND BIBLICAL SCHOLARSHIP

In the previous section it was noted that the Bible plays a crucial role in the life and ministry of Akan AICs, particularly in shaping the understanding of who Jesus is. It was also established that the vernacular apprehension of Scripture plays a vital role in the development of an indigenous hermeneutics, which—as this research has shown—is relevant for an African context. Furthermore, this vernacular hermeneutic in which the Bible is seen as the dominant point of reference for biblical interpretation (and not the theologies or ideologies of missionary Christianity) is actually a point of departure for biblical interpretation.

A crucial question that needs to be asked at this juncture is "what are the critical tools used by the indigenous reader to assess whether the Christ encountered through vernacular reading and apprehension is the biblical Christ?" Essentially this question has to do with the validity of the methodology employed by what Gerald West calls "the ordinary reader."[16] John Parratt, in an article entitled "African Theology and Biblical Hermeneutics," questions this validity, asserting that it lacks scholarship and academic prowess:

Mbiti's claim that "African Christianity" has the Bible at its forefront, and the Bible is shaping much of its theological development both explicitly and implicitly, is only partially correct. At a popular level this may be so but at the level of biblical scholarship it is a long way from being the case.[17]

15. Sanneh, "The Horizontal," 170.

16. West, "Local is Lekker," 37.

17. Parratt, "African Theology," 89.

Although Parratt acknowledges that the Bible is the main source of African theology, he infers that the lack of scholarship somehow diminishes its qualitative value. The lack of academic infrastructure for the development of biblical studies in Africa, chiefly the study of Greek and Hebrew, according to Parratt, severely undermines the credibility of the claims that African Christianity is rooted in the Bible.[18]

His assessment of the course that vernacular biblical reflection should take in Africa is based on a number of assumptions and therefore raises a number of important issues. The idea (suggested by Parratt) that western style scholarly theological reflection or interpretative methods should be the goal of African vernacular theology is an imposition of a western theological and ideological framework upon the African Christian context. First of all the widespread assumption that western-style biblical scholarship, the result of interpretation, is value free (neutral and also universal) is a false one. Although one would not support a non-literary approach to theological reflection in Africa or give the impression that anti-intellectualism prevails in the African context, it is important to locate the ideological framework to which the kind of theological scholarship, advocated by Parratt, belongs.

Laurenti Magesa enunciates these assumptions eloquently in his article "From Privatised to Popular Biblical Hermeneutics in Africa":

> In accepting and attempting to apply the result of biblical interpretation worked out on the basis of different ideologies, some of them hostile to Africa, the interpretation of the Bible in mainline Churches has tended to ignore economic and social class biases which impinge upon the Christian faith in the continent.[19]

Such western hermeneutical schooling, according to Magesa, cannot help but make African Christians internalize key ideological presuppositions and viewpoints of the same northern hemisphere as the basis for hermeneutics. African biblical scholars who are schooled in the western ideological framework, and therefore hold biases inimical to Africa, also hold these ideological biases. Hermeneutics is thus indicative of specific cultural, economic, political, social, and religious situations and constitutes the very backbone of any meaningful application of what the text means and how it should be applied to a given context. It should therefore

18. Ibid.

19. Magesa, "From Privatised to Popular," 25.

use methods that relate to and are understood by those for whom it is intended and to whom it is targeted.

The hermeneutical motivation for western biblical interpretation, which is part and parcel of a broader western ideological framework, is therefore perhaps unsuited to the African situation. The ideological framework to which western hermeneutics belongs is rationalistically based. It holds that contemplative and academic reflection for its own sake is its own reward which, as Megesa, Schreiter, and Éla would contend, is the hermeneutics of privilege and not necessity. This research found that the Christology of Akan AICs advances a biblical hermeneutics that is functionally driven to ultimately enhance life and well-being. The hermeneutics relevant for Africa must therefore speak to the structures of poverty and death that African people have to confront daily. This means a hermeneutic for Christology which goes beyond the dichotomy between African theologies of liberation and inculturation to deal realistically with the pains, suffering and poverty that rule the lives of millions of Africans today.

Abraham Akrong believes strongly that the temptation to erect a wall of separation between socio-political oppression and cultural alienation, which has dominated the methodologies of African theology, must be resisted because in the existential reality of millions of African people such distinction does not exist.[20] For the West, biblical hermeneutics is by and large the product of the social elite of which the institutional church is an integral part. Their hermeneutics represent, therefore, the views of a particular class of people who have a particular view of the world.

This point is effectively stated by B. Tihagale and I. Mosala who maintain this kind of hermeneutics represents a "privatised interpretation":

> Privatised [sic] interpretations are usually the options with a reasonable amount of social security. They usually emanate from that class of people who had a reasonably well off life with middle class care. Thus, such an interpretation is more a revelation of the class positions of the interpreters, than the understanding of the text from the social position determined by an option for the oppressed classes.[21]

20. Akrong, "Empowering Christ."
21. See Tihagale and Mosala, (eds.), *Hammering Swords*, 185.

The hermeneutic for African Christology exemplified in the African indigenous churches, whose peoples' lives are often ruled by structures of death manifested through oppression, starvation, exploitation, military brutality, and tribal massacres, which continue to distort their humanity, is therefore one that must promote life. This quest for life exemplified through the vernacular hermeneutics of AICs must therefore be able to illuminate the present with the light of God with us. It is a hermeneutic that should enable life through the life-giving message of Christ. In this regard, vernacular hermeneutic must be liberative and existential in its application to the lives of the faith community.

This is not to say, however, that there is no room for the "scholarly readership." Gerald West argues that there is an important role for what he calls the "socially engaged scholar" to play in vernacular hermeneutics which is one of creating a genuine dialectical interaction between themselves and the popular reader and only then can the "popular reader" and the "socially engaged scholar" move beyond "speaking for" and "listening to" towards a place where they are hearing together and differences are expressed.

He states,

> The call of ordinary indigenous readers, particularly the vast majority who are in poor and marginalized communities, is a call to participate *with* them, *against* the forces of death and destruction and *for* the forces of survival, liberation and life. When we work and struggle together we are engaged in vernacular hermeneutics because they have invited us to do so.[22]

Additionally, the questions posed by Magesa regarding the motive behind biblical hermeneutics therefore ring very loud:

> Does biblical interpretation emanating from today's economic North show sufficient sensitivity to the plight of the South, specifically, to those elements in scripture most relevant to this situation? What are these elements? Are they explicit or implicit in the Bible? Do indigenous interpreters, either scholarly or "pastorally orientated," actually relate these elements to specific local situations in their work? If not, or seldom, an issue of ultimate significance arises: What is the effect of such interpretation on, in our case, the people of Africa? Does it empower them or does it rather integrate them inextricably into an ideology and concrete system of

22. West, "Local is Lekker," 42.

self-negation and helplessness in every aspect of life, and all in the name of the "Word of God"?[23]

In summary, the quest for suitable and relevant hermeneutics for Africa is linked to an absolutely basic question asked by Éla and referred to earlier, namely, "how can the gospel become the leaven which leads to a new meaning in life, but always with reference to Jesus of Nazareth who is *par excellence*, both the other and one's closest neighbour?" It is here that the hermeneutical Christology of the AICs comes into sharp focus. Their engagement with the biblical text at the level of the local assembly has created a hermeneutical boldness that enables them to apply the Bible to their own situation, without feeling the need to be legitimized by western mission Christianity.

Another issue that is highlighted by Parratt's critique of biblical hermeneutics in Africa is the issue of ownership. His assertion that "African theology has the Bible as its forefront only at the popular level but at the level of biblical scholarship it is far from the case"[24] reveals another assumption, namely, the dichotomizing of the educational elite and the faith community. This too is an assumption borne out of western presuppositions based upon class and educational elitism.[25] Magesa differentiates between "privatized" hermeneutics and the "popular" hermeneutics. Privatized interpretation is the tool used primarily by a small group of people (usually the educated elite) and popular interpretation the majority of the faithful. Parratt's distinction between the "popular level" and the "scholarly level" is indicative of this division. The question then arises: by whom can biblical hermeneutics best be done? In order to ascertain who is best qualified or suited to do biblical hermeneutics, a supplementary question is necessary: what is the purpose of African hermeneutics?

According to Carlos Mesters, speaking from a Brazilian context,

> Interpreting the Bible ceased to be thought of as the transmission of information exclusively by the exegete who has studied for this

23. Magesa, "Biblical Hermeneutics," 26.

24. Parratt, "African Theology," 89

25. Govender observes that the Bible and preaching are often the main instruments used to preserve the status quo: whether it be the privileged position of the intellectuals or the power of the clergy or the seizure of power by men within the structure of the church. He argues that racism, sexism, oppressive capitalism, and the marginalization of various groups and classes of people have all found a safe haven in dominant biblical hermeneutics. See Tihagale and Mosala, (eds.), *Hammering Swords*, 185.

purpose, but a community activity to which all should contribute, each in his or her own way, including the exegete. The aim of popular interpretation is no longer to interpret the Bible, but to interpret life with the help of the Bible.[26]

Also, Robert Schreiter, a Catholic theologian and author of the highly acclaimed *Constructing Local Theologies*, affirms that the purpose of hermeneutics is to serve the community:

> The experience of those in small Christian communities who have seen the insight and the power arising from the reflections of the people upon their experience and the Scriptures has prompted making the community itself the prime author of theology in local contexts. The Holy Spirit, working in and through the believing community, gives shape and expression to Christian experience. Some of these communities have taught us to read the Scriptures in a fresh way and have called the larger church back to a fidelity to the prophetic word of God.[27]

He continues:

> Theology is certainly intended for a community and is not meant to remain the property of a theologian class. The expression of faith in theology should make a difference in people's lives; otherwise it is a mere beating of the air. Reflection for its own sake may lead to contemplation, but contemplation should lead to action as well.[28]

It therefore seems obvious that contextual cultural hermeneutics can hardly be accomplished by ministers of the Church on their own in their studies or in the Sunday sermon or homily. Nor can it be done by biblical studies scholars alone in institutes of higher learning; it is the work of whole community. It is also crucial that the understanding of the popular reader be harnessed. Carlos Mesters notes that the faithful themselves

26. Mesters, "Use of the Bible," 48; Adamo maintains that African cultural hermeneutics is an approach to biblical interpretation that makes the African social cultural contexts subjects of interpretation. This means that African cultural hermeneutics, like any other Third World hermeneutic, is contextual since interpretation is always done in a particular context. Specifically it means that analysis of the text is done from the perspective of African worldview and culture. The purpose is not only to understand the Bible and God in our African experience and culture, but to break the hermeneutical hegemony and ideological stranglehold that Euro-centric biblical scholars have long enjoyed. See "African Cultural Hermeneutics," 67–68.

27. Schreiter, *Constructing Local Theologies*, 16–17

28. Ibid.

sometimes with the help of an "expert" should voice what the Word of God in Scripture means to them and their descendents; their experiences and expectations must not be ignored. They must be taken seriously by the official Church as part of the process of God's self-revelation through the Scriptures to a given community, the people.[29]

VERNACULAR HERMENEUTICS IN AKAN AIC CHRISTOLOGY

The Akan AIC Christology that emanates from the experience of Christ from the perspective of indigenous culture and the hearing of Scripture is based upon vernacular hermeneutics. This is a means of interpreting Scripture without having to "filter" it from the imposed western interpretive universalities and the barriers of language. In this section, how this vernacular apprehension of Christ is used as a hermeneutical tool for biblical discourse will be explored. The word *hermeneutics* is derived from the Greek word *hermēneutikos*, which means *the study of the principles and methodology of interpretation.*

When referred to the Bible, it means the art or technique of interpreting a biblical text in order to understand its original context and then finding its contemporary meaning. In Severino Croatta's definition of hermeneutics there are three aspects to interpretation: the privilege locus, pre-understanding arising from a particular context, and the interpreter's enlargement of the meaning of the text being interpreted.[30] Nthamburi and Waruta argue that hermeneutics seeks to perform two tasks: the first is to determine valid modes of understanding a biblical text in its own setting, and the second is to determine a valid mode of expressing that meaning in the contemporary situation.[31] In other words it addresses the problem of how an interpretation can bridge the gap between biblical meaning and the contemporary application.

---

29. During my work with the OAIC in Ghana, in which I taught Theological Education by Extension (TEE), I was involved in conducting Bible studies with local people from different AICs. These lessons brought together people from different backgrounds and educational standards: some had no formal education while others had gained senior secondary school certificates; others were graduates from the Good News Theological College and Seminary where I taught. These lessons served as good examples of the community doing theology together and learning from each others' experiences.

30. Croatto, *Biblical Hermeneutics*, 1.

31. Nthanburi and Waruta, "Biblical Hermeneutics," 40.

The hermeneutical tools the AICs employ are not philosophical and rationalistic but are rather far more pragmatic in applying the Bible to people's daily lives. The questionnaire survey clearly illustrated this by revealing that the Christological concerns of respondents were matters of health, healing, and protection from evil spirits and witchcraft, which have the capacity to bring chaos on family life and well-being. The Christological prophylactics that are deemed helpful are understood in visual and literal terms such as saving, healing, delivering, and restoring life. This hermeneutical approach is based upon a literal interpretation of Scripture, but not the biblical literalism of fundamentalism associated with western Christianity.[32]

The driving force behind AIC hermeneutics is not "unquestioning" literalism, which is one of the hallmarks of western fundamentalism, but rather pragmatic need to "concretize" and appropriate the Bible to "living faith." Mesters speaks of a "dislocation" that occurs when "common people" read the Bible, in which emphasis in not placed upon the text *per se* but upon the meaning of the text for the people reading it.[33] This "concordistic approach" to biblical hermeneutics seeks to apply the Bible to real life situations of the ordinary people.[34]

The hermeneutical approach employed by AICs is also pre-critical. Gerald West, drawing upon his research based upon four case studies of ordinary indigenous readers reading the Bible, states:

> Ordinary readers read the Bible pre-critically. My use of "pre-critical" is not pejorative; ordinary indigenous readers have little choice in how they read the Bible. They read it pre-critically because they have not been trained in the critical modes of reading that characterise biblical scholarship.[35]

Similarly, Severino Croatto seems to argue that the poor and oppressed engage in an "in-front-of-the-text mode of reading" the Bible.[36]

---

32. Anderson, *African Reformation*, 220.

33. Mesters, *Use of the Bible*, 14.

34. This term is taken from the word *concord*, which means *to be in agreement* or *harmony*; it is used by Croatto to mean finding common ground between the Bible and life situations. See Croat's *Biblical Hermeneutics*, 6.

35. West, "Local is Lekker," 38.

36. Croatto, *Biblical Hermeneutics*, 50.

Vernacular hermeneutics employed by AICs bring the African worldview into the foreground, therefore commissioning indigenous concepts to express the meaning of biblical objects and thought forms. In cases where there is no vernacular equivalent the lingua franca of the missionary hermeneutics or the nearest equivalent in the local vernacular is used. For the most part, however, AICs are hearing the "word of God" in their own language and are responding in a way that their needs are addressed and their questions are answered. To this extent AICs represent African Christianity coming of age.

According to Bediako the ability of Africans to respond in this way is a crucial landmark, which expresses that Christianity is now truly an African's religion:

> If hearers of the word in their own language may then be presumed to respond in their own terms, this is another way of saying that it is not others'" but their own questions, which they would bring to the Bible, taking from it what they would consider to be its answers to their questions.[37]

Within the context of vernacular apprehension, Christ is not accessed through a third party, namely "western mission agencies," but he makes himself known through the "mother tongue" of his African brethren. That he comes to them in the vernacular creates an instant rapport; the veil erected by western missionary Christianity is lifted and there is a revelation of a Christ previously unknown.[38] This revelation discloses a Christ who is not a stranger to them, but who through the vernacular feeds the 5000 and walks among the poor in African villages. Yet it also reveals a Christ who is distinctly "other,"[39] one who confronts them with a truth that transcends culture and transforms the familiar. It is this dialectical process between the immanence and the transcendence of Christ that makes the religiosity of AICs a dynamic and fluid phenomenon.

The direct access to "the Jesus of Holy Scripture" through the vernacular has not only allowed AICs to respond in their own terms and through their own cultural matrix, but it has also introduced a different

---

37. Bediako, *Christianity in Africa*, 63.

38. I am using the term *revelation* here to mean *illuminating disclosure* or *revealed truth*.

39. Christ is yet distinctly "other" because he is not from their ethnic or tribal group and is not totally confined to their cultural setting.

hermeneutical slant in biblical interpretation. This is another example of "hermeneutics from the underside of society" in which the "ordinary" people take the task of interpreting the Bible into their own hands. This re-reading of the biblical text through the eyes of the local people has been providing fresh insight to the studies of vernacular hermeneutics, particularly in Two-Thirds-World countries. One of the prominent areas where this kind of re-reading can be seen is in the liberation theologies of Gutierrez, Boff, and Sobrino. Although these theologies do represent a grassroots re-reading of the Bible which is very context sensitive, their articulation nonetheless falls largely within the western intellectual tradition.[40]

African vernacular hermeneutics is by no means a recent phenomenon but goes back as far as the translation of the Bible into African languages; yet it has been highly undervalued as an important source for the development of Christianity in Africa. The reason for this is as much due to the "theological elitism" of the African mission Churches as it is to not conforming to the set of ground rules and theological protocol set by the academies and educational institutions.

AKAN AIC CHRISTOLOGY AND THE HERMENEUTICS OF ORALITY

One of the most memorable events witnessed during the course of the research was a recital of the birth, death and resurrection of Christ using the traditional *atumpan* or talking drum. The recital was accompanied with dancers who moved skilfully as they graphically and movingly narrated through choreography the life and death of Christ. Though "wordless" the language of the drums and the choreography of the dances spoke vividly to all who could hear.[41] In this discussion of Akan AIC hermeneutics it is important to take cognisance of the need to interpret the non-literary sources of Christology, legitimately called "oral theology (Christology).

---

40. Sugirtharajah *Vernacular Hermeneutics*, 12.

41. Within the traditional context, the talking drum is not essentially just a form of telegraph, although it is used to announce important events. Primarily the talking drum is an instrument of prayer and of mediation with the sacred order of the gods and the ancestors. The drummer, *okyerema*, in the very language of the drum summarizes the myth of creation, represents the stages of creation and life. The drummer stands for knowledge for he knows the history and lore of the community and he recites it on the talking drums. See Fisher, *West African Tradition*, 34.

This oral theology, as Pobee has observed, is the stream in which the vitality of people of faith in Africa, illiterate and literate, is mediated.[42]

42. Pobee, "Oral Theology," 87–92.

7

Healing and Wholeness

CHRIST AS HEALER *PAR EXCELLENCE*

IN RECENT YEARS WRITERS and observers of the development of Christianity in Africa have become increasingly aware of the two distinct realms in which African Christians now live. Pobee identifies these realms as the new world of modern technology and the old world of traditional values,[1] pointing out that Africans have two different names and using them on the basis of the worldview they are operating in at a given time. Tutu highlights the same dualism that has arisen in Africa, calling it "a split in the African soul," which leads to what he calls "religious schizophrenia."[2] Bosch believes that this split, or dualism, in African Christianity is caused by the failure of the western mission to integrate Christianity to the 'whole life' of the African people.[3] One area in which this dualism is patently clear is the area of healing. While this issue has affected Christianity across the continent, the AICs have been at the forefront in tackling it, insisting on a brand of Christianity that is more integrated to the African worldview and way of life. Kofi Appiah-Kubi explains:

> Whilst in the established Churches, medical practice has become so specialised [sic] and secularised [sic] that the ordinary pastor has become radically excluded from the service of the sick, healing and worship becoming separated, in the Indigenous African Christian Churches, there has been a reintegration of healing and worship. This is in fact in the line of thinking and understanding

1. Pobee, "Church in West Africa," 139.
2. Tutu, "Whither African Theology?" 365–66.
3. Bosch, *Het Evangelie*, 43.

of health, for religion in the Akan mind is to do with health and fertility of man, animal and land.[4]

In my earlier discussion on *Healer* I observed that after *Saviour, Messiah*, and *Lord*, Christ as Healer was by far the most popular Christological option (55.3% of respondents).[5] I argued that this was significant because it was the only non-biblical umbrella term that was chosen by respondents. Harvey Cox observed that healing is the area in which the African Indigenous Churches have most to offer to other Christians and to the world at large.[6] I concur with this view. The notion of Christ as healer is by no means a novel one, but one that has been variously explored, particularly in relation to health, wholeness, sickness, the causes of sickness, witchcraft, and healing in relation to traditional religious practices.[7] My interest in this section is to explore how Christ is understood as healer among Akan AICs at the level of the local assembly.

In African tradition, healing is much more than merely swallowing medicine. Kofi Appiah–Kubi's distinction that "man cures, God heals" highlights the major difference between the western and African perspective on healing.[8] The appeal of Christ as *Healer* within an Akan AIC context is predicated upon a worldview that healing and health are inextricably connected to social behaviour, moral conduct and spiritual forces. Appiah-Kubi comments, "One can be cured from a sickness but

4. Appiah-Kubi, *Healing in Indigenous*, 55.

5. See ch. 5.

6. Cox, *Fire From Heaven*, 255; Daneel states that no single factor has been mentioned more by members of AICs as the reason for their joining these movements than the healing treatment performed by African prophets (*Old and New in Southern*, 186); Kubi says that healing is the most common reason given for the emergence of these Churches, *Man Cures, God Heals*, 86.

7. *Man Cures, God Heals*, by Kofi Appiah-Kubi is an excellent book which gives an Akan perspective on healing. The main thesis of the book argues that there is a difference between 'man curing' diseases and sickness, which is to address the biological aspects of healing, as opposed to having a holistic and comprehensive understanding of healing and sickness which is linked into both the natural and spiritual world. In Shorter's excellent book *Jesus and the Witchdoctor*, he argues that Jesus of Nazareth in many ways could be likened to the African witchdoctor. Healing in the context of AICs has been explored by Oosthuizen et al (eds). The article "Indigenous Healing" by Oosthuizen gives a good overview of the healing practices of AICs (albeit from a South African perspective), while the article by Dube, "Search for Abundant Life," provides interesting insights to the African view of healing and health.

8. Appiah-Kubi, *Man Cures, God Heals*, 14.

still remain unhealed. Healing implies restoring the equilibrium in the otherwise strained relationship between man, his fellowmen, environment, ecology and God."[9]

In spite of the wonderful achievements of modern western medicine in Africa, there is still the tendency to perceive it as tackling the manifestations of disease but not its cause. Africans therefore look for someone who will tackle its cause as well as provide healing. In my earlier elucidation of *healer* in chapter 5 based on the findings of the survey, I argued that salvation is essentially freedom from sickness and affliction of all kinds and the agents that bear them. This understanding of healing and wholeness therefore goes beyond symptomatic healing but addresses the causal factors also. Though healing is based upon the African understanding as to the cause of sickness and the nature of healing, AIC leaders will be the first to point out that this perspective on healing is also grounded in the teaching and practice of Jesus as well as the Old and New Testaments. It is this strong scriptural backing that legitimizes healing practices of Akan AICs, who otherwise would be bombarded with even further accusations of syncretism.[10]

Having established the holistic and integrated premise of healing among Akan, an important question is *what qualifies Christ as Healer?* The answer to this question lies in part with the African understanding of the role of the ancestors in healing, an issue explored by Charles Nyamiti. He argued that, among the supernatural powers ascribed by Africans to their ancestors, the capacity to heal bodily ailments is one of the most important.[11] During my visits to the northern region of Ghana, I personally witnessed sick people visiting their ancestral shrines to implore their ancestors for restoration of health as well as for protection from further diseases. Healing power is thus an important ancestor function in Akan

---

9. Ibid., 12.

10. A few examples of healing in the Gospels often cited by AIC leaders include Mark 8:22–26, (note that Christ both touched the patient and used saliva), the paralytic at Capernaum (Matt 9:1–8; Luke 5:18–26), and is an eloquent illustration of a physical disability being cured by a new spiritual relationship. The curative factor here is the forgiveness of sins. This also illustrates the involvement of the bystanders and the faith of friends. Christ repeats three times: "seeing their faith." The centurion's servant and the nobleman's son (Matt8:5–13; Luke 7:1–10; John 4:46 –54) are examples of a paranormal cure by absent or remote treatment.

11. Nyamiti, *Christ as our Ancestor*, 55.

traditional beliefs.[12] The basis of ancestral authority to heal is their close-ness to God—the absolute source of healing—gained through their death and elevation to a higher realm of existence.

Charles Nyamiti goes on to argue that Christ has superseded the role of the ancestors in this regard: "It is, therefore, appropriate and even useful to examine Christ's healing function in connection with his ancestorship, especially because Holy Scripture allots to this function a place of impor-tance in the life of Jesus."[13] Nyamiti cites a number of interesting parallels between Christ's healing function and that of the ancestor.[14] The main difference, however, is that unlike the ancestors, who are obligated to heal members of their ethnic group, Jesus offers healing to all. In this respect Jesus universalizes the healing power of God. The means by which Jesus accomplishes this—through his death, resurrection and glorification—resonates most powerfully with the African spirit.

Abraham Akrong asserts:

> The salvific functions of Jesus are based on the roles with which we identify him in Akan religion. Jesus as an ancestor is a hero ancestor, a mediator ancestor and a tutelary ancestor because of his own status as saviour of the world and his dual nature as God-man. Jesus, the ideal ancestor of the human race, has broadened the scope of the family to include all beings in order to remind us of the realty of God's family that embraces all human beings. In Jesus Christ therefore our kinship obligations become obligations to our fellow human beings.[15]

In his comparison between Christ's approach to healing and that of the African witchdoctor, Shorter maintains that both used an "integrated ap-proach" to healing, which emphasized the moral and social as well as the physical aspects of human healing needs. The strength of the approach adopted by the Akan AICs is that it combines the biblical healing method of Christ in the Bible (along with its spiritual implications) with that of the traditional practice.

---

12. For a detailed analysis of the healing function of the ancestor, see Nyamiti, *Christ as our Ancestor*, 55–57.

13. Ibid., 55.

14. Ibid.

15. Akrong, "Christology from an African," 125–26.

HEALING AND WHOLENESS: TOWARD
AN INTEGRATED WORLDVIEW

The AIC leaders I met during the course of my research share a biblical vision of healing and wholeness in which sickness is viewed as the result of personal sin and where the link between sickness and the demonic is established through the ministry of Jesus.[16] The approach to sickness adopted by AIC's methodological and theological approaches to such sickness is one that goes beyond the symptomatic reductionist approach of clinical medicine and touches the existential realities of everyday life. This outlook on healing and wholeness (demonstrated variously throughout this work) provides valuable insight in addressing some of Africa's pressing needs by adopting an integrated approach. Questions of nutrition and health are inseparable from the economic and social system. Disease and malnutrition do not exist in a vacuum; rather they are the results of human beings existing in a state of "disharmony" with each other and with the world they inhabit.

For AICs sickness is associated with the presence and activity of evil forces, and healing is seen as deliverance from their hold by the superior power of Jesus Christ. This "naming" and thus "concretizing" of the forces of evil—which, though hidden, inflict real pain on real people—calls for a re-evaluation of the "principalities and powers" that operate in the visible universe where men and women are their chief victims. In this respect concrete historical responses must be given to the scourge of sickness and disease in Africa. Confining its source to the realm of the inner life and treating sickness as nothing more than the effect and consequence of original sin is not good enough. In doing so we gloss over the real devastation of sickness by not accepting its real form.[17]

Éla asseverates:

> If we consider the violence being done to life in the conditions in which we live, and localise it in the invisible relationship of the soul with God, we spiritualise it to a dangerous degree. We "sacral-

16. This view was strongly enunciated by Apostle Entwi of the Gethsemane Grace Healing Church, who maintained that the churches that do not practice spiritual healing are going against the Bible and the teachings of Jesus. For a detailed discussion on the similarities between sickness and healing in African tradition and the Bible that leans toward the African perspective, see Éla, *My Faith*, 77–80; see also Onunwa, "The Biblical Basis."

17. Éla, *My Faith*, 80.

ize" [sic] it. We constantly risk transforming sin into a structure of mythical existence against which we can do nothing, except ritually in the church through the sacramental and religious activity that is used to symbolise our faith.[18]

To AICs, healing and wholeness suggests reciprocity between individuals and society and the invisible forces of the universe. Individuals are able to "hurt" the community by their failure to act in the interest of the "whole" and in turn collective sin results in sickness within the bodies of individuals or in the dysfunction of the natural order. The "oral Christology" of AICs is therefore one that does not just concern itself with the healing and liberation of individuals but the healing and liberation of all creation. The need to heal and liberate creation is a response to the impact that a "wounded" creation is having upon the community: sickness, death, poverty, famine and other such devastation.[19]

AICs, by asserting the supremacy of Christ over the forces of sickness and death, propound a Christology that abandons the idea that sickness is a matter of fate—the invasion of an imaginary "adversary" beyond human responsibility or beyond the reach of any strategies. AICs believe that personal morality and responsibility has been flouted, thus precipitating a state of abnormality and dis-equilibrium. Locating the behavioral deviance and acting toward re-harmonization completes the circle of cause and effect, the cause being "failure to act in the interest of the whole"; the effect being "sickness and disharmony," and the restoration being "confession and re-building of relationships." Christ as the healer *par excellence* is the solution to the apparent contradiction that exists between sickness (anti-life) and the will of God. In a world which is vastly coming to terms with the perceived constancy of suffering, famine, injustice, misery, and the structures of death on the African continent, the Christology of healing and wholeness propounded by AICs exposes this situation as being radically incompatible with the plan of God. This contradiction is an effective hermeneutical starting point in confronting the economic and social conditions that are currently dogging the African continent.

In his book *African Earthkeepers*, Marthinus Daneel explores the idea of Christ the earth keeper. He argues that the idea of our being good earth stewards has received little attention by African theologians so

18. Ibid.

19. The idea of a wounded creation is explored in Daneel, *Earthkeepers*, 8–11.

far. Drawing upon the ecological practices of the Association of African Earthkeeping Churches (AAEC) (an organization he founded) he sets forth good praxis of earth-stewardship by AICs which complements and enhances not only African Christianity generally but written African Christologies in particular. He states, "Instead of being presupposed in the prophets' Spirit-filled outreach to afflicted humanity, Christ now emerges more decisively than before as the healer of all creation, as the one who deals consistently with both human and environmental illness."[20] He continues: "By perceiving Christ as earthkeeper, the new family or tribe—the extended family of churches who accept earthkinship and give expression to it by constantly proclaiming the unity of the shoots (churches) in Christ, the vine—receives a new leitmotif: a ministry of earth-care."[21] The incorporation of the created order as a means of echoing the "integratedness" and the continuity between the invisible and visible dimensions is providing fresh insight in Christology.[22]

The AICs holistic approach to healing and wholeness is further relevant in that it is multidimensional and integrated—*multidimensional* in the sense of its 'simultaneous geography' comprising both the physical and the spiritual universe, *integrated* in the sense that it does not fragment the cause, effects, and the need for restoration but believes them to be interrelated. It does not seek to heal the body without accessing and rooting out the cause of the sickness because the two are related. Neither does it transform its sick members into objects of care, pity or sympathy. Rather, in the face of sickness and death it proclaims the source of all life and health, pointing toward a Christ who comes in the name of *Onyame* the Supreme One, empowered to heal all sickness and disease and protect from all those who are its perpetrators.

An examination of the socio-economic situation in regards to health in Africa reveals a system that encloses human beings in a circle of misery and sickness. Issues of nutrition and health are indivisible from the economic and social system. AIDS, disease, poverty, and malnutrition never exist by themselves; rather they are the effects or products of social organisations.[23] The position of sickness in Africa is therefore a decisive reality

20. Daneel, *Earthkeepers*, 225.

21. Ibid., 18.

22. See Ott, *African Theology in Images*, 371–433.

23. For a discussion on the impact of human behaviour on the environment, see Daneel, *Earthkeepers*, 16–35.

of our time and an historic condition in which sickness is the result of the abuse of power in the allocation of resources. It comes from a system characterized by violence, by a pattern of impoverishment of the majority, and by the monopoly by a minority of the means to live with dignity. The application of the integrated and multidimensional worldview in regards to healing and wholeness is effective when extended to addressing the social and economic crises in Africa. To begin with the refusal to normalize the manifest disharmonies within the society or to "spiritualize" the daily misery that manifests itself in the suffering of the community is a motivation to seek a concrete causation.

Further, the link between "wrong behavior" (behavior not in harmony with the rest of the community) and suffering is to locate the individual or group who is "hurting" the community and to proclaim the Good News of the Christ who confronts the enemies of life. This dynamic of socio-religious relation portrays the drama of sin and salvation through Christ at the heart of the concrete realities of the suffering, pain and death that rule the lives of millions of Africans.

In Akan AIC's cosmology, the visible creation of humans and many objects are intricately interwoven with the invisible realm. Like many other African ethnic groups Akans have a paradoxical relationship with the environment. On one hand there is a deep respect and even fear of the trees, hills, rivers, etc., yet on the other hand, there is wanton destruction of the bush through widespread burning, especially for firewood and timber, often raping and denuding the land for a long time.[24] In spite of this, the cosmology of Akan AICs challenges us to re-examine the way we interact with our natural environments.

CONCLUSION

Healing is perhaps the very essence of Akan AIC Christology. Behind the quest for healing is the pursuit of life and happiness. In this regard healing and the Bible converge. The hermeneutic that is characteristic of the Akan AICs is one that has the enabling of life as its primary task. Healing is also tied up with the theme of salvation or soteriology. As has been noted, for Akan AICs to be "saved" is to be "healed."

---

24. In recent years people have begun to plant fruit, shades, and/or firewood trees but only in the vicinity of their compounds.

8

Toward a Post-missionary African Oral Christology

INTRODUCTION

SO FAR IN THIS study the development of AICs in Ghana and the impact of an imposed western Christology have been explored. The findings of the national survey have also been quantified and discussed. The first major theme identified was the prominence of the Bible in the life and worship of Akan AICs. The second was that of healing; the quest for healing, I have argued, is the overall driving force behind the Christology of Akan AICs. Tied into this quest for healing is the soteriological and eschatological ethos of Akan AICs. The last theme to be identified was the "lived" nature of this Christology, in which the transcendent and the imminent experience of Christ converge in the everyday life of the Akan AIC believer.

A closer look at the research as a whole reveals some significant dynamics that seem to permeate the Christological outlook of Akan AICs. Firstly, there is a distinct bias toward an "oral Christology" experienced through the resources of Akan oral tradition. The bias toward a Christology of "orality" is demonstrated through the preference of song, prayer, preaching, and testimonies as means of expressing faith.[1]

The oral nature of the spirituality of Akan AICs was evident in the questionnaire survey, which showed a preference toward oral expressions as significant means of experiencing Christ.[2] This is particularly evident in the prominence that is given to the Bible, which the vast majority of adherents engage with orally rather than textually. The Bible, as we have seen, is far more than a literary document; it is experienced through hear-

---

1. We shall explore these modes of orality later in this chapter.
2. These will be explained in more detail later in this chapter.

ing and not through reading only. Another important dynamic, related to orality, is that of the "lived" nature of the Akan experience of Christ. The importance of experiencing Christ in the "everyday," in the "banal," is an integral part of their spirituality. Akan AICs present us with a "this world" Christology in which Jesus aids in overcoming the challenges thrown up by everyday life. Earlier in this study I discussed the immanence and the transcendence of Christ in the experience of the Akan AIC worshipping community, and concluded that the immanence of Christ is not only an abstract presence, but also a concrete one in which Christ is understood as being near through the created order as well as through human culture.[3]

The other important dynamic revealed by this research—which is also integral to an outlook of orality—is the quest for healing. Healing is indeed the essence of Akan AIC Christology. In my discussion of healing in the last chapter I argued that Akans ultimately put their trust in Christ for their healing. I also argued that healing is integral to Akan AIC's idea of salvation, redemption, and their perception of the universe. For the Akan AICs faith in Christ touches on the totality of existence.[4] In a continent suffering with the structures of death through AIDS, poverty, famine, social alienation, economical ruin, and political fragmentation, any discussion about Christ must have healing and wholeness at its very heart in order for it to really appeal to the African.

These important dynamics present us with some essential "indicators" of what a Christology that is suited for an African context must employ. In this chapter a Christology which draws upon the wellsprings of the oral dimensions of African culture and tradition will be posited as a model for inculturating Christ into African soil. The essential thesis is

---

3. The idea of encountering God or knowledge of a being close to us in and through nature is an ongoing theological debate within western academic theology. It argues principally that the natural environment bears witness to the existence of a Supreme Being outside revelation and grace. In the last twenty years or so there has been an upsurge stimulated particularly by the New Age Movement, and Eco-theology. See Steven and Bowman, *Beyond New Age*; Hanegraaff, *New Age and Western*; Alcock, "Dwelling Lightly"; Hallman (ed.), *Ecotheology*; Bouma-Prediger, *The Greening*; and Birch, Eakin, and McDaniel (eds.), *Liberating Life*.

The notion of God experienced through nature in this work, is however not a part of this debate, although there may be some similarities and interesting connections. The existence of God is not on trial here but rather the degree in which He reveals Himself through the natural order beyond that of human beings.

4. Éla, *My Faith*, 67.

based upon "orality," which it will be argued, is the principal medium of Christological discourse.

AKAN AIC CHRISTOLOGY AS ORAL DISCOURSE

Researchers engaged with Akan AICs soon discovers that their time will not be spent churning through endless documentation or deconstructing doctrinal propositional statements, but rather immersed into a living tradition in which faith is lived out on a daily basis. I would like to posit an approach to Christology, which has come as a result of four years of living, teaching, researching, and sharing fellowship with Akan AICs, because of which, I have found myself forced to explore against all my own western propositional theological pedagogy.

My research found that, on the whole, Akan AICs do not possess a propositional Christology—by which I mean a Christology based upon written creeds, doctrine or theological formulae, that form the basis of a western epistemology—but rather an implicit and enacted Christology which draws upon the wellsprings of oral tradition. This Christology is perhaps best described as an "oral Christology."[5] The issue of orality is usually associated with oral tradition. Oral tradition can be defined in various ways. Here I employ the definition of Theodorson and Theodorson that it is "culture that is transmitted from one generation to the next by word of mouth rather than through written account."[6] Oral tradition according to Vansina is described as "historical sources of a special nature, which are derived from the fact that they are unwritten sources couched in a form suitable for oral transmission."[7]

Thus, oral theology is the encounter of God through the language that is heard and spoken by the visible and invisible participants of the African universe. The starting point of this orality is not the message or the form in which the oral tradition exists, which could be narrative, song, proverb etc., but rather the invisible domain or dimension in which it emerges. My usage of the term *orality* therefore will not be limited to "oral communication" but will also include the wider framework that gives these forms meaning. My reason for preferring *orality* instead of other

5. The idea of an "oral Christology" is a derivative of "oral Theology" which we will explore later in this chapter.

6. Theodorson and Theodorson, *Modern Dictionary of Sociology*, 285.

7. Vansina, *Oral Tradition*, 1.

terms such as *narrative, enacted, symbolic,* or *local* (all of which are re-lated) is, I would argue, that *orality* is the actual "structure" or the "fabric" of the African universe of which narrative, story, myth, etc., are modes in which it is expressed or voiced.[8]

Oral theology is described by Pobee as the stream through which the vitality of the people of faith in Africa, literate and illiterate, is mediated.[9] A detailed discussion regarding the non-written historical sources, which make up the oral tradition among the Akan AICs falls, outside the scope of this presentation.[10] The main concern here is to examine what the Akan AIC's bias toward "oral expression" and orality as a "dimension of existence" can teach us about how Christ is experienced by Akan AICs.

Mbiti voicing the value of oral theology maintains: "African oral theology is a living tradition. We must come to terms with it. We must ac-knowledge its role in the total life of the church. It is the most articulate ex-pression of theological creativity in Africa. This form of theology gives the church a certain measure of theological selfhood and independence."[11]

This idea of "oral theology" as a particular appropriation of Christ within an indigenous Akan culture has been explored by Kwame Bediako:

> We ought to speak positively of oral, spontaneous, implicit or grassroots theology, as a theology which comes from where faith lives, in the life-situation of the community of faith. Accordingly this grassroots theology is an abiding element of all theology, and therefore one that is essential for academic theology to be in touch with, to listen to, to share in, and to learn from – but never replace.[12]

John Mbiti came to appreciate the importance and relevance of this type of theological idiom for Africa:

> The Christian way of life is in Africa to stay, certainly for the fore-seeable future, [and] much of the theological activity in Christian Africa is being done as oral theology (in contrast to written theol-

8. Jehu-Appiah argues for the term "Narrative" over the term "Oral." He maintains that "narrativity" refers to the essential character of the theological system, whereas "oral-ity" simply refers to the manner of transmission. See "African Indigenous," 29.

9. Pobee, "Oral Theology," 88.

10. For a detailed discussion on this issue, see Vansina, *Oral Tradition*, 1–18.

11. Mbiti, "Cattle Are Born," 35–51.

12. Bediako, "Cry Jesus," 23.

ogy) from the living experience of Christians. It is theology in the open air, from the pulpit, in the market place, in the room as people pray or read and discuss the scriptures . . . African Christianity cannot wait for written theology to keep pace with it . . . academic theology can only come afterwards and examine the features retrospectively in order to understand them.[13]

The term "oral theology" has been variously discussed in relation to the means through which the oral sources communicate God.[14] In this section I am concerned with the means through which this orality communicates Christ in the context of Akan AICs.

The Akan AICs distinct bias toward orality is evident in the priority given to prayer, reading (hearing) the Bible, sermons, testimonies and worship by the Akan AIC adherents. These are evidently some of the main sources that characterize the shape of the Christology of the Akan AICs. "Orality" is therefore the essence of oral expression, which represents the ultimate reality in all its aspects, visible and invisible. Akan "oral Christology" which follows on from this, is therefore the encounter and experience of Christ primarily through the means of the Akan culture of orality.

THE MAJOR AREAS OF ORALITY
IN AKAN AIC CHRISTOLOGY

Within the worship tradition and community life of Akan AICs, a wide range of sources drawn from oral culture is employed within their religious discourse. These include proverbs, myths, stories, folklores, legends and oratory.[15] Akan tradition is rich with these oral forms, particularly in the area of storytelling (the "Ananse spider" stories are internationally known),[16] drumming (talking drums), and oratory (royal courts).[17] Akan AICs employ these vehicles of orality in different ways and to different

13. Mbiti, *Bible and Theology*, 229.

14. See Mbiti, "Cattle Are Born"; Pobee, "Oral Theology"; and Vansina, *Oral Tradition*.

15. Healey and Sybertz explore African proverbs, sayings, riddle, stories, myths, plays, songs, cultural symbols, and real life experiences as the guide for exploring African narrative theology. See *Towards an African Narrative*, 13. See also Fisher, *West African Religious*, 34.

16. See Jehu-Appiah, "African Indigenous Churches," 24, for an example of this type of storytelling.

17. See Yankah, *Speaking for the Chief*, 3–24.

degrees. The place of these individual forms of oral expression in the life of Akan AICs *per se* will not be examined, but rather I will seek to establish that this is a dimension of Christological discourse. In this research a number of areas in which the "oral Christology" of Akan AICs is communicated is identified and I now turn to them.

Preaching

For Akan AICs preaching is given a very central place in the service. It is through the preached "word" that the Bible is "re-oralized" into Akan oral culture and worldview. Sermons and homilies on the Christian faith are preached every Sunday and weekdays by pastors, priests, lay people, catechists, teachers, evangelists, and a host of untrained preachers.[18] It is here the most articulate expression of "oral Christology" is found. The survey indicated that 1440 (57.6%) of respondents to the national questionnaire believe that the sermon was the primary means by which they experienced the power of Christ. The significance of preaching as an aspect of Akan AIC "oral Christology" is based upon the centrality of the Bible, and the importance of Akan vernacular apprehension of the Bible. The Bible as we have seen in the examination of the source of Akan AIC Christology, emerged as pivotal, with 1918 (77%) of the sample indicating that it is their main source of experiencing Christ.

A total of 75 out of the 98 churches surveyed also held their services exclusively in the Twi vernacular and the rest used Twi as the dominant language but translated into one other language. The vernacular sermons of Akan AICs, which draw heavily upon the biblical narrative, are preached in church buildings, in school classrooms, under trees, in market places, in hospitals, buses, people's homes, in the open air, over the radio, and almost everywhere people gather.

---

18. Turner, in his analysis of 8,000 sermon texts preached in Aladura churches across West Africa, concluded that the text preferred by preachers were (in order of priority): a) Wisdom, and practical teaching, moral or religious; b) Gospels and Epistles, with the emphasis on the didactic, including ethical; c) Mythological, as in Genesis 1–11; d) Apocalyptic books; e) Prophetic literature; and f) Historical, legal and personal material, whether in the Old Testament, the Gospels, Acts, or the Epistles. This research demonstrates an AIC preference for books of the Bible more suited to African oral discourse such as, Wisdom books: Proverbs and Ecclesiastes, and books that provide moral, ethical and practical teaching and guidance such as the Gospels and the Epistles. See Turner, *Profile Through Preaching*, 78–79.

In his discussion on preaching in the context of oral theology Mbiti states,

> Sermons teach people new truths; some remind them what they already heard before. Sermons interpret the Gospel, and retell parts of the Bible record. Others challenge hearers to follow particular ideas and codes of behaviour; and some remind people of the promises of God. Others stimulate people to face life's situations with courage and hope. In short, sermons are the most influential means of shaping African Christianity.[19]

Preaching as an oral art form plays a crucial role in retelling the biblical story.[20]

In my discussion of the Christological categories in chapter 3 it was shown that the biblical "umbrella" titles *Saviour, Messiah, Lord* were the dominant titles used by Akan AICs to describe Jesus. Dominant among these was the title *Saviour*, selected by 1867 (74.7%) of respondents. Preaching plays a significant role in interpreting these biblical Christological concepts and recasting and retelling their meaning in vernacular form. *Saviour*, for example, as I have enumerated in chapter 5, is interpreted as *Osagyefo*, literally meaning *one who saves the battle*. Symbolically the term refers to a chief or a warrior. It is through the orality of preaching using the vernacular medium, therefore, that the symbolism of *chief* or *warrior*—and all that this means to the Akan—is transferred to Christ who is able to save within an African universe.[21]

The Bible

Earlier in this chapter I established that the dominant role the Bible plays among Akan AICs and maintained that the Bible is "re-oralized" through preaching. One way in which this is demonstrated is very similar to stories, folklores and proverbs. Apart from the text on which the sermon is based the majority of the quotations are not assisted with the chapter and verse in which they are found but are often quoted loosely or para-

19. Mbiti, "Cattle are Born," 18.

20. Opoku observes that the preacher's concern through his preaching is essentially to show the audience that the Bible demonstrates the importance and need for deliverance by its own witness of such occurrences taking place. Believers are therefore encouraged to emulate those who have been delivered in the Bible. See, "Akan Witchcraft," 265.

21. I will be discussing symbolism in more detail later in this chapter.

phrased. An example of this is in a sermon preached at the Bethel Faith Temple entitled "The Living Water":

> ... Bible says, when he met the woman of Samaria at the well, the woman, after a little chat with him, said give me some of that living water so that I don't have to come and fetch water here again. Again the Bible says, Jesus said if any man thirst let him drink of the water that I will give him to drink.[22]

A sermon preached at the MDCC Accra New Town provides another example:

> You may think that there is no way out and therefore you are worried, my friend let me talk to you, do you believe the Bible, the *Bible says* Jesus was wounded for you and bruised and by his stripes you are healed. *Bible says* his blood was poured out for you so that you can have life.[23]

The informal quoting and paraphrasing of the Bible locates the biblical text within the matrix of oral tradition, which can be accessed for the purpose of preaching.

Oral Tradition

Oral tradition is another source in the preaching of Akan AICs, and includes a range of oral sources drawn from songs, myths, proverbs and oral history. A typical example is seen in a sermon preached by one of the elders at MDCC, Accra New Town in which the Akan lore based upon Kwaku Ananse was referred to:

> Some of you are not living a pleasing life to God but you tried to pretend that all is fine. When you are at home you are fighting with your wife, fighting with your husband fighting with your children and then you come to church and pray for healing and ask for blessing. You cry because you are suffering and can't be healed but you won't do the right thing; you want to be like *Kwaku Ananse* and use your brain on God because you think that he only sees you on Sundays when you come to church. You remember *Kwaku Ananse, the spider* that we heard about in school (laughs). My friend, if you want God to bless, you do the right thing in your house, at work and anywhere you go. God will see that you are

22. Sermon recorded on February 25, 2001.
23. Sermon recorded on April 1, 2001.

faithful and therefore when you are in trouble he will come and help you; he will surely bless you ... Hallelujah![24]

Kwaku Ananse is a spider from an ancient Akan folklore who has a repetition for mischief. Though the stories are now collated into books, their main mode of transmission is still oral.

In addition to folklore, perhaps the most common aspect of oral tradition used in AIC sermons is proverbs. Illustrated below are two sermons, the first preached at MDCC, Accra New Town and the second at Gethsemane Grace healing Church:

> Bible says, Behold how good and how pleasant it is for brethren to dwell in unity. We see it is God's will that we do everything together; when we are together then the Devil cannot cause division among us because we are praying together, worshiping together, and fasting. When we are together then everything will be in order and there will not be any confusion. In our [Akan] tradition, we have a saying: *Onyankopɔn mpɛ asɛmmɔne nti na okyɛ din maako-maako,* which means, "God does not like disorder therefore he has given a name to everything."[25]

> The Devil tried to trap Jesus when he was tempted in the wilderness. He said I will give you all of this world if you fall down and worship me, and although Jesus was physically very weak because he had been fasting forty day and nights he rebuked the Devil and told him to go away. When we are in trouble we can call upon Christ because he knows what it feels like to be tempted by the Devil. It does not matter where you are you can call upon God. We have a saying in our culture *obi nnkyere abofra Onyame,* "no one needs to point out God to a child" because God is everywhere.[26]

Another source that is drawn upon is the oral history of the Church. This is particularly the case when churches have a long and rich history like the MDCC and the Ossa-Madih. During a service at a Ossa-Madih Church adherents were encouraged to persevere in the face of persecution and hardship:

> Beloved we must listen to the Holy Spirit and obey Christ's voice; don"t be like Peter and doubt or like Thomas and doubt Jesus, but be like Mary who said to the people at the wedding in Cana when

24. Sermon recorded on April 11, 1999.
25. Sermon recorded on June 4, 2000.
26. Sermon recorded on March 21, 1999.

the wine had got finished; do everything he tells you. We must obey God. When God told Samuel Dankwa and his group to move from the Central Region to a place that God would give them as a settlement, they did not doubt or question God but obeyed. The group was guided by five birds provided by God to travel from Muzano in the central region through the eastern Ashanti region and finally to Bromaa in the Brong Ahafo region. The group spent the entire year of 1928 walking to accomplish the second missionary journey. Although it was hard they struggled and because of that we are here in this place.[27]

Narratives such as the one quoted above are important reference points for the church faithful and are significant events for the church's solidarity. Orally transmitted and often reinforced through preaching, they reside in the collective memory of the worshippers.

Existential Context

Mbiti maintains that the contemporary life of the congregation figures prominently in preaching.[28] AIC's sermons are highly contextual and therefore as such draw heavily upon the real life setting of their members. A sermon entitled "The Living Water" preached at the Church of the Lord is a classic illustration:

Water is a very essential mineral, even in the world; when one is about to die of thirst water is what you need. Praise the Lord, Hallelujah! When Jesus was on the cross he was dying for a drink of water. Even in our daily lives you may have electricity light and all the social gadgets, yet the moment one is thirsty all these things mean nothing to him because he needs water. Hallelujah! In our locality, when Ghana Water Corporation closes or shuts the taps for two or three days, see how people search for water. We have to walk far and buy water from people who are selling it for very extortionate prices, and yet we have to buy it because we need water to survive. We need it to bathe to make our food and do everything. Even this mineral water being sold here in Ghana, see how people patronize it when the water is not flowing . . . Praise the Lord, Hallelujah! So water is very essential . . . So when Jesus

27. Sermon recorded on June 6, 1999.
28. Mbiti, *Bible and Theology*, 86.

was asking for water on the cross you can imagine how he was suffering.[29]

The preacher illustrates his point on the importance of water by referring to the struggle with which all of his members would be familiar namely, the struggle to find water when the taps are closed.

A sermon on the woman with the issue of blood in Luke chapter eight preached at the Church of the Lord Brotherhood in Tamale provides another example:

> . . . this woman went to all the doctors and spent all her money on medicine and the Bible says she even got worse after their treatment. In Ghana here many of the doctors will not even know your problem, but all the time they will look at you and give you prescription to go and buy medicine and tell you to come back in two days time. All the time you will be coming and going, up and down, until you have no money left, and then they will tell you to get money before they can talk to you. This is what happened to this woman until she went to doctor Jesus who did not tell her to go up and down, but just by touching him she got healed.[30]

In our earlier treatment of the source of Akan AICs Christology in chapter 4, I explained that for Akan AICs preaching is not monological but dialogical, in ways reminiscent of the call and response of the *atumpan* (talking drums).[31] The *dialogical* nature of preaching among Akan AICs occurs when someone in the audience, resonating with something the preacher says, stands and begins singing a song in which the whole congregation joins. The preacher would continue after the song had been sung two or three times,[32] though there have been times when the congregation would get so carried away into the song as to necessitate the intervention of the preacher or the moderator.

An example of the use of song in response to the preaching was observed in a service attended at the MDCC in Cape Coast:

<hr>

29. Sermon recorded on March 19, 2000.

30. Sermon recorded on March 20, 1999.

31. See Fisher, *West African*, 34.

32. Beckmann maintains that an Eden Revival preacher never begins without the inspirational of a song, and he calls for hymn breaks again and again throughout the sermon; see *Eden Revival*, 82.

Preacher: If you want God to heal you must not be proud but humble, because the Bible says a broken and humble heart the Lord will listen to, but the proud he will turn away. Jesus wants us to be humble . . .
(Song interjection by a member of the choir, subsequently sung in concert)

Make me whole, my Lord;
Make me whole.
You know what I am,
You know what I need.
All my life, all my prayer
Shall be, shall be:
Make me whole, my Lord;
Make me whole.[33]

This pattern of what Yankah calls "formal speech interaction,"[34] which underscores the importance of mediative "oral consensus building" through the means of verbal response by the audience or, as Yankah puts it, "answering," serves two main functions. The first is that it establishes the agreement of the people with God's word, and thus the maintenance of harmony in the community; secondly it lends a measure of objectivity to the "oralized" message of the preacher's interpretation of the Bible, implying that the speaker's view-point is not a subjective one, but one based upon "oral consensus" and shared experience of Jesus Christ through the Holy Spirit.

The Christological content of the preaching of Akan AICs forms part of their message which will determine the extent to which Christ is encountered and expressed. On the surface it would appear that the sermons are low in Christological content; however, on closer examination it is evident that Akan AICs often use the term *Onyankopong* (God) and *Yesu Kristo* (Jesus Christ) interchangeably and often together as in *Yesu Christo Onyankopong*.[35] Harold Turner, in his small book analyzing 8,000 sermon texts preached by members of the Church of the Lord (Aladura), maintained that Aladura preaching did not lack in Christological content.[36]

33. Sermon recorded on November 21, 1999. Song from *Songs of Inspiration 135*.

34. Yankah, *Speaking for the Chief*, 19.

35. I have personally heard *Onyankopong* referred to as "dying on the cross" and also "raising from the dead."

36. Turner noted that the three main areas distinctly favored by Aladura preachers were "the Temptation of Christ," "The triumphal entry of Christ," and the "Resurrection

Although one must be careful not to force comparisons when exploring the significance and meaning of AIC practices in relation to traditional religious practice, it is highly probable that the idea expressed in Akan "royal oratory" can give meaningful insights into the role and function of the preaching of Christ within Akan AICs. In cultures where writing is only a recent development, but which have operated within a framework of pristine orality, the practice of using speech intermediaries attains an added significance. This is partly due to the socio-political significance of orality in such cultures, but also because of the potency they often attached to the spoken word.

Of the spoken word in an Akan traditional context, Kwesi Yankah maintains that "[b]eing the embodiment of acoustic energy and ordinarily enjoining co-presence, to all participants in the communicative enterprise the spoken word has immediate impact."[37] In an Akan context the spoken word has performative powers or magical potency—the power to alter reality.

This was demonstrated to me in the most personal of ways while I was attending a funeral in Kumase, in the Ashanti region. Simply wishing to convey my condolence, I mistakenly asked one of the relatives of the bereaved family, "Is it your son who has died?" However, the man I spoke to, who happened to be the brother of the man whose son had passed away, looked at me with great trepidation and said, "No, it is my brother's child who has died." When I enquired of my host why he looked at me with such consternation, he said to me, "By simply asking whether he is the bereaved one, you may have inadvertently spoken it into being."

Prayer

Within Akan AICs (as elsewhere in Africa) prayer is fundamentally about communication between the visible and the invisible realms of reality and constitutes a significant factor in the development of Akan oral Christology.[38] Tokunboh Adeyemo describes prayer as "the commonest

of Christ." See *Profile Through Preaching*, 32.

37. Yankah, *Speaking for the Chief*, 10.

38. Taylor suggests that the communication link between the living and the dead is prayer; see Taylor, *The Primal Vision*, 154–71; Sundkler argues that prayers are the point of contact between the living and the world of the spirit ancestor; see *Bantu Prophets*, 192–93; Mfusi believes that prayer in Africa is perhaps recognized as the major form of verbal communication with the supernatural; see "Religious Communication," 183.

act of worship" in Africa,[39] while Mbiti characterizes the practice as "one of the most ancient items of African spiritual riches."[40] Among the Akan AICs prayers are not normally silent and contemplative, but audible, expressive, and spontaneous.[41]

The investigation of the source of Akan AIC Christology revealed that 33% of respondents indicated that prayer was a very important means of experiencing Christ. Prayer therefore is a significant and integral aspect of Akan AIC "oral Christology" primarily because it is through prayer that requests are made for personal and family needs: requests for health and healing, protection from danger, safety in journeys and undertakings, guidance in finding a good wife or husband, success in undertaking examinations and business, gratitude for answered prayers and other blessings, good welfare of members of the family and relatives or friends.

In the examination of the function of Akan AIC Christology in chapter 5, the Devil (1770; 70.8%), sickness (1408; 56.3%) and evil spirits (1123; 45%) were the main reason for which protection through prayer was sought. Most Akan AIC's prayers are not recorded; nonetheless, these oral expressions are the raw materials of an Akan AIC Christology. Through prayers people pour out their hearts before God. Prayers often expose the innermost being and concerns of a person before God and provide clues to the nature of their Christology.

Four different types of prayers were observed among the Akan AICs visited for this research. These are *petition prayers* (earnest requests), *adoration prayers* (praising and honouring the Supreme Being, as well as expressing devotion and dependence), *supplication prayers* (lamentations, particularly for forgiveness for wrong doing or extreme frustration of a persistent problem), and *gratitude prayers* (prayers of thanksgiving).[42] The orality that characterizes the Akan AICs practice of prayer is seen in their pragmatic approach in petitioning for practical needs to be met. It is useful to cite some prayers recorded during the field research that highlight this characteristic.

---

39. Adeyemo, *Salvation in African Tradition*, 35.

40. Mbiti, *Prayers of African Religion*, 2.

41. Wyllie, *Spiritism in Ghana*, 39.

42. The Akan AICs devotion to prayer has been a very challenging and enriching learning curve for me. During my visits to these churches, I often took part in their prayer meetings and all-night prayer services, which has deepened my own prayer life.

A prayer by a member of MDCC in Accra New Town is especially illuminating of the theology and basic expectation of Akan AIC's Christology:

> *Onyame* (God) you are the God of Abraham, Isaac and Jacob;
> You made all things and all things belong to You
> I pray to you to make a way for me and my family.
> *Onyame*, you know that the rent on our house is due and
> The landlord is worrying us for the money;
> You know I am not working and my wife is sick.
> We beg you to please have mercy upon us and help.
> In the Name of Jesus we claim by faith the money that we need
> All money belongs to You, and not to the devil and all his people
> Please bless us and meet our need we are really suffering.... (*sic*).[43]

A very common feature of Akan AIC prayer is petition for God to aid a particular undertaking, such as the following one recorded at an all-night prayer meeting:

> *Onyankopͻn ntafowayifo* (God who performs wonderful deeds)
> Please, I want to travel and I will be going to the Embassy tomorrow
> By myself I cannot make it and do not know the question that they
> will use to trap me. I have spent my entire money going up and down to
> prepare well. I beg you do not allow them disappoint me. Remove all
> the powers that want to frustrate me and open all the doors that are
> closed.
> I want to visit my daughter whom I have not seen for a long time in the UK.
> You are Jehovah the mighty One please bless me ...[44]

The following is a typical prayer of supplication from a member of the Pentecostal Healing Church:

> Lord I have come to hear what you have to say to me,
> I have been waiting and praying for a long time. My husband
> has gone and my children has travelled and my business has gone down.
> Everyday I pray and cry to you but nothing is happening.
> I have come today and my heart is very heavy.
> *Yesu Kristo* you rose from the dead to give us life,
> Your blood gives us power and heals us.

---

43. A prayer extracted from a recording of a service at MDCC, Accra New Town on July 4, 1999.

44. Ibid.

I know you will hear my cry and so I am waiting to
see what you will do for me . . .[45]

As well as prayer being an important means of African people oral-
izing the challenges of everyday life, it also allows the African to communicate with Christ using the language of African culture and to draw upon
symbolism of African worldview. This type of Christological discourse as
a model for Africans to articulate their faith is well illustrated in Madam
Afua Kuma's book *Jesus of the Deep Forest.*

Afua Kuma—a native of the forest town of Obo-Kwahu on the Kwahu
mountain ridge in the Eastern Region of Ghana where she lives, farms,
and also practices as a traditional midwife—has written some liberating
prayers and praises which have been translated into English from Akan-
Twi by Fr. Jon Kirby. Interestingly, since these texts were first published in
1981, the Twi version *Kwaebirentuw ase Iesu* has been far more popular
than its English counterpart. Her prayers and praises in her vernacular
provide a liberating expression of faith in Christ, which mirror the Akan
affinity with the natural world, demonstrating that the Christian faith becomes, in the words of Andrew Walls, "culturally infinitely translatable."[46]
Below are some examples of Madam Kuma's prayers and praises:

> Jesus you are solid as a rock!
> The green mamba dies at the sight of Jesus
> Iron rod that cannot be coiled into a head-pad:
> the cobra turns on his back, prostrate before you!
> Jesus, you are the Elephant hunter, Fearless One!
> You have killed the evil spirit, and cut off its head!
> The drums of the king have announced it in the morning.
> All of your attendants lead the way with joy.[47]

Again:

> *Tutugyagu*: the Fearless One!
> You have pulled the teeth of the viper, and there he lies
> immoveable as a fallen tree, on which children play!
>
> *Adubasapɔn*: Strong-armed One!
> You are the one who has tied death to a tree

45. Recorded in a service at the Pentecostal Healing Church in Tamale on January
30, 2000.

46. Walls, "Gospel as the Prisoner," 39.

47. Kuma, *Jesus of the Deep*, 7.

so that we may be happy.
Just as you have done in the days of old
Today, you continue to work your wonders![48]

In a worldview which is beleaguered with spirits who operate in and through material objects, thus bringing terror to the Akan heart, Christ is the Fearless One who is not afraid of even the notorious viper, which is often perceived as being the embodiment of the most dangerous of evil spirits. Christ is the strong-armed one, the one who through His resurrection has conquered death. For the Akan death is not the end of a person's existence but the great disrupter of life. Death hinders the Akan from reaching his potential in life for wealth, fame, children, peace, long life, position and so on, here on earth; these are what one prays for and never for death.

> Jesus blockades the road of death with wisdom and power.
> He, the sharpest of all great swords
> has made the forest safe for the hunters.
> The *mmoatia* he has cut to pieces
> he has caught *Sasabonsam* and twisted off his head.[49]

Mmoatia, the mysterious creatures with supernatural powers that live deep in the forest, are believed to be tiny, with feet that point backwards. Suspending themselves from trees, they wait for the tired hunter in pitch darkness of the night. At their head, as in their head-spirit, is *Sasabonsam* with blood-shot eyes. This *Sasabonsam* has found its way in Akan AIC's (and Akan Christianity generally) vocabulary to designate the Devil. In the vivid language of the Akan, Jesus has twisted off its head.

> He is the Hunter gone to the deep forest.
> *Sasabosam*, the evil spirit,
> has troubled hunters for many years.
> They ran in fear
> Leaving their guns behind.
> Jesus has found these same guns,
> and brought them to the hunters
> to go and kill the elephant.
> Truly, Jesus is a Man among men!
> He stands firm as a rock. [50]

48. Ibid., 7.
49. Ibid., 19.
50. Ibid.

Jesus is the Hunter gone to the forest: the forest of the Akan world-view that has the *Sasabonsam* lurking and waiting for its next prey. Jesus has become a Hunter in order to deliver his own fellow hunters from that which they fear the most. Here we see a tremendous appropriation of the incarnation of Christ and His victory over evil spirits in the invisible realm of the *Sasabonsam* and his *mmoatia,* and in the visible realm of the wild creatures like elephants, who can be manipulated by evil spirits to wreak havoc upon a local village and take away a child. Jesus not only rescues the hunters, but also gives them back the power to subdue and conquer the animals possessed by these evil spirits.

This next praise clearly indicates that Madam Kuma is fully aware of the biblical Christ:

> A thousand thousands people give thanks to your Name.
> Angels of Heaven lift their praises.
> They say Hosanna!
> Men of earth; all of them
> Proclaim your Name in glory,
> you who cleanse us with your blood.
> Therefore take us and do what you like.[51]
> This Jesus of the deep forest is here clearly identified as the biblical
> Christ; the one who shed His own blood. The One who is glorified
> by the heavenly host of angels who cry "Hosanna"! But the "Jesus of
> the deep forest" is also the Jesus of the Gospels, the miracle worker
> who has compassion for those who are hungry and destitute.
> Wonderworker, you are the one
> who has carried water in a basket
> and put it by the roadside
> for travellers to drink for three days.
> You use the kono[52] basket to carry water to the desert,
> then you throw in your net and bring forth fish!
> You use the net to fetch water and put it into a basket
> We ride in canoes on the water's surface and catch our fish.[53]

Prayer therefore is one of the key aspects of an Akan AIC "oral Christology," representing the ultimate expression of a believer's personal encounter with Christ using their own language and from within their perception of the world.

51. Ibid., 14.
52. This is a large basket usually used to carry foodstuff in bulk.
53. Kuma, *Jesus,* 5.

Testimony (adansezi)

Orality within Akan Christological discourse is also expressed in *adansezi*, "testimony." Earlier in this chapter it was noted that for Akan AICs words have performative power and magical potency. Verbalization is therefore an essential means of releasing the favor of God. Through testimony, adherents publicly declare what the Lord has done for them, and for which, they want to give thanks and invite the community to share in their rejoicing.[54] Although there are different types of testimonies,[55] their essence is to express gratitude and thanksgiving, and this is sometimes accompanied with an offering.[56]

The following are testimonies recorded in different Akan AICs:

> I want to thank the Lord because I went for a job and although I didn"t have the necessary qualifications for the work I still got the job. Halleluiah![57]

Also another short testimony:

> For the past three weeks I have been very ill and could not come to church, but Hallelujah the Lord has touched me and I am here today.[58]

Another type of testimony observed is what I refer to as "special testimony." This is a testimony of thanksgiving for something that would be classified as potentially a very serious problem, which might have led to tragic consequences. An occasion for celebration and dancing, it attracts family and friends to the front of the church before the congregation with the "testifier" wearing the same traditional cloth that was worn at the time of the brewing problem. After the testimony is given, the celebration con-

54. Examples of these kinds of testimonies are found in Onyinah, "Akan Witchcraft," 263–64.

55. Wyllie outlines five different types of testimonies: unspecified benefits, healing, protection, petition and difficult problems that have been solved. See *Spiritism in Ghana*, 40.

56. Wyllie maintains that during the testimony service the pastor calls members to come forward and "witness to God's goodness," or "tell what the Lord has done for you," *Spiritism in Ghana*, 34.

57. This is a short testimony given by a member of MDCC, Abeka Junction Branch, February 7, 1999.

58. Recorded at the Church of the Lord in Labone, Accra, March 25, 2001.

tinues at the home of the one who gave the special testimony to which many are invited.

An example of this kind of "special testimony" was recorded at Emmanuel Healing Church in Tamale:

> Brethren I stand here with my family to tell the Lord thank you and also to thank all of you for your prayers and support. Many of you know my story, how I have been sick with diabetes, which was resulting in my leg being amputated. For a long time I kept on delaying because I really feared losing my leg. Things really got worse and my doctor said if I didn"t amputate it would spread to other parts of my body. I prepared everything to go into the hospital for an extended time. Brethren, when I got to the hospital the doctor said that the diabetes had gone and that the blood was now flowing into my leg. I really want to thank the Lord Jesus because I don"t have to lose my leg anymore. Hallelujah!![59]

Another "special testimony" at MDCC, in Kumase follows as such:

> Four days ago my son was very ill with malaria; we gave him all the medicine but still he did not get better. Yesterday pastor came and he organised a prayer meeting and we all prayed and fasted. Today he is feeling much better. Praise the Lord.[60]

Testimonies are therefore another feature of "oral Christology" that drew upon the traditional means of communication, which is indicative of the African oral tradition.

Worship

In various places throughout this inquiry I have sought to illustrate the integral function of worship in Akan AIC religiosity. It has been noted earlier in this research that "worshipping and praising God in Church," of which singing and dancing are the most prominent aspects, was the second highest option (71%) as the means of respondents experiencing the presence of Christ. In the context of Akan AICs, the orality of "worship" gives clear expression to their "oral Christology."[61] What M. Xulu says of the Zionist churches in South Africa, is also true of Akan AICs:

59. Recorded at the Emmanuel Healing Church Tamale, June 12, 1999.

60. Recorded at the MDCC, Kumase Branch, January 31, 1999.

61. For a detailed examination of the development and function of hymns in one particular AIC, see Krabill, *The Hymnody*; see also Turner, *History of African*, 294–314;

Spiritual singing is marked by speaking in tongues, prophesying and a general state of transformation. Often it is at the height of spiritual singing when people are sweating and some are even crying, while others may be lying low on the ground, that the Holy Spirit is felt to be present. At this point those who are opened up to the Holy Spirit receive enormous power from God through the priest or bishop and they are capable of doing things they would normally not do because their trance state reveals to them such secrets of the world as cannot be revealed in any other way. It is at this stage that personifications of Christ and even God in human form of priests and archbishops can be witnessed.[62]

The egalitarian nature of worship means that everyone present can take part and become a part of the "movement" of the Holy Spirit. In my previous treatment of this issue I argued that researchers who tend to focus on the pneumatological often overlook the Christological dimension of worshipping and praising God. I also noted observations of believers expressing intimacy with Christ during the "moving of the Holy Spirit" in worship. The Christological nature of AIC worship was also noted in the songs that are used during the communion service in which singing and dancing played an important part.[63] Further to these Christological insights of AIC worship is the idea that through singing and dancing the environment for the supernatural presence of Christ is created, and at the height of the worship, there is strong belief that he is present. The distinction between the presence of Christ and that of the Holy Spirit in the context of AIC worship and how these elements interact is one that is often overlooked by researchers and is certainly an area for further investigation.

Music expressed through singing and dancing is, however, the language of the transcendent; the conduit line through which the presence of the supernatural may be invoked. The essence of music as "orality" is seen in its ability to project the worshipper into the spirit-world. In the "trance" of song "all is spirit." The "song" and the "dance" therefore are not just a means by which Christ becomes imminent within the context of the worship but also a means by which the worshipper becomes transcended

---

Molyneux, "Oral Dimension," 24. Also see Beckmann, *Eden Revival*, 74–83, which gives some meaningful insights into Eden Revival's worship.

62. Xulu, "Music and Leadership."

63. Ibid.

into the realm of the spirit-world. It is at this point the worshipper is at one with Christ, who reigns over this realm, and the believer is therefore at his/her most powerful. The capability of music and song to transcend itself in this way is based upon it being a medium of pristine orality and its ability to be "inter-dimensional."

RESTORING THE TREASURES: TOWARD AN AFRICAN ORAL CHRISTOLOGY

So far we have discovered that Akan AIC Christology is clearly expressed through orality and have established that Akan AICs have a bias toward experiencing and communicating Christ through preaching, praying, song, testimony, and through hearing the Bible, which has been re-oralized principally through preaching, prayer and singing. These are ultimately the raw materials of Akan oral tradition. Orality therefore is the medium through which Akan AIC Christology is interpreted.

The tendency toward a Christology based upon western rationalistic paradigms in Africa has come under more and more scrutiny in recent years.[64] In spite of the advances that have undoubtedly taken place in the area of Christology in Africa, to a large extent there still remains a conscious and/or a sub-conscious desire for theological approval by the western theological intelligentsia. This has led to a number of theologians to call for a more radical overhaul of the African Christological approach. Among those theologians calling for a redefinition of the Christian faith in Africa is the Cameroonian theologian Jean-Marc Éla. He insists,

> If Christianity wants to reach Africans, to speak to their hearts and enter into their consciousness and the space where their soul breathes, it must change. To do so, Christianity must do violence to itself and break the chains of western rationality, which means almost nothing in the African civilisation of symbols. Without some form of epistemological break with the Scholastic universe, Christianity has little chance of reaching the African.[65]

African theologians are now increasingly demanding that the nature of "theologizing" in Africa take more account of the African oral resources, as we have seen with Mbiti, Appiah, Bediako, and Éla. Innovative and new ways are now being explored in order to tell the story of God's

64. Bediako, "Biblical Christologies," 115–61, is a good example.
65. Éla, *My Faith*, 41.

revelation in Christ using the language of Africa, which is the language of orality. This is the realm where orality is expressed through the language of symbols, metaphor, and analogy. In this realm God surges up from symbolic discourse as an absent subject whom we can neither grasp nor appropriate, but evoke. It is not unusual for an African to see things moving from the visible to the invisible through symbolism and it is therefore possible for Africans to develop a new symbolic understanding of their relationship with God. Symbolism makes the African Christian into a converted narrator, storyteller, theologian poet, God's *okyeame* (linguist), and singer.

Éla states further,

> In order to evangelise black Africa, we must establish a relationship with the "living revelation" where God begins to speak through an apostle of a base community using an African style to speak to Africans. The pedagogy of faith must develop a method of integrating the narrative of the passion and resurrection of Christ into the memory of our people. The art of the black African storyteller can be of service. We must talk about God in lands where the millet granary is the very image of the world and says far more to people than the vine or the wheat field. We dream of a church where God speaks to these people with images and symbols rooted in the hard soil of the grassland and the trees of the forest.[66]

The language that is employed by orality in articulating AIC Christology is symbolism.

AIC Oral Christology and Symbolism[67]

Africans live in what Éla calls a "forest of symbols,"[68] which is a unique way of maintaining their relationship to the universe. The employment of symbolic discourse within the context of this pristine orality is therefore essential for inculturating Christ in post-missionary Africa. Symbols in Africa are however usually "preloaded" with meaning and significance and any association with them carries the risk of misrepresentation or accusations of syncretism. This is particularly risky when attempting to

66. Ibid., 45.

67. A thorough treatment of the issue of symbolism, which proved very useful, was Dillistone, *Christianity and Symbolism*; For a discussion on symbolism in the context of AICs, see also Beckmann, *Eden Revival*, 80–82.

68. Ibid., 35.

appropriate Christ into a context that operates with a myriad of divinities. Since Akan AIC Christology is overwhelmingly oral, religious language is therefore the language of symbols.[69] Akans, as do Africans generally, express themselves through an infinite variety of symbols drawn from the concrete universe of their experience wherein language finds it meaning.

Taylor perceptively observes, "We shall need to remember that if we seriously intend to understand this African vision of reality, we shall find ourselves entering a world of strange perspective and relationships, marked with symbols."[70] This symbolic perception of reality implies that meaning is attached to words and objects beyond themselves and relates to the whole drama of existence that expresses relationship between human beings and the invisible realities. Symbolic language is therefore based upon consensus of meaning between the visible and invisible entities of reality. This is the level of "meaning" and "reality" which the western cerebral missionary outlook has failed, in part, to connect with and appropriate Christ into.

In the earlier discussion on the source and function of Akan AIC Christology it was concluded that the Bible was the ultimate authority as well as the source for moral and ethical guidance. It also noted the essential symbolic quality attributed to the Bible. The Bible is given a prominent place within the church and also used as an instrument of healing. The Bible serves "visibly" as a moral and ethical guidebook, and as a symbol, it serves "invisibly" as a symbol of power and authority, having the capacity to access the realms of the natural and the supernatural. This two dimensional function of Akan AIC's oral symbols is a dialectical discourse strikingly revealed in their Christology.

For Akan AICs, words have power and often point to a reality greater than themselves. This is the reason why the Bible as the "spoken" or "preached" Word of God takes precedence over the written texts. This distinction between words as "symbol" and the word as "text" is an important one for the development of an Akan "oral Christology." This incantatory power of the spoken word as symbol, preached, prayed, sung, danced, and communicated through the language of the drum, is the medium through which the power of Christ the "Great Ancestor" and protector in the invisible world of the spirit-realm, can be evoked.

---

69. Éla, *My Faith*, 36.

70. Taylor, *Primal Vision*, 41.

In chapter 5 Christ as Saviour was symbolically represented as *Osagyefo,* a term which carries with it the concrete symbolic meaning of "one who saves the battle." As *Osagyefo,* Jesus is the one who saves from the "enemies of life" or the "anti-life forces." As a symbol of protection, *Osagyefo* is the protector and provider within the visible realm and also the one who soars above the invisible realm of the spirit-world as Lord and Supreme Ancestor. In an African context ravished by AIDS, famine, and sickness, *Osagyefo* is a symbol of hope and life. It is perhaps not surprising that this title was selected by 74% of respondents as the title that best describes Jesus.

Bishop Peter Sarpong, the Catholic Bishop of the Diocese of Kumasi, states, "If Christianity's claim to be universal is to be believed, then it is not Africa that must be Christianised, but Christianity that must be Africanised."[71] *Sasabonsam* as a mystical representation of the "Devil" and "a worker of witchcraft" (as illustrated in the treatment of "Christological prophylactic") is another effective example of translating the message of the gospel of Christ into the language of African culture.[72]

For most Akans the fear of evil spirits and witchcraft is a very real one and one from which they seek protection and relief. Translating the concept "Devil" into the mystical concept of *Sasabonsam* is first of all to begin with the reality of the African culture and, secondly, to take the symbolic language of Akan culture seriously.[73] It is within this dimension that the language of symbolism becomes a means of communication through metaphor and helps speak to the One who exists beyond words. This is the Christ who it is believed is able to enter the realm of the mystical world of spirits and the concrete universe of symbols without contradiction or discontinuity.

What Father Placide Temples says of the Bantu is equally true of the Akan of Ghana:

> They cannot conceive a man as an individual existing by himself, unrelated to the animate and inanimate forces surrounding him. It is not sufficient to say he is a social being; he feels himself a

71. Sarpong, as quoted in Healey and Sybertz, *Towards a Narrative Theology,* 19.

72. For a detailed delineation of *Sasabonsam* in relation to the practice of witchcraft, see Onyinah, "Akan Witchcraft," 53.

73. See Meyer, *Translating the Devil,* 80.

vital force in actual intimate and permanent rapport with other forces—vital force both influenced by and influencing them.[74]

The "spirit-world" in which these "other forces" live along with human-kind is communicated on the level of symbolism.

Sasabonsam therefore, as a symbol of evil, is overcome through the Akan symbol of *Osagyefo*—the symbol of a great warrior. Christ therefore as *Osagyefo* draws from the concrete universe of their experience, where language finds its meaning. This "foregrounding" of the subliminal world, which underlines much of the Akan religious consciousness—even in modern Africa—is the realm in which the Akan AICs seek to bring into the captivity of Christ, through the effective employment of symbols, the "anti-life" forces of the spirit-world. Their inclusion and adaptation of selective symbols from local and foreign sources is a feature for which Akan AICs are known. Being sensitive to the close affinity between traditional symbols and traditional religion, however, Akan AICs are keen to avoid accusations of syncretism and sectarianism from the wider church community whose distancing of traditional practice is a part of their Christian piety.[75]

AKAN AIC ORAL CHRISTOLOGY AS METAPHOR

In the realm of the African symbolic universe, symbolism finds clear expression through metaphor. A metaphor, according to F. W. Dillistone, "[w]idens, transcends, overcomes, gives birth to the new, creates. It is a process of tension and energy. It begins with symbols but it transcends and transforms all symbolic fixation and reductions."[76] S. K. Langer remarks, "Metaphor is our most striking evidence of *abstractive seeing*, of the power of the human mind to use presentational symbols." Every new experience, or new idea about things, evokes first of all some metaphori-

---

74. Tempels, *Bantu Philosophy*, 30.

75. This could possibly provide an explanation for the findings of the research, which surprisingly showed that the Christological title "ancestor" was one of the least favored options selected by the respondents, in spite in being a popular Christological metaphor for African academics. As we have noted in our treatment of this title in chapter 5 it was the association of ancestor with "traditional religion" that caused Akan AICs to distance themselves from this as a Christological title though the function of "ancestor" was very much part and parcel of their experience of Christ.

76. Dillistone, *Christianity and Symbolism*, 28.

cal expression.[77] Sallie TeSelle says, "in the simplest formation, when we use a metaphor we have two thoughts of different things active together and supported by a single word, or phrase, whose meaning is a resultant of their interaction."[78]

Metaphor in this sense is a form of inculturation of Christianity that allows us to visualize God's revelation in Christ in an African environment. Although it begins with the known, namely "African culture," it also makes room for the unknown, "revelation of Christ." The unknown subject is therefore made available to us through the known. Another important aspect of the metaphoric discourse is that it operates in both the visible and the invisible dimensions of the African worldview. Through the metaphor the two subjects, ordinary life and the transcendent, are so intertwined that there is no way of separating them, and in fact, what we learn is not primarily something about God but a new way to live an ordinary life.

A good example of this type of theological discourse, which articulates the Akan AICs expression of faith in Christ, is seen in one of the recorded prayers for healing at the Church of the Lord Brotherhood in Bolgatanga:

> Jesus you are the Chief healer
> Your medicine is the strongest of all
> The Devil is afraid of you; *mmoatia* flees at your coming
> All workers of witchcraft know your name.
> You have beaten down the devil with your pestle.
> You have crushed the head of Satan.
> Lay your hands on this woman and heal her of all her problems.[79]

Among the Akan, healers are many. Declaring Jesus as the chief healer whose medicine is more potent than all others is to acknowledge the connection between healing and deity. The Devil and *mmoatia*, who both have powers to heal are afraid of the medicine that is used by Jesus. In a realm in which hierarchy of powers is indicative of the potency of medicine (healing), witchcraft and curses, Jesus is acknowledged as Supreme. The idea that Jesus has beaten down the Devil with a pestle and has crushed the head of Satan demonstrates the importance of integrating

77. Langer, *Philosophy in a New Key*, 141.
78. TeSelle, *Speaking in Parables*, 43.
79. Recorded on March 14, 1999.

the "ordinary with the transcendent," which is a significant aspect of this metaphorical Christology. Fufu pounding symbolizes the realm of Satan and all other spirits. The idea of the Devil's head being crushed is possibly a re-oralization of Genesis 3:15, which is a passage often quoted by Akan AIC preachers.

Songs are a primary cradle and medium of the metaphoric symbolic language in which Akan AIC oral Christology is nurtured and expressed. Praises offered to Christ during an Easter Celebration Service at MDCC, Cape Coast branch, are a case in point:

> Jesus you are our King, *ose, ose*
> Walk slowly because you are holy
> Walk gently and take your seat among us
> You are majestic. You are majestic and holy
> You died and rose from the dead and now you have been given the highest stool
> Walk gently, walk slowly, walk majestically, we have come to worship you.[80]

The idea of kingship is very important for Akan, as for Africans generally, intoning multidimensional implications in both the visible and the invisible realms. Declaring Jesus as King is a metaphor that draws upon the Kingship of Christ (the reign of Christ) as well as the Akan notion of kingship.

This is vividly demonstrated in the request for the king (Jesus) to walk slowly and majestically. In traditional Akan culture—particularly in Ashanti—the king walks slowly and graciously to his seat;[81] the congregation rises in deference, while the herald in a shrill voice proclaims his arrival. It is into this ambience that the sovereignty of Christ, the one who died and rose again, is appropriated and celebrated.

> Jesus, you are the rock that hid us and the big tree that we lean on. You are the great King who protects all of your people and you died for our sins. Your blood gives us life. Death is afraid of you because you can break it. You are the fearless God *(Tutugyagu)*.[82]

---

80. Recorded on April 15, 2001.

81. The king traditionally walks slowly as a sign of grace and also for the king to trip or to fall is a sign of a bad Omen.

82. Prayer recorded at MDCC Accra New Town branch, May 23, 1999.

In this prayer the familiar Akan symbols of a "rock" and a "tree" are employed. As a rock Christ is strong and as a tree he is dependable. The Twi appellation often applied to Christ is *Tweaduampɔn,* which literally translated means "lean against a tree, it will not fall." Christ is therefore the dependable one. In this prayer the significance of blood within an Akan traditional context has been metaphorically linked to the death of Christ. Christ as the one who defeated death is therefore the ultimate source of life, the "eldest son" of *Nyame* the Supreme God.

Éla's observation that "Christianity's victory over traditional religion was a deadly blow to its credibility," is very revealing.[83] Revealing most of all because, as well as ostensibly triumphing over the ancestral belief and traditional deities, it also rejected the oral paradigm which "sees" through intuition, symbolism, and metaphors. What is seen through the Christological discourse of Akan AICs is a rediscovery of this African unspoken language.

Éla, quoting French savant Bachelard, makes the point forcibly:

> We need to "reawaken the wellsprings" to rediscover the path that will free humanity, currently suffocating with narrow rationalism, for openness and participation. If we are to live our context marked by basic symbolism of life and death, we must find our way back to the pool of Siloam (John 9:7) where, like the blind man who washed his eyes and had his sight restored, we can once again claim our primordial language. Symbolic language is not an historical avatar or a cultural accident of revelation; rather, faith can be expressed only symbolically, and every other type of discourse must be subordinated to this symbolic expression.[84]

To a large degree the scholastic and academic pedagogy of the West penalizes symbolism and ridicules metaphor.[85] Christianity, however, cannot dispense with the symbolic language that scholasticism eliminated from Christian theology. It is rather ironic that the first Christians and the Fathers of the Church did not disdain the use of symbols to express their faith and make it intelligible to others.

What is seen in the Christology of Akan AICs is a re-actualizing of the significance of Christ within a cultural structure of orality, where symbolism expresses the destiny of humanity through metaphors of ev-

83. Quoted in Éla, *My Faith,* 33.

84. Ibid., 42

85. Ibid.

eryday life. At the heart of this approach to Christology is the idea that we cannot attain to Christ by lifting ourselves out of the world, or by isolating ourselves from time and space; we cannot attain God in the pure transcendence of the spirit, or in absolute. Rather we find Christ concretely at the human level, there where we are most genuinely ourselves. In this African realm of reality all is united—the natural and the supernatural, the invisible and the visible, the physical and the spiritual, the transcendent and the immanent, the "now" and the "hereafter"—in a tangible existence where salvation takes on flesh and every aspect of Christ crucified penetrates the most physical aspects of our daily lives.

Another important aspect of metaphorical discourse in relation to African Christology is the fact that it unites Africans and their world at a level below "subject—object"; it is the nexus of humanity in the "being" of the world, the intimation of our original unity with all that is. This is significantly an African perspective of the universe, which far from being static is very dynamic—ever evolving as new connections are made between the familiar and the unfamiliar, so that new possibilities can be glimpsed.

This was evident in the treatment of vernacular hermeneutics, where important connections were made between placing the biblical narrative into an African vernacular outlook.[86] Through the process of what Sallie TeSelle calls in another context a "dialectic of imaging," new frames of reality are made.[87] These frames of reality are established through associations and connections within their familiar environment, dislocating it sufficiently so that "what is." For example, African perception of reality is seen in a new light as what it "might be" in the light of the metaphorical relationship between "Jesus of the deep forest of Africa" and "Jesus as the biblical Christ. This metaphorical association in African Christological discourse provides a valuable source for new insights, of seeing the "new world" which is also the "old world," thus "seeing," "hearing," and "reading" the story of Jesus as a new story, as story which is the prolepsis of God's revelation in Christ in an African milieu.

---

86. See ch. 6.
87. TeSelle, *Speaking in Parables,* 43.

Implications for Written "Academic" Christology

One of the significant aspects of AIC Christology, to which this research has attested, is its highly "functional"[88] rather than merely ontological nature.[89] The field research itself demonstrated that Akan AICs seek Christ for protection and benefits that will enable them to live more effectively. Theirs is a theology that is enacted, "lived," and communicated primarily through orality. Theirs is an "oral Christology" which articulates African theological creativity and gives the Church in Africa a certain measure of theological self-hood.[90]

Yet we must recognize that however rich and lively "oral Christology" is, it has certain limitations. For example, "oral Christology" cannot sustain a long theological argumentation or discourse. The audience of "oral Christology" is generally very limited, being confined to local group situations, and occasions to which it addresses itself. So far as it is orally disseminated, it cannot be easily put through the scrutiny of scholarly and critical evaluation and analysis. Further, it is also difficult, if not impossible, to transport specific formations of "oral Christology" from one place to another, from one period to another, without changes and alterations that go with oral transition of information. Nevertheless, as it has been explained above in my treatment of "oral Christology" and "re-oralizing," this oral process will not be a permanent substitute for written Christology but a foundation and basis upon which a written tradition will be built. It also provides ample material for the evaluation of written Christology, not only in terms of its content but also in terms of its method of operation.

Written theology by comparison is mainly systematic academic reflections on the mystery of Christ in the midst of African realities.[91] One of the weaknesses of the academic theological approach to Christology in Africa—espoused by both African and western theologians alike—is that it imposes the epistemological framework of a western mindset and pedagogy. At its heart is the separation of the mind (or spirit) and body, the invisible and the visible. This theology is therefore often abstract and detached from the daily necessities and banality of life, valuing contem-

88. Healey and Sybertz, *Towards an African Narrative*, 76.
89. By "ontological" I refer to God being seen in purely contemplative terms.
90. Mbiti, "Cattle Are Born," 23.
91. Daneel, *African Earthkeepers*, 205.

plation as something that is an end in itself. Thought is considered greater than action and the abstract superior to concrete realities. As such it inadvertently devalues the pedagogical essentialities that African thought construct is predicated upon: symbolism, mythology, song, gesture, metaphor, analogy, the co-existence of the visible and the invisible, and transcendent and imminent realities.

In order for the academic Christology to have value for Africans at a grassroots level it will have to re-engage with the language of culture within the framework of orality. It must rethink Christ taking into account the words and gestures through which African people negotiate the drama of life and death. African academics must translate their relationship with Jesus of Nazareth into the language of the masses that seek him. The "oral Christology" presented in this work, as a model shaped through the researching of the Christology of Akan AICs, is an invitation to replace the Christological method that is based upon western rationalism with one that begins with and allows itself to be shaped by the oral dimensions of African culture. Since it is the living church that produces its own theology,[92] oral Christology takes us to the fields where the Christians who make up the living church are found. It is these fields in which the bulk of written Christology will have to germinate and grow in order for Christ to be meaningful for Africans.

Implications for African Christologies

The methodological dichotomy between the Christologies of inculturation and liberation highlights the degree to which African theologians have adopted western methods of theological reflection.[93] The Christology suited for the African context, however, must seek to go beyond theoretical distinction between inculturation and liberation to deal realistically with the pain, suffering, and death structures that rule the lives of millions of Africans today. The dualism between the theologies of liberation and inculturation operates on the same basis as the evolutionary epistemology

---

92. Schreiter argues that the Church community is a key source for theological development and expressions. *Constructing Local Theologies*, 16–18.

93. For an analysis of African Christologies of inculturation and liberation, see the following references: Schreiter, *Faces of Jesus in Africa*; Mugambi and Megesa (eds.), *Jesus in African Christianity*; for analysis of the inculturation and liberation perspective of African Christology, see Martey, *African Theology*.

that justified colonial exploitation in the name of civilising mission.[94] The integrated universe in which cause and effect can even translate between the dimension of the visible and invisible realms refutes any approach that draws a line of demarcation between socio-political oppression and cultural alienation. In the lives of millions of suffering Africans there is no such distinction.

J. José Alviar states,

> In contrast with the modern western accent on human nature in terms of liberty, self-determination, autonomy and self-fulfilment, the African mind refuses to conceive the human being separately from his social and cosmic environment. A person is in the measure in which he/she simultaneously belongs to a community and to the universe. Human nature in this respect, appears as "being situated in" a mesh of relationships among discrete existence which taken together, make up a unified whole.[95]

The African liberation and inculturation Christologies discussed in chapter 2 must of course be seen as genuine creative contribution to African Christology so far as they are the personal reflections of Africans.

Charles Nyamiti celebrates the originality of these Christologies by pointing out that they introduced a whole new systematic categorization that expounds upon the mystery of Christ such as Christ as chief, healer, master of initiation and ancestor, just to name a few.[96] However as a developing written tradition, African Christological paradigms have struggled to make their theological reflection on the mystery of Christ a corollary of African grassroots or local theological reflection from which an entire reservoir of words, images, symbols, and concrete categories can cause a new Christian vocabulary to burst forth. This comment is not meant to disparage other ways of doing African Christology but rather to call attention to the practical advantages of a Christology of orality, which draw upon African symbol, imagery, and metaphor. This "oral Christology" therefore challenges African theologians to rediscover the oral dimensions of theology, which is no less important than the *summae* and the great treatises. Perhaps this could help liberate African theology from the

---

94. This ideology could be traced to the evolutionary epistemology, which separates political ideas from their cultural forms.

95. Alviar, "Anthropological Foundations."

96. Nyamiti, "African Christologies," 14.

cultural system that sometimes conveys the impression that the "Word has been made text, and not flesh."[97]

The oral dimension in which this Christology can be seen is represented in the singing, preaching, testimonies, prayers, and healing practices; for the most part these are not recorded in books or stored in ways that they can be readily retrieved, but they are heard echoing from the daily lives of people in community. It is here in the market place of life that people can be seen making sense of, and appropriating the meaning of, the mystery of Christ. It is here where their Christology is being "oralized" and lived out. The challenge of this "oral Christology" is to call African theologians away from the isolationist approach to theology in which an individual engages in theological reflection from the confinement of his/her study or in a library, to one in which the community participates together.

Éla astutely states, "I dream of a "theology under the tree," which would be worked out as brothers and sisters sit side by side wherever Christians share the lot of peasant people who seek to take responsibility for their future and for transforming their living conditions."[98] This "oral Christology" in which Christ is encountered within the open space of the African rural environment—which, in spite of the rapid expansion of urbanisation spreading across the continent is still the milieu with which most Africans are familiar—challenges us to discover fresh and innovative language for expressing the mystery of Christ.

Earlier in this chapter I discussed the idea of a metaphorical Christology, which draws upon the natural environment as a means of expressing through the language of symbolism and metaphor that which cannot not be illuminated in any other way. This fresh theological language which draws upon metaphor and symbolism in the natural environment—exemplified in the *Prayers and Praises* of Madam Kuma and the recorded prayers outlined in chapter 4—delivers the African academic theologian from the burden that he or she is expected to construct an African Christology unaided.[99] The raw material of orality that makes up this grassroots Christology has a renewed appreciation for the meta-narrative of God's creation as telling the story of God's revelation through

97. Éla, *My Faith*, 180–81.

98. Ibid., 180.

99. Bediako, *Christianity in Africa*, 60.

Christ. Ott's analysis of the KuNgoni Art Craft Centre's portrayal of Christ as a "Kachere Tree" depicted in wooden sculpture,[100] and Daneel's Earthkeeping Christology (mentioned above) are good examples of how this kind of "oral Christology" expressed through symbolism and metaphor and drawn from the roots of African society, are able to provide new ways of talking about the mystery of Christ in a post-missionary African context.

Revisiting the Sacraments: Holy Communion and Baptism

My assessment of the sacraments of Holy Communion and Baptism in chapter 4 showed that these practices were infrequently observed and were also among the lowest categories selected as means of experiencing Christ. One of the reasons noted for the infrequent practice of the sacraments was that in some cases the use of the symbolic elements such as water, wine, and the implication of the blood of Christ clashed with some very deep cultural symbolic association and meaning.[101] In spite of the somewhat inconsistent and fragmentary use of the symbolism of sacraments in expressing the mystery of Christ, I would argue that the "symbolic approach" indicated in the use of the sacraments as pointing toward "transcendent mystery" expressed through "immanent concrete realities" represents the language that speaks to the African soul.

African theologians and church leaders are increasingly adopting oral Christological methods to express through the use of sacrament symbolisms the meaning of the incarnation narrative of Christ.[102] Christology as sacrament is a valuable area of Christological inculturation in an African setting that has the potential for further exploration. It will provide both dialogue and exchange between academic Christology and the "oral Christology" that is more indicative of grassroots Christology and the Bible. The theological reflection on a symbolic representation of

---

100. "Kachere" is a local Malawian name for a much branched evergreen tree up to fifty feet in height. The decision to use this was because of its many metaphoric association with the Christ-figure. See Ott, *African Theology*, 371–433.

101. One of the examples cited was the idea of drinking the blood of Christ unworthily, tantamount to imposing a curse on yourself. See section on Holy Communion, chapter 4.

102. For examples of inculturation of the sacraments in different African contexts, see Healey and Sybertz, *African Narrative Theology*, 254–76; Daneel, *Earth Keepers*, 227; and Tovey, *Inculturation*, 17–27.

Christ further provides common ground for the academic scholar and the illiterate or semi-illiterate African Christian. This common ground is established on the basis that the starting point for reflection is not the epistemological and theological presuppositions of western academia—which form the tutelage of many of the African scholars—but rather the symbol or the metaphor which does not communicate through the rational mind alone but speaks the language of intuition—the language of orality—gleaned through the eyes of the African worldview.

Implications for Theological Language

From the Christology of Akan AICs we have seen that language and theological concepts are an integral part of appropriating Christ. The language of theology must be taken seriously, because it is through language that thoughts and ideas are formulated in regard to the mystery of Christ. The pertinent questions to be considered here are: Does theology through vernacular hermeneutics communicate more than just the meaning of words? Do churches that use the vernacular respond more effectively and appropriately to issues than those who use a *lingua franca*?

In my exploration of vernacular hermeneutics in chapter 6, it was discovered that where the language of the hearer was used to communicate the Bible or theological concepts it allowed the speaker to enter the hearers" world and also encouraged them to base their interpretation on vernacular concepts and ideas. In the Bible studies conducted in English and Twi mentioned in the same chapter, we discovered that the group using the Twi vernacular drew more readily upon vernacular culture and indigenous symbols and concepts when interpreting the text. They were also the group that had a more active involvement from a cross-section of the group. The group using the English translation had limited participation, involving only those who were privileged to have had a secondary education and therefore had a better command of English and were therefore more confident to contribute.

Although English is the *lingua franca* of Ghana the dominance of the English language is still only in the cities and usually just among those who have had formal education in English. The research showed that 75 percent of the churches in the survey used only the Twi vernacular for their services.[103] The research also showed that less that 50 percent of

---

103. This number is generally higher in the newer charismatic churches in Ghana,

the surveyed population had achieved Primary and Secondary formal education. The vernacular therefore is still the dominant language among the Akan AICs. This then raises the issue, if Christian education occurs only in English, will the person in training for ministry learn effectively how to transmit the mystery of Christ in their mother tongue? The vital importance of this is appreciated when orality as the dominant medium through which the message of Christ is communicated in Africa is seen as the channel for optimally communicating the gospel message in Ghana.

Implications for Health, Healing and Wholeness

The Akan AIC concept of healing speaks forcefully to the African continent itself as well as to the understanding of healing and wholeness in other contexts. Within Africa, the adoption of a western-style democratic ideological structure is increasingly insisting that religion and socio-economic issues be polarized. Although we are now familiar with the idea of Africa being the centre of gravity for Christianity, having the fastest growing number of converts to Christianity in the world,[104] it is still a continent plagued with poverty, famine and political and economic chaos. The Akan AIC integrated and holistic Christology of healing highlights the inherent contradiction that we can be a people that are "spiritually well" but "socio-economically sick." According to this conception of reality there can be no polarization of socio-economic health (or well-being) and religious favor (well-being) and vice versa; the health of the nation economically is contingent on the health of the nation spiritually and therefore the socio-economic dysfunction is connected to moral and spiritual behavior.

As we have noted above, the Akan AIC approach to personal illness is one of determining the root cause of the illness and then seeking the appropriate means whereby harmony may be restored. This approach provides us with a vision of overcoming the social ills that are caused through the "anti-life" forces controlling the economic and structural dimensions of society. In the same manner in which Christ is enlisted in the battle against the unseen evil forces that seek to bring disharmony and death, Jesus should be identified as the one who dominates evil forces working against the socio-economic well-being of society. In this respect the gospel of Christ is the enemy of corruption, injustice, poverty and

---

which are influenced by American charismatic Christianity.

104. Bediako, *Christianity in Africa*, 3.

all who work against the well-being of the society as a whole. These are perhaps signs of a liberation motif based upon AICs understanding of healing and wholeness which is at the heart of their notion of the meaning of salvation in Christ.

The AIC's understanding of healing is also a vision of health and wholeness that is contrasted to that which is portrayed by western societies, which has a more fragmented view of the relationship between people and nature. Harvey Cox perceptively remarks:

> Paradoxically, the traditional African cosmology, which the indigenous Christian churches incorporate so inventively, may be more in tune with the "quantum world" than western theology . . . While the western churches still seem mired in a theology that separates man from nature and grants him "dominion" over the beast and the plants, Africans are evolving theology that locates human life within the web of nature and views violation of the natural order—which is the domain of the "Earthkeeping Spirit"—as a serious sin.[105]

In a world in which we are now accustomed to hearing alarm bells rung in regard to the extent to which human behavior through abuse and excesses is "hurting" the planet through abuse such as pollution and deforestation,[106] the worldview of the AICs which sees humankind as stewards of the earth speaks powerfully.

As well as the harmony between humankind and nature, AICs also present a vision of the interconnection between the physical world and the metaphysical world beyond "matter." Harvey Cox again purports: "While western medicine has just begun to scramble for a new understanding of the place of altered states of consciousness in curing human diseases, and the mysterious link between mind and body, the indigenous African churches have never given up the powerful bond between prayer and healing."[107]

For many, the healing practices and worldview of AICs may present a picture of "primal" behaviour and a worldview that is outdated and irrelevant. However, their experience of living through the most dreadful crises such as famine, ethnic genocide, religious strife, economic chaos,

---

105. Cox, *Fire*, 258.

106. For a discussion of African ecology, see Daneel, *African Earthkeepers*, 8–15.

107. Cox, *Fire*, 258.

political turmoil, and the most recent scourge AIDS, may, as Cox suggests,[108] provide insights into the precious resources that keep the spirit alive and give the soul hope in the face of these enemies of life.

CONCLUSION

The shift of focus away from the manner in which missionaries have historically sought to proclaim Christ—particularly the shortcoming of their endeavours—to the effective methods that are being employed by African Church movements such as the AICs and, more recently, the new Charismatic churches, in inculturating the gospel should now be the starting point of our main theological discourse. It is by focusing upon the methods Africans have used to talk about God and live out their faith meaningfully that academic theologians are forced to enter once again the world of symbolism and metaphor. Restoring the treasures of symbolic discourse into the arena of theology has made it possible to speak about the revelation of God in the language of African culture. The oral Christology of Akan AICs is a rereading of the gospel on the actual scene where people seek reconciliation with the invisible powers and protection from occult forces. The whole symbolic structure of the African universe therefore challenges our theological reflection. Healing and wholeness is a case in point, the symbolic universe providing renewed connections between faith and health, and the integration and interaction between both the invisible and the visible realms of reality. Oral Christological discourse is not just a nostalgic return to African "authenticity" but offers insights that can be valuable, not only for African theological reflection, but challenging theologians everywhere to reread the gospel of Christ in the face of socio-cultural transition.

108. Ibid.

9

Summary and Conclusions

A T THE BEGINNING OF this study I posed the question whether the call for an African Christology was a legitimate one, or nothing more than a storm in a tea cup brewing among the African intellectual elite vying for a Christology in the vein of western Christological construct. This research has made clear that Christology in Africa is present and developing, but perhaps African theologians and western scholars with interest in African Christianity have been looking in the wrong places for it. In very much the same way that the first century Jewish people were expecting the Messiah to hail from the upper echelons of their society, only to realize that he was to be found among the common people of their day, perhaps those expecting that a clear picture of the Jesus of Africa would essentially be found on the pristine pages of scholastic literature lodged in the halls of academia are also mistaken. The most significant outcome of the research carried out for the present study is the discovery of a vibrant and living faith in Christ that is present in the worship communities of Akan AICs. This in-depth and thorough inquiry into the way Akan AICs experience and appropriate Jesus Christ has served to bring to light a number of significant conclusions regarding the complex issue of Christ and culture as well as those between the universality and the particularity of Christ.

INCULTURATION

This study is placed within the context of the ongoing discussion about Christ and culture. Put more specifically, it concerns how best to inculturate Christ in a post-missionary African society without minimising his universal significance, while at the same time not constructing a purely objectified faith that has little local appeal. The term selected by this research that best articulates this task is "inculturation," which as we have seen in our introduction, Shorter defines as "the ongoing dialogue between faith and culture."[1]

The "anthropological poverty" inflicted on Africa through a prolonged programme of slavery and colonization has made more urgent the task of rediscovering some of the generic values of African culture at the local level.[2] At the heart of our research stands Christ as encountered, experienced, reformulated, lived, and expressed anew through the culture, language, and worldview of the Akan AICs in Ghana. Our research takes seriously the need to understand how faith works at the grassroots level and debunks the notion that Christology—and theology for that matter—is a monopolistic understanding of a select few, instead of a joint enterprise that includes even those ordinary men and women who have had no formal training in the scientific handling of God's word. The result of this inquiry suggests that the clearest expression of Akan AIC Christology is conveyed through orality. Orality, as I have maintained in this work, is more than verbalism or speech and is a means of experiencing and communicating what is not fixed in time or space. It is the multi-dimensional matrix, the web that brings together the past the present and the future as well as the visible and the invisible realm of the African worldview.

In both the qualitative and quantitative research it is clear that there is a strong proclivity toward an oral epistemology and pedagogy. In particular, the Bible, which is not understood in purely literary terms, is re-oralized through preaching, giving it a multiplex function and power as outlined in chapter 8. Testimony, prayers, songs, worship and praise were all considered to be crucial sources for articulating their experience of Christ. The use of symbolism and metaphors in Christological apprehension, as well as proverbs, myths and the existential context of believers as seen in chapter 8, are all part and parcel of this oral orientation. It would, however, be wrong to deduce from this that this is by implication an anti-text or anti-literary approach. The fact that the Bible plays such a promi-

1. Shorter, *Theology of Inculturation*, 11.

2. The term "Anthropological Poverty" was introduced by Per Frostin to mean "the general impoverishment of the people." Colonialism brought about a loss of their identity and a diminishment of their creativity. It is understood as a process that discriminately disrupted African identity, communal tribal life and organisation, and destroyed their indigenous values, religious beliefs and traditional culture. This wholesale pauperization is now maintained by economic and cultural neo-colonialism. See Frostin, *Liberation Theology*, 15.

nent role reveals that the methodology is far more complex than a binary literary-oral bifurcation.

What has been deduced from this study of the faith of the Akan AICs is that it is a living faith with present realities and significance. A Christ who is a mere historical figure of the past is therefore of little consequence; what really matters is his ability to impact their world in the here and now. This realized eschatology does not prioritize "text" which, after being written down, is no longer a part of the present but the past, but rather orality, which applies to the continuous present realities.

Making Christ relevant to Africa, as described here in the oral Christology of the Akan AICs, points toward a dimension of inculturation that is often overlooked in the inculturation Christologies referred to in the second chapter of this work, where Christ is looked at as *ancestor, chief, healer* and so forth. One of the revealing findings of the research is the degree to which the concept of "Christ as ancestor" was by and large ignored as a Christological title that Akan AICs would adopt. This is so in spite of the popularity of this concept among a number of African academic theologians.[3] Although the theological value of academic titular Christologies is not in question here, the propositional theological construct upon which they are predicated is a point of departure for the grassroots or local theologian. Put another way, *ancestor* is a concept that is familiar to the African, but the discourse in which Christ is inculturated as ancestor is foreign to the African setting.

The "oral Christology" of Akan AICs undertaken in this work avoids this pitfall because it bases Christological discourse upon the language of oral tradition such as preaching, song, proverbs, mythology, dance, testimony and prayer, which tell the story of Christ using the language of African oral culture that speaks through symbolism and metaphor. This study advocates that the Christology articulated in the testimonies, prayers, preaching, and singing of Akan AICs, which draws upon the symbols and metaphors of the African worldview, should be used as the starting point for inculturating Christ in Africa. The Prayer and Praises of Madam Kuma, the Christological image of Christ as a *Kachere Tree* presented by Martin Ott, and Christ the Earthkeeper Christology championed by Daneel, provide good examples of such a Christology.

3. See Pobee, "Christ as Nana," 94; Nyamiti maintains Christ as "Our Ancestor" (see *Christ as Our Ancestor*); Bujo posits Christ as the "Proto-Ancestor" (see *African Theology in its Social Context*).

It is not the intention of this work to romanticize traditional African culture or to take a nostalgic view of the bygone days of pre-colonialism; indeed, African societies are rapidly and irreversibly changing. With increasing urbanization and the proliferation of western cultural, linguistic, and economic influence, a new Africa is on the horizon ready to embrace and to replicate the best of the West. With the shifting sands of African tradition and cultural values there are still, however, some fundamental philosophical principles that undergird the African worldview. The usefulness of such symbols as crosses, water, staffs of office, vestments, candles, and oil (chapter 8) is in their ability to reflect a Christology from below as well as a Christology from above. On one hand they resonate with African culture through their usage and meaning culturally (below) while also having biblical grounding and significance (above). What such Christological symbols achieve is a genuine realisation of mission through dialogue. Put another way, the authentic Akan AIC inculturation of Christ provides a local and cultural repertoire of motifs and symbolism that can mediate between African culture and the biblical Christ.

THE HEALER OF AFRICA

Throughout this work it has been argued strongly that healing is an area in which the Christology of the Akan AICs has a great deal to contribute. Although on the whole I have purposely avoided the methodology of merely taking African titles and applying them to Christ, the notion of Christ as healer *par excellence* deserves a special mention. The questionnaire survey revealed that most of the traditional titles for Christ such as *Chief, Elder Brother, Ancestor* and *Conqueror* were given a low priority; however, besides the biblical umbrella terms of *Saviour, Lord,* and *Messiah,* the title *Healer* was selected by the majority of respondents. The ethnographic evidence also corroborated this view. The strength of this Christological-healing paradigm, I have argued, is based upon the idea that healing and wholeness is a result of harmony between the invisible world of the spirits and the visible world of human activity. The oral Christology outlined in chapter 8 is a means that allows a dialogue between these two realms.

The Akan AIC perspective on healing presents us with a realistic vision of the world, and indeed the universe as a whole, in which, we are not called to exploit or to subdue but to live in harmony with. By placing healing and wholeness at the heart of their salvation in Christ and view-ing sin as that which violates harmonious living within the world (visible and invisible), Akan AICs have opened up the possibility for a whole new starting point for theological reflection in Africa. A theological discourse not wholly driven by, and reacting against, the inequalities of the past colonial missionary era but one that seeks to re-establish and redefine the way of African harmonious living in the light of Christ is possible. Such a redefinition of African holistic living will bring order and integrity into African politics and socio-economic life as well as providing a measure of African selfhood.[4]

The theological task then is to develop a new vision of living in harmony with God and each other in the light of the kingdom of God, of which Christ is sovereign ruler, and approach the creation of a new perspective of the African personality in the new life of Christ's healing power. It is this power that transcends and contradicts the distorted image of Africa created by European oppression—a painful reality often inter-nalized by Africans. The healing Christology of the Akan AICs indicates where the resources for this new African health and wholeness must be found: the moral and spiritual heritage of African oral culture, and cosmological outlook. This means our theology must revisit the cosmo-logical and soteriological presuppositions that define our questions and concerns for Christology. Such an atavistic quest means exorcizing the internalized Christ of missionary apprehension who deals narrowly with only individual sin and guilt and inviting in the African Christ, presented to us by Akan AICs, who point a finger of accusation at collective sin and structural evil as the source for the suffering and sickness of the oppressed peoples of Africa. The Akan AIC notion of Christ as healer *par excellence* could therefore be extended beyond that of physical and spiritual healing to the healing of the African wounded personality as well as the healing of the African continent.

MARKETPLACE CHRISTOLOGY

In this study we have revealed that Akan AIC experience of Jesus Christ is not one that is confined to personal piety or private devotions, but rather one that is shared and experienced in the public arenas of life. Through it

---

4. The term selfhood is used to mean here "a sense of self" against the background of anthropological poverty mentioned above.

we have learnt that Akan AICs possess a functional Christology that aids life and protects from anti-life forces. They have no concept of religion as a mere philosophical or theological construct; they know only how to serve God through their daily encounter with Him through daily living. Akan AICs have defined Christ as the empowering one to whom they can address their questions and concerns like their benevolent ancestor. Theirs is not a Christology of aloof ecclesiastical pietism but a Christology of the marketplace bustling with the sound of trade. In an African context, where often the Church occupies a position of power and wields influence, this Christology reminds us of the simplicity of the Jesus of Scripture who moved among the common people of his day. It invites us to once again integrate faith in Christ into our everyday living; it also challenges the thinking that insists that faith can be a private affair and religion can be divided into the compartments of the sacred and the secular.

Bibliography

Abraham, William E. *The Mind of Africa*. The Nature of Human Society. Chicago: University of Chicago Press, 1962.

Adeyemo, Tokunboh. *Salvation in African Tradition*. Nairobi: Evangelical, 1979.

Akrong, Abraham. "Christology from an African Perspective." In *Exploring Afro-Christology*, edited by John Pobee, 119–36. Studien zur interkulturellen Geschichte des Christentums 79. Frankfurt: Lang, 1992.

———. "The Empowering Christ: A Postcolonial African Christology." Unpublished paper, 1999.

Alcock, Peter. "Dwelling lightly on the Earth: Towards a Dialogical Ecotheology." PhD diss., University of Birmingham, 2000.

Allen, Robert E. *The New Penguin English Dictionary*. London: Penguin, 2000.

Alviar, José. "Anthropological Foundations of African Christology." *African Christian Studies* 13 (March 1997) 9–27.

Anderson, Allan. "Challenges and Prospects for Research." *Missionalia* 23 (1995) 283–94.

———. *African Reformation: African Initiated Christianity in the 20th Century*. Trenton, NJ: African World, 2001.

———. *An Introduction to Pentecostalism*. Cambridge: Cambridge University Press, 2004.

Anderson, Allan, and Samuel Otwang. *TUMELO: The Faith of African Pentecostals in South Africa*. Studia Originalia 17. Pretoria: UNISA, 1993.

Antubam, Kofi. *Ghana's Heritage of Culture*. Leipzig: Koehler & Amelang, 1963.

Appiah-Kubi, Kofi. *Man Cures, God Heals: Religion and Medical Practice Among the Akans of Ghana*. Totowa, NJ: Allanheld, Osmun, 1981.

———. "Christology." In *A Reader in African Christian Theology*, edited by John Parratt, 69–81. London: SPCK, 1987.

———. "Jesus Christ: Some Christological Aspects from an African Perspective." In *African and Asian Contributions to Contemporary Theology*, edited by John S. Mbiti, 56–72. Geneva: W.C.C. Ecumenical Institute, 1997.

Appiah-Kubi, Kofi, and Sergio Torres, editors. *African Theology En Route: Papers from the Pan-African Conference of Third World Theologians, December 17–23, 1977, Accra Ghana*. Maryknoll, NY: Orbis, 1979.

Asamoah-Gyadu, J. "Renewal within African Christianity: A Study of some Current Historical and Theological Developments within Independent Indigenous Pentecostalism in Ghana." PhD diss., University of Birmingham, 2000.

Asempa Hymns: With Orders for Holy Communion and Mass. Accra: Asempa, 1980.

Baëta, C. G. *Prophetism in Ghana: A Study of Some "Spiritual" Churches*. World Mission Studies. London: SCM, 1962.

———, editor. *Christianity in Tropical Africa*. London: Oxford University Press, 1968.

Bahemuka, Judith M. "The Hidden Christ in African Traditional Religion." In *Jesus in African Christianity: Experimentation and Diversity in African Christology*, edited by J. N. Kanyua Mugambi and Laurenti Megesa, 1–14. 2nd ed. Nairobi: Acton, 1998.

Bannerman-Richter, Gabriel. *The Practice of Witchcraft in Ghana*. Winona, MN: Apollo, 1982.

Barrett, David B. *Schism and Renewal in Africa: An Analysis of Six Thousand Contemporary Religious Movements*. Nairobi: Oxford University Press, 1968.

Bartels, Francis Ludowic. *The Roots of Ghana Methodism*. Cambridge: Cambridge University Press, 1965.

Beckmann, David. *Eden Revival: Spiritual Churches in Ghana*. St. Louis: Concordia, 1975.

Becken, Hans-Jurgen. *Relevant Theology for Africa*. Paperbacks of the Missiological Institute at LTC, Mapmulo 1. Durban: Lutheran Publishing House, 1973.

Bediako, Kwame. "Biblical Christologies in the Context of African Traditional Religion." In *Sharing Jesus in the Two Third World: Evangelical Christologies from the Context of Poverty, Powerlessness, and Religious Pluralism: The Papers of the First Conference of Evangelical Mission Theologians from the Two Thirds World, Bangkok, Thailand, March 22–25, 1982*, edited by Vinay Samuels and Chris Sudgen, 115–75. Grand Rapids: Eerdmans, 1984.

———. "Roots of African Theology." *International Bulletin of Missionary Research* 13 (April 1989) 58–65.

———. *Jesus in African Culture: A Ghanaian Perspective*. Accra: Asempa, 1990.

———. *Theology and Identity: The Impact of Culture upon Christian Thought in the Second Century and Modern Africa*. Oxford: Regnum, 1992.

———. "Cry Jesus." *Vox Evangelica* 23 (1993) 7–23.

———. *Christianity in Africa*. Edinburgh: Edinburgh University Press, 1995.

———. "How is Jesus Christ Lord?: Aspects of an Evangelical Christian Apologetics in the Context of African Religious Pluralism." *Exchange* 25 (1996) 27–42.

———. *Jesus in Africa*. Accra: Regnum, 2000.

Bediako, Mary Gillian. "The Relationship Between Western Missions and Indigenous Christian Prophets of West Africa: William Wade Harris, John Swatson, and Sampson Oppong, and its Significance for Christian Mission." MA thesis, University of Aberdeen, Scotland, 1980.

Beecham, John. *Ashantee and the Gold Coast: Being a Sketch of the History, Social State, Superstitions of the Inhabitants of Those Countries, with a Notice of theState and Prospects of Christianity among Them*. London: Mason, 1841.

Birch, Charles, William Eakin, and Jay B. McDaniel, editors. *Liberating Life: Contemporary Approaches to Ecological Theology*. Maryknoll, NY: Orbis, 1990.

Blakely, Thomas D., W. E. A. van Beek, and Dennis L. Thomson, editors. *Religion in Africa: Experience & Expression*. Monograph Series of the David M. Kennedy Center for International Studies at Brigham Young University 4. Portsmouth, NH: Heinemann, 1994.

Boahen A. "The Origins of the Akan." *Ghana Notes and Queries* 9 (1966) 3–10.

Boesak, Allan Aubrey. *Farewell to Innocence: A Socio-Ethical Study on Black Theology and Black Power*. Maryknoll, NY: Orbis, 1977.

Boomershine, Thomas E. "Biblical Megatrends: Towards a Paradigm for the Interpretation of the Bible in Electronic Media." *SBL Seminar Papers* 26 (1987) 144–57.

Bosch, David. "God in Africa: Implications for Kerygma." *Missionalia* 1 (1973) 3–21.

Bibliography

————. *Transforming Mission: Paradigm Shifts in Theology of Mission.* American Society of Missiology Series 16. Maryknoll, NY: Orbis, 1991.

Botchway, Frank. "The OSSA-Madih Church." *Journal of African Christian Thought* 3 (2000) 2–15.

Bouma-Prediger, Steven. *The Greening of Theology: The Ecological Models of Rosemary Radford Ruether, Joseph Sittler, and Jürgen Moltmann.* American Academy of Religion Academy Series 91. Atlanta: Scholars, 1995.

Brown, Colin. *Jesus in European Protestant Thought: 1778–1860.* Studies in Historical Theology 1. Durham, NC: Labyrinth, 1985.

Bujo, Bénézet. *African Theology in Social Context.* Translated by John O'Donohue. Maryknoll, NY: Orbis, 1992. Reprint, Eugene, OR: Wipf & Stock, 2006.

Bulmer, Martin. *The Uses of Social Research: Social Investigation in Public Policy-Making.* Contemporary Social Research Series 3. London: Allen & Unwin, 1982.

Burnett, David. "Charisma and Community in a Ghanaian Independent Church." PhD diss., School of Oriental and African Studies, University of London, 1997.

Busia, K. A. "The Ashanti of the Gold Coast." In *African Worlds:Studies in the Cosmological Ideas and Social Values of African Peoples,* edited by Daryll Forde, 190–209. London: Oxford University Press, 1954.

Buthelezi, Manas. "Violence and the Cross in South Africa Today." *Journal of Theology for South Africa* 29 (December 1979) 51–55.

Carr, Burgess. "The Relation of the Union to Mission." In *Third World Theologies,* edited by Gerald H. Anderson and Thomas F. Stransky, 158–68. Maryknoll, NY: Orbis, 1976.

Claridge, William Walton. *A History of the Gold Coast and Ashanti: From the Earliest Times to the Commencement of the Twentieth Century.* 2nd ed. London: Frank Cass, 1964.

Clarke, Clifton. *The Reason Why We Sing: Introducing Black Pentecostal Spirituality.* Grove Spirituality Series 61. Cambridge: Grove, 1997.

Cook, Thomas, and Charles Reichardt. *Qualitative and Quantitative Methods in Evaluation Research.* Sage Research Progress Series in Evaluation 1. Beverly Hills, CA: Sage, 1979.

Cox, Harvey. *Fire From Heaven: The Rise of Pentecostal Spirituality and the Reshaping of Religion in the Twenty-First Century.* London: Cassell, 1996.

Croatto, J. Severino. *Biblical Hermeneutics: Toward a Theory of Reading as the Production of Meaning.* Maryknoll, NY: Orbis, 1987.

Crollius, Roest. "What is so New about Inculturation?" *Gregorianum* 59 (1978) 721–38.

Dakubu, M. E. Kropp, editor. *The Languages of Ghana.* African Languages: Occasional Publication 2. London: Kegan Paul International, 1988.

Daneel, M. L. *African Earthkeepers: Wholistic Interfaith Mission.* Maryknoll, NY: Orbis, 2001.

————. "Communication and Liberation in African Independent Churches." *Missionalia* 12:2 (1984) 57–93.

————. *Old and New in Southern Shona Independent Churches.* Vol. 1, *Background and Rise of the Major Movements.* Change and Continuity in Africa. The Hague: Mouton, 1971.

————. *Old and New in Southern Shona Independent Churches.* Vol. 2, *Church Growth—Causative Factors and Recruitment Techniques.* Change and Continuity in Africa. The Hague: Mouton, 1974.

———. *Quest for Belonging: Introduction to a Study of African Independent Churches.* Mambo Occasional Papers, Missio-pastoral Series 17. Gweru, Zimbabwe: Mambo, 1987.

Danquah, J. B. *The Akan Doctrine of God: A Fragment of Gold Coast Ethics and Religion.* Lutterworth Library 16. London: Lutterworth, 1944.

Debrunner, Hans. W. *A History of Christianity in Ghana.* Accra: Waterville, 1967.

———. *The Story of Samson Oppong, The Prophet.* Accra: Waterville, 1967.

———. *Witchcraft in Ghana.* Accra: Waterville, 1978.

Dickson, Kwesi. *Theology in Africa.* Maryknoll, NY: Orbis, 1984.

Dickson, Kwesi, and Paul Ellingworth, editors. *Biblical Revelation and African Beliefs.* London: Lutterworth, 1969.

Dillistone, I. W. *Christianity and Symbolism.* Philadelphia: Westminster, 1955.

Dodd, C. H. *The Apostolic Preaching and its Developments.* London: Hodder & Stoughton, 1936.

Dolphyne, F. Abena. "The Volta-Comoe Language." In *The Languages of Ghana,* edited by M. E. Kropp Dakubu, 30–43. Kegan Paul International, 1988.

Dube, D. "A Search for Abundant Life: Health, Healing and Wholeness in Zionist Churches." In *Afro-Christian Religion and Healing in Southern Africa,* edited by G. C. Oosthuizen, S. D Edwards, W. H. Wessels, and I. Hexham, 109–136. African Studies 8. New York: Mellen, 1989.

Edet, Rosemary, and Bette Ekeya. "Church Women of Africa: A Theological Community." In *With Passion and Compassion: Third World Women Doing Theology,* edited by Virginia Fabella and Mercy Amba Oduyoye, 4–20. Maryknoll, NY: Orbis, 1988.

Éla, Jean-Marc. *My Faith as an African.* Maryknoll, NY: Orbis, 1988.

Ellis, A. B. *The Tshi-Speaking People of the Gold Coast of West Africa: Their Religion, Manners, Customs, Laws, Language, etc.* London: Chapman & Hall, 1887.

Evan-Pritchard, E. E. *Witchcraft, Oracles and Magic Among the Azande.* Oxford: Clarendon, 1937.

Fabella, Virginia, and Mercy Amba Oduyoye, editors. *With Passion and Compassion: Third World Women Doing Theology.* Maryknoll, NY: Orbis, 1988.

Fashole-Luke, E. "The Quest for African Christian Theologies." *Scottish Journal of Theology* 29 (1976) 159–75.

Fasholé-Luke, Edward W., Richard Gray, Adrian Hastings, and Godwin Tasie, editors. *Christianity in Independent Africa.* London: Rex Collings, 1978.

Ferguson, Sinclair B., David F. Wright, and J. I. Packer, editors. *New Dictionary of Theology.* The Master Reference Collection. Downers Grove, IL: InterVarsity, 1988.

Fisher, Robert B. *West African Religious Traditions: Focus on the Akan of Ghana.* Faith Meets Faith. Maryknoll, NY: Orbis, 1998.

Ford, David, editor. *The Modern Theologians: An Introduction to Christian Theology in the Twentieth Century.* Vol. 2. Oxford: Blackwell, 1989.

Forde, Daryll. *African Worlds: Studies in the Cosmological Ideas and Social Values of African Peoples.* Oxford: Oxford University Press, 1954.

Frostin, Per. *Liberation Theology in Tanzania and South Africa: A First World Impression.* Studia Theologica Lundensia 42. Lund: Lund University Press, 1988.

Geertz, C. *Interpretation of Culture: Selected Essays.* New York: Basic, 1973.

Gelfand, Michael. *Witch Doctor: Traditional Medicine Man of Rhodesia.* London: Harvill, 1964.

Bibliography

Ghana Evangelism Committee. *National Church Survey: Facing the Unfinished Task of the Church in Ghana.* Accra: Ghana Evangelism Committee, 1989.

Gibellini, Rosino, editor. *Paths of African Theology.* Maryknoll, NY: Orbis, 1994.

Gifford, Paul. *African Christianity: Its Public Role.* Bloomington: Indiana University Press, 1998.

Goodacre, David. *World Religions and Medicine.* Religion and Medicine 4. Oxford: Institute of Religion and Medicine, 1983.

Gottwald, Norman K, editor. *The Bible and Liberation: Political and Social Hermeneutics.* Rev. ed. Maryknoll, NY: Orbis, 1993.

Greenberg, J. H. "Languages of Africa." *Research Centre for the Study of Language Science, Publication* 25 (1963) 7–15.

Gyekye, Kwame. *An Essay on African Philosophical Thought: The Akan Conceptual Scheme.* Cambridge: Cambridge University Press, 1987.

Hahn, Ferdinand. *The Titles of Jesus in Christology: Their History in Early Christianity.* Lutterworth Library. London: Lutterworth, 1969.

Haliburton, Gordon. "The Calling of a Prophet: Samson Oppong." *The Bulletin of the Society for African Church History* 2 (1965) 84–96.

———. *The Prophet Harris.* London: Longman, 1971.

Hallman, David G., editor. *Ecotheology: Voices from the South and North.* Maryknoll, NY: Orbis, 1994.

Hanegraaff, Wouter J. *New Age Religion and Western Culture: Esotericism in the Mirror of Secular Thought.* SUNY Series in Western Esoteric Traditions. Albany: State University of New York Press, 1998.

Hastings, Adrian. *The Church in Africa 1450–1950.* The Oxford History of the Christian Church. Oxford: Oxford University Press, 1994.

Healey, Joseph G., and Donald Sybertz. *Towards an African Narrative Theology.* Nairobi: Pauline Publications Africa, 1996.

Hesselgrave, David. *Communicating Christ Cross-Culturally: An Introduction to Missionary Communication.* Contemporary Evangelical Perspectives. Grand Rapids: Zondervan, 1978.

———. "Worldview and Contextualisation." In *Perspective on the World Christian Movement: A Reader,* edited by Ralph D. Winter and Steven C. Hawthorne, 398–409. Pasadena: William Carey Library, 1981.

Hollenweger, Walter. *The Pentecostals.* London: SCM, 1972.

Idowu, Bolaji. *Olódùmarè: God in Yoruba Belief.* London: Longmans, 1962.

———. *Towards an Indigenous Church.* Students' Library 3. Oxford: Oxford University Press, 1965.

Jehu-Appiah, J. "African Indigenous Churches in Britain." PhD diss., University of Birmingham, 2001.

John Paul VI. "Address to the All Africa Bishops' Symposium July 31, 1969." *AFER* 10:4 (1969) 302–5.

Jorgensen, Danny L. *Participant Observation: A Methodology for Human Studies.* Applied Social Research Methods Series 15. Newbury Park, CA: Sage, 1989.

Jules-Rosette, Bennetta. *African Apostles: Ritual and Conversion in the Church of John Maranke.* Symbol, Myth, and Ritual Series. Ithaca: Cornell University Press, 1975.

Kabasele, F. "Christ as Chief." In *Faces of Jesus in Africa,* edited by Robert Schreiter, 103–113. London: SCM, 1991.

Bibliography

Kalu, Ogbu, *African Pentecostalism: An Introduction*. New York: Oxford University Press, 2008.

Kelly, J. N. D. *Early Christian Doctrines*. London: Adam & Charles Black, 1958.

Kimble, David. *The Political History of Ghana: The Rise of Gold Coast Nationalism, 1850–1928*. Oxford: Clarendon, 1963.

Kant, Immanuel. *Critique of Pure Reason*. Translated by Norman Kemp Smith. London: Macmillan, 1968.

Kinoti, Hannah W., and John Mary Waliggo, editors. *The Bible in African Christianity*. African Christianity Series. Nairobi: Acton, 1997.

Kitshoff, M. C., editor. *African Independent Churches Today: Kaleidoscope of Afro-Christianity*. African Studies 44. Lewiston, NY: Mellen, 1996.

Kolié, C. "Jesus as Healer." In *Faces of Jesus in Africa*, edited by Robert Schreiter, 128–49. London SCM, 1991.

Krabill, James R. *The Hymnody of the Harrist Church Among the Dida of South-Central Ivory Coast (1913–1949): A Historico-Religious Study*. Studien zur Interkulturellen Geschichte des Christentums 74. Frankfurt: Peter Lang, 1995.

Kraft, Charles H. *Christianity in Culture: A Study in Dynamic Biblical Theologizing in Cross-Cultural Perspective*. Maryknoll, NY: Orbis, 1979.

Krentz, Edgar. *The Historical-Critical Method*. Guides to Biblical Scholarship. Philadelphia: Fortress, 1975.

Kuma, Afua. *Jesus of the Deep Forest*. Accra: Asempa, 1980.

Larbi, E. K. *Pentecostalism: The Eddies of Ghanaian Christianity*. Studies in African Pentecostal Christianity 1. Accra: Centre for Pentecostal and Charismatic Studies, 2001.

Lindbeck, George. "Ecumenical Theology." In vol. 2 of *The Modern Theologians: An Introduction to Christian Theology in the Twentieth Century*, edited by David Ford, 255–73. Oxford: Basil Blackwell, 1989.

Lindars, Barnabas, and Stephen S. Smalley, editors. *Christ and the Spirit in the New Testament: Essays in Honour of C. F. D. Moule*. London: Cambridge University Press, 1973.

McCaskie, T. C. "Anti-Witchcraft Cults in Asante: An Essay in the Social History of an African People." *History in Africa* 8 (1981) 125–54.

Magesa, Laurenti. *African Religion: The Moral Traditions of Abundant Life*. Maryknoll, NY: Orbis, 1997.

———. "Christ the Liberator of Africa Today." In *Jesus in African Christianity*, edited by J. N. K. Mugambi and Laurenti Megesa, 79–92. Nairobi: Acton, 1998.

———. "From Privatised to Popular Biblical Hermeneutics." In *The Bible in African Christianity*, edited by Hannah Kinoti and John Waliggo, 25–30. Nairobi: Acton, 1997.

Maimela S. S. "Salvation in African Traditional Religions." *Missionalia* 13:2 (1985) 63–77.

———. "Jesus Christ: The Liberator and Hope of Oppressed Africa." In *Exploring Afro-Christianity*, edited by John Pobee, 31–42. Frankfurt: Peter Lang, 1992.

Makhubu, Paul. *Who are the Independent Churches?* Johannesburg: Skotaville, 1988.

Martey, Emmanuel. *African Theology: Inculturation and Liberation*. Maryknoll, NY: Orbis, 1994.

Martin, Marie-Louise. *The Biblical Concepts of Messianism and Messianism in Southern Africa*. Morija, Lesotho: Morija Sesuto Book Depot, 1964.

———. *Kimbangu: An African Prophet and his Church*. Oxford: Basil Blackwell, 1975.

Bibliography

Mbiti, John Samuel. *African and Asian Contributions to Contemporary Theology: A Report of a Consultation Held at the Ecumenical Institute, Bossey, 8–14 June 1976*. Céligny: The Institute, 1977.

———. *African Religions and Philosophy*. London: Heinemann, 1969.

———. *Bible and Theology in African Christianity*. Nairobi: Oxford University Press, 1986.

———. "Cattle Are Born with Ears, Their Horns Grow Later: Towards an Appreciation of African Oral Theology." In *All Africa Lutheran Consultation on Christian Theology in the African Context: Gaborone, Botswana, October 5–14, 1978*, edited by Alison Bares, 35–51. Geneva: Lutheran World Federation, 1978.

———. "Is Jesus Christ in African Religion?" In *Exploring Afro-Christianity*, edited by John Pobee, 21–29. Frankfurt: Lang, 1991.

———. *The Prayer of African Religion*. Maryknoll, NY: Orbis, 1975.

———. "Some African Concepts of Christology." In *Christ in the Younger Churches: Theological Contributions from Asia, Africa, and Latin America*, edtied by Georg F. Vicedom, 51–62. Theological Collections 15. London: SPCK, 1972.

McFague, Sallie. *Speaking in Parables: A Study in Metaphor and Theology*. Philadelphia: Fortress, 1975.

Menkiti, Ifeanyi A. "Person and Community in African Traditional Thought." In *African Philosophy: An Introduction*, edited by Richard A. Wright, 171–80. Lanham, MD: University Press of America, 1984.

Mesters, Carlos. "The Use of the Bible in Christian Communities of the Common People." In *The Bible and Liberation*, edited by Norman Gottwald, 119–33. Maryknoll, NY: Orbis, 1993.

Meyer, Birgit. "If You Are a Devil, You Are a Witch, and If You Are a Witch You Are a Devil. The Integration of 'Pagan' Ideas into the Conceptual Universe of Ewe Christians in Southeastern Ghana." *Journal of Religion in Africa* 22 (1992) 98–132.

———. *Translating the Devil: Religion and Modernity among the Ewe in Ghana*. International African Library 21. Edinburgh: Edinburgh University Press, 1999.

Meyerowitz, Eva Lewin-Richter. *The Akan of Ghana: Their Ancient Beliefs*. London: Faber & Faber, 1958.

———. *The Sacred State of Akan*. London: Faber & Faber, 1951.

Mfusi, S. K. "Religious Communication: Prayer, Sacrifice and Divination." In *African Independent Churches Today: Kaleidoscope of Afro-Christianity*, edited by M. C. Kitshoff, 183–200. Lewiston, NY: Mellen, 1996.

Migeod, Fredrick. *Language of West Africa*. London: Kegan Paul, 1872.

Milingo, Emmanuel. *The World in Between: Christian Healing and the Struggle for Spiritual Survival*. Edited by Mona Macmillan. Maryknoll, NY: Orbis, 1984.

Mofokeng, T. A. *The Crucified Among the Crossbearers: Towards a Black Christology*. Kampen: Kok, 1983.

Molyneux, Gordon. "The Oral Dimensions of Theological Expression: The Place and Function of Hymns in EJCSK [Kimbanuist Church]." Ph.D. diss., School of Oriental and African Studies, London University, 1986.

Momen, Moojan. *The Phenomenon of Religion: A Thematic Approach*. Oxford: Oneworld, 1999.

Moore, Basil, editor. *Black Theology: The South African Voice*. London: Hurst, 1973.

Mugambi, J. N. N., and Laurenti Magesa, editors. *Jesus in African Christianity: Experimentation and Diversity in African Christology*. Nairobi: Initiative, 1989.

Musama Disco Christo Church. *Songs of Inspiration*. London: MDCC Publication Committee, 1992.

———. *Some Common Elements of Power*. Accra: Musama Evangelistic Committee, 1994.

Musopole, Augustine. "Witchcraft Terminology, the Bible and African Christian Theology: An Exercise in Hermeneutics." *African Christian Studies* 8 (1993) 347–54.

Muzorewa, Gwinyai H. *The Origins and Development of African Theology*. Maryknoll, NY: Orbis, 1985.

Myles, Kwasi. *Musama Disco Christo Church: An Introduction to its Main Doctrine*. Accra: Midland, 1987.

———. *Studies on Musama Church: Reflections on Key Devotional Prayer Ritual of Musama Disco Christo Church*. Accra: Catholic Mission Press, 1998.

Nasimiyu-Wasike, A. "Christology and African Women's Experience." In *Jesus in African Christianity*, editors J. N. K. Magumbi and Laurenti Megesa, 123–35. Nairobi: Acton, 1998.

Neuman, Lawrence. *Social Research Methods: Qualitative and Quantitative Approaches*. New York: Allyn & Bacon, 2000.

Nkrumah, Kwame. *Consciencism: Philosophy and Ideology for Decolonisation*. London: Panaf, 1964.

Nthanburi, Zablon, and Douglas Waruta. "Biblical Hermeneutics in African Instituted Churches." In *The Bible in African Christianity*, edited by Hannah Kinoti and John Waliggo, 40–47. Nairobi: Acton, 1997.

Nusbaum, S. "Rethinking Animal Sacrifice." *Missionalia* 12:2 (1984) 49–63.

Nyamiti, Charles. "African Christologies Today." In *Faces of Jesus in Africa*, edited by Robert Schreiter, 3–19. London: SCM, 1991.

———. *African Tradition and the Christian God*. Spearhead 49. Eldoret, Kenya: Gaba, 1977.

———. "Ancestral Kinship in the Trinity: An African Theology of the Trinity." *Inculturation: Working Papers on Living Faith and Culture* 9 (1987) 29–40.

———. "Contemporary African Christologies: Assessment and Practical Suggestions." In *Paths of African Theology*, edited by Rosina Gibellini, 62–76. London: SCM, 1994.

———. *Christ as our Ancestor*. Gweru, Zimbabwe: Mombo, 1984.

———. "The Mass as Divine and Ancestral Encounter between the Living and the Dead." *African Christian Studies* 1 (1985) 28–48.

———. "Uganda Martyrs: Ancestors of all Mankind." *African Christian Studies* 1 (1986) 41–66.

Odamtten S. K. *The Missionary Factor in Ghana's Development up to the 1880s*. Accra: Waterville, 1975.

Oduyoye, Mercy. "Women and Christology: An African Women's Christ." Paper presented at EATWOT Continental Consultation on Theology from the Third World Women's perspective at Port Harcourt, Nigeria, August 19–23, 1986.

Olupona, Jacob K., editor. *African Traditional Religions in Contemporary Society*. New York: Paragon, 1991.

Onyinah, Opoku. "Akan Witchcraft and the Concept of Exorcism in the Church of Pentecost." PhD diss., University of Birmingham, 2002.

Oosthuizen, Gerhardus Cornelis. *The Theology of a South African Messiah: An Analysis of the Hymnal of "The Church of the Nazarites."* Oekumenische Studien 8. Leiden: Brill, 1967.

———. *Post-Christianity in Africa: A Theological and Anthropological Study*. London: Hurst, 1968.

Bibliography

―――. *The Healer-Prophet in Afro-Christian Churches.* Studies in Christian Mission 3. Leiden: Brill, 1992.

Oosthuizen, G. C., S. D. Edwards, W. H. Wessels, and I. Hexham, editors. *Afro-Christian Religion and Healing in South Africa.* Lewiston, NY: Mellen, 1989.

Opoku, Kofi Asare. "A Brief History of the Independent Church Movement in Ghana since 1862." In *The Rise of Independent Churches in Ghana,* 12–21. Accra: Asempa, 1990.

Ott, Martin. *African Theology in Images.* Kachere Monographs 12. Blantyre, Malawi: Christian Literature Association in Malawi, 2000.

Parrinder, Geoffrey. *African Traditional Religion.* 3rd ed. London: Sheldon, 1974.

Parratt, John. "African Theology and Biblical Hermeneutics." *Africa Theological Journal* 12:2 (1983) 88–94.

―――. *A Reader in African Christian Theology.* SPCK International Study Guide 23. London: SPCK, 1987.

Patterson, K. David. "The Influenza Epidemic of 1918–1919 in Gold Coast." *Transactions of the Historical Society of Ghana* 16 (1995) 205–25.

Peel, J. D. Y. *Aladura: A Religious Movement among the Yoruba.* Oxford: Oxford University Press for the International African Institute, 1968.

Pobee, John. "The Church in West Africa." In *The Church in Africa, 1977: Papers Presented at the Symposium at Milligan College, March 31–April 3, 1977,* edited by Charles R. Taber, 139–53. South Pasadena, CA: William Carey Library, 1977.

―――. "Confessing Christ in *A LA* African Instituted Churches." In *Exploring Afro-Christology,* edited by John Pobee, 145–51. Frankfurt: Lang, 1992.

―――. "In Search of Christology in Africa: Some Considerations for Today." In *Exploring Afro-Christology,* edited by John Pobee, 9–20. Frankfurt: Lang, 1992.

―――. *Kwame Nkrumah and the Church in Ghana 1949–1966.* Accra: Asempa, 1988.

―――. "Oral Theology and Christian Oral Tradition: Challenge to our Traditional Archival Concept." *Journal of the International Association for Mission Studies* 6:1 (1989) 87–92.

―――. *Towards an African Theology.* Nashville: Abingdon, 1979.

―――, editor. *Exploring Afro-Christology.* Frankfurt: Lang, 1992.

Rattray, Robert Sutherland. *Ashanti.* Oxford: Clarendon, 1923.

―――. *Ashanti Law and Constitution.* Oxford: Clarendon, 1929.

―――. *Ashanti Proverbs.* Oxford: Clarendon, 1969. First published 1916.

―――. *Religion and Art in Ashanti.* Oxford: Oxford University Press, 1927.

Reason, Peter, editor. *Participation in Human Inquiry.* Thousand Oaks, CA: Sage, 1994.

Ricoeur, Paul. *Interpretation Theory: Discourse and Surplus of Meaning.* Forth Worth, TX: Texas Christian University Press, 1976.

Rise of Independent Churches in Ghana, The. Accra: Asempa, 1990.

Ross, Kenneth. "Current Christological Trends in Northern Malawi." *Journal of Religions in Africa* 17:2 (1997) 160–76.

Sackey I. "A Brief History of the A.M.E Zion Church West Gold Coast District." *Ghana Bulletin of Theology* 1:3 (1957) 6–20.

Salvodi, Valentino, and Renato Kizito Sesana, editors. *Africa, the Gospel Belongs to Us: Problems and Prospects for an African Council.* Ndola, Zambia: Mission, 1986.

Samuel, Vinay, and Chris Sugden, editors. *Sharing Jesus in the Two Thirds World: Evangelical Christologies from the Contexts of Poverty, Powerlessness, and Religious Pluralism.* Bangalore: Partnership in Mission-Asia, 1983.

Bibliography

Sanneh, Lamin. "The Horizontal and the Vertical in Mission: An African Perspective." *International Bulletin of Missionary Research* 7:4 (1983) 165–71.

———. *Translating the Message: The Missionary Impact on Culture*. American Society of Missiology Series 13. Maryknoll, NY: Orbis, 1989.

Santon, Anselme T. "Jesus, Master of Initiation." In *Faces of Jesus in Africa*, edited Robert Schreiter, 85–102. London: SCM, 1991.

Sarantakos, Sotirios. *Social Research: A Toolkit for Quantitative Data Analysis Using SPSS*. 2nd ed. New York: Palgrave, 1998.

Sarpong, Peter. *Ghana in Retrospect: Some Aspects of Ghanaian Culture*. Tema, Ghana: Ghana Publishing Corporation, 1974.

Saton, A. T. "Jesus, Master of Initiation." In *Faces of Jesus in Africa*, edited by Robert Schreiter, 85–102. London: SCM, 1991.

Sawyerr, H. *Creative Evangelism: Towards New Christian Encounter with Africa*. London: Lutterworth, 1968.

———. "Sin and Salvation." In Relevant Theology: Soteriology Viewed from the Africa Situation." in *Relevant Theology*, edited by Hans-Jurgen Becken, 126–37. Durban: Lutheran Publishing House, 1973.

Schineller, Peter. *A Handbook on Inculturation*. New York: Paulist, 1990.

Schoffeleers, M. "Christ in African Folk Christology: The Nganga Paradigm." In *Religion in Africa*, edited by Thomas D. Blakely, Walter E. A. van Beek, and Dennis Thomson, 73–88. London: Heinemann, 1994.

Schreiter, Robert J. *Constructing Local Theologies*. Maryknoll, NY: Orbis, 1985.

———, editor. *Faces of Jesus in Africa*. Faith and Culture Series. Maryknoll, NY: Orbis, 1991.

Seale, Clive, editor. *Researching Society and Culture*. Thousand Oaks, CA: Sage, 1998.

Segundo, Juan Luis. *Liberation of Theology*. Maryknoll, NY: Orbis, 1976.

Senghor, Léopold Sédar. *On African Socialism*. New York: Praeger, 1964.

Shank, David. "A Prophet for Modern Times: The Thoughts of William Wada Harris, West African Precursor of the Reign of Christ." 2 vols. PhD diss., University of Aberdeen, 1980.

Shorter, Aylward. *African Christian Theology: Adaptation or Incarnation?* Maryknoll, NY: Orbis, 1977.

———. *Jesus and the Witchdoctor: An Approach to Healing and Wholeness*. Maryknoll, NY: Orbis, 1985.

———. *Toward a Theology of Inculturation*. Maryknoll, NY: Orbis, 1989.

Silverman, David. *Doing Qualitative Research: A Practical Handbook*. Thousand Oaks, CA: Sage, 2000.

Souga, Thérèsa. "The Christ-Event from the viewpoint of African Women: A Catholic Perspective." In *With Passion and Compassion: Third World Women Doing Theology*, edited by Virginia Fabella and Mercy Oduyoye, 22–29. Maryknoll, NY: Orbis, 1998.

Spencer, Herbert. *Principles of Sociology*. Vol. 1. London: William and Norgate, 1885.

Stiver, Dan R. *Theology After Ricoeur: New Directions in Hermeneutical Theology*. Louisville: Westminister John Knox, 2001.

Sugirtharajah, R. S., editor. *Vernacular Hermeneutics*. The Bible and Postcolonialism 2. Sheffield: Sheffield Academic, 1999.

———. "Vernacular Resurrection: An Introduction." In *Vernacular Hermeneutics*, edited by R. S. Sugirtharajah, 11–16. The Bible and Postcolonialism 2. Sheffield: Sheffield Academic, 1999.

Bibliography

Sundkler, Bengt G. M. *Bantu Prophets in South Africa*. 2nd ed. Oxford: International African Institute by Oxford University Press, 1961.

————. *Zulu Zion and Some Swazi Zionists*. London: Oxford University Press, 1976.

Sutcliffe, Steven, and Marion Bowman, editors. *Beyond New Age: Exploring Alternative Spirituality*. Edinburgh: Edinburgh University Press, 2000.

Taber, Charles R., editor. *The Church in Africa, 1977: Papers Presented at the Symposium at Milligan College March 31–April 3, 1977*. South Pasadena, CA: William Carey Library, 1977.

Taylor, John. *The Primal Vision: Christian Presence in African Religion*. Christian Presence Series. London: SCM, 1963.

Tempels, Placide. *Bantu Philosophy*. Translated by Colin King. Paris: Présence Africaine, 1958.

Theodorson, Achilles G., and George A. Theodorson. *Modern Dictionary of Sociology*. New York: Crowell, 1969.

Tihagale, Buti, and Itumeleng J. Mosala, editors. *Hammering Swords into Ploughshares: Essays in Honour of Archbishop Mpilo Desmond Tutu*. Johannesburg: Skotaville, 1986.

Toren, Benno van den. "Kwame Bediako's Christology in its African Evangelical Context." *Exchange: Journal of Missiological and Ecumenical Research* 26 (1997) 218–31.

Tovey, Phillip. *Inculturation: The Eucharist in Africa*. Grove Liturgical Study 55. Nottingham: Grove, 1998.

Turner, Harold W. *History of an African Independent Church*. Vol. 1, *The Church of the Lord (Aladura)*. Oxford: Clarendon, 1967.

————. *History of an African Independent Church*. Vol. 2, *The Life and Faith of the Church of the Lord (Aladura)*. Oxford: Clarendon, 1967.

————. *Profile Through Preaching*. IMC Research Pamphlet 13. London: Edinburgh House, 1965.

————. *Religious Innovation in Africa: Collected Essays on New Religious Movements*. Boston: Hall, 1979.

Tutu, Desmond. "Whither African Theology?" In *Christianity in Independent Africa*, edited by Edward Fasholé-Luke, Richard Gray, Adrian Hastings, and Godwin Tasie, 364–69. London: Collings, 1978.

Twum-Baah, K. A., and T. K. Kumekpor. *Analysis of Demographic Data*. Vol. 2, *Detailed Analysis Reports*. Accra: Ghana Statistical Service, 1995.

Tylor, Edward. *Primitive Culture*. Vol. 1, *Researches into the Development of Mythology, Philosophy, Religion, Art, and Custom*. London: Murray, 1903.

Udobata Onunwa. "The Biblical Basis for some Healing Methods in African Traditional Religion." *Africa Theological Journal* 15:3 (1986) 187–94.

Ukpong, Justin. *African Theologies Now: A Profile*. Spearhead 80. Eldoret, Kenya: Gaba, 1994.

————. "The Immanuel Christology of Matthew 25:31 in African Perspective." In *Exploring Afro-Christianity*, edited by John Pobee, 55–64. Frankfurt: Lang, 1992.

Vansina, Jan. *Oral Traditions: A Study in Historical Methodology*. London: Routledge & Kegan Paul, 1961.

Vicedom, Georg F., editor. *Christ and the Younger Churches: Theological Contributions from Asia, Africa, and Latin America*. Theological Contributions 15. London: SPCK, 1972.

Vinay, Samuels, and Chris Sugden, editors. *Sharing Jesus in the Two Third World: Evangelical Christologies from the Context of Poverty, Powerlessness, and Religious Pluralism: The*

Bibliography

Papers of the First Conference of Evangelical Mission Theologians from the Two Thirds World, Bangkok, Thailand, March 22-25, 1982. Bangalore: Partnership in Mission-Asia, 1983.

Wachege, P. N. *Jesus Christ Our Mūthamaki (Ideal Elder): An African Christological Study Based on the Agĩkũyũ.* Nairobi: Phoenix, 1992.

Waliggo, J. M. "African Christology in a Situation of Suffering." In *Jesus in African Christianity,* edited by J. N. K. Mugambi and Laurenti Magesa, 93-111. Nairobi: Acton, 1998.

Walls, Andrew F. "The Gospel as the Prisoner and Liberator of Culture." *Faith and Thought* 108:1-2 (1981) 39-52.

Ward W. E. F. *History of the Gold Coast.* London: Allen & Unwin, 1948.

Welbourn, F. B. "Some Problems of African Christianity: Guilt and Shame." In *Christianity in Tropical Africa,* edited by C. G. Baëta, 182-194. London: Oxford University Press, 1968.

Wessels, Anton. *Images of Jesus: How Jesus is Perceived and Portrayed in Non-European Cultures.* Translated by John Vriend. London: SCM, 1990.

West, Gerald. "Local is Lekker but Ubuntu is Best: Indigenous Reading Researches from a South African Perspective." In *Vernacular Hermeneutics,* edited by R. S. Sugirtharajah, 11-16. Sheffield: Sheffield University Press, 1999.

West, Martin Elgar. *Bishops and Prophets in a Black City: African Independent Churches in Soweto, Johannesburg.* Cape Town: David Philip, 1975.

Williamson, S. G. *Akan Religion and the Christian Faith: A Comparative Study of the Impact of Two Religions.* Accra: Ghana University Press, 1965.

Winter, Ralph D., and Steven C. Hawthorne, editors. *Perspectives on the World Christian Movement: A Reader.* Pasadena: William Cary Library, 1981.

Wiredu, Kwesi. "Death and the Afterlife in African Culture." In *Person and Community,* edited by Kwesi Wiredu and Kwame Gyekye, 137-152. Ghanaian Philosophical Studies 1. Washington, DC: Council for Research in Values and Philosophy, 1992.

Wiredu, Kwesi, and Kwame Gyekye, editors. *Person and Community.* Ghanaian Philosophical Studies 1. Washington, DC: The Council for Research in Values and Philosophy, 1992.

Wright, Richard A. *African Philosophy: An Introduction.* 3rd ed. Lanham, MD: University Press of America, 1984.

Wyllie, Robert. *Spiritism in Ghana: A Study of New Religious Movements.* AAR Studies in Religion 21. Missoula, MT: Scholars, 1980.

Xulu, M. "Music and Leadership in the Zionist Churches." In *African Independent Churches Today: Kaleidoscope of Afro-Christianity,* edited by M. C. Kitshoff, 173-80. African Studies 44. Lewiston, NY: Mellen, 1996.

Yankah, Kwesi. *The Proverb in the Context of Akan Rhetoric: A Theory of Proverb Praxis.* Sprichwörterforschung 12. Bern: Lang, 1989.

———. *Speaking for the Chief: Okyeame and the Politics of Akan Royal Oratory.* African Systems of Thought. Bloomington: Indiana University Press, 1995.

Yates, Walter. "History of the African Methodist Episcopal Church in West Africa: Liberia, Gold Coast (Ghana) and Nigeria, 1900-1939." PhD diss., University of Hartford, 1967.

Young, Josiah U. *Black and African Theologies: Siblings or Distant Cousins?* The Bishop Henry McNeal Turner Studies in North American Black Religions 2. Maryknoll, NY: Orbis, 1986.

Index

Index

Index

Inculturation, xi, 9, 10, 35–37, 39, 113, 156, 161, 162, 164, 170, 171, 172
Indigenous prophets, 51
Islam, 16
Ivory Coast, 11, 16

Jehu-Appiah, 14, 53, 65,
Jesus Christ, x, 3–5, 10, 22, 24, 33, 35, 38, 39, 41, 53, 57, 59, 68, 82, 83, 86, 87, 91, 94, 101, 110, 125, 126, 141, 169, 173

Kabasélé, François, 93
Kalu, Ogbu, 32
Kirby, Fr. John, 145
Kuma, Afua, 145

Langer, S. K., 155
Libation, 26, 77, 79, 81
Libation prayers, 26
Liberation, 8, 35, 37, 53, 54, 74, 88–90, 113, 114, 120, 127, 161, 162, 167, 170

Magesa, Laurenti, 13, 99
Marty, Emmanuel, 34
Mbiti, John, 1, 2, 12, 26 67, 133
Mennonite Mission, 61
Messiah, 1, 4, 53, 82–85, 87, 90, 104, 105, 123, 136, 169, 172
Mesters, Carlos, 115, 116
Metaphor, 53, 72, 152, 154–59, 161–65, 168, 170, 171
Methodist Church, 45, 46, 50, 56, 57
Meyer, Birgit, 99, 101
Meyerowitz, Eva, 15
Mother tongue, 17, 47, 119, 166
Mugambi and Magesa, 4
Musama Disco Christo Church, xiv, 56, 97
Mythology 161, 171

National Baptist Church, 45, 62
Nicaea in AD 325, 6
Nkrumah, Kwame, 52–54
Nyame, Gye, 21
Nyamiti, 2, 124, 125, 171
Nyamiti, Charles, 124, 125, 162

Old Testament, 47, 59, 70, 78
Onyame, 18–23, 38, 85, 86, 100, 128, 138, 144
Onyankopong, 141
Oral theology, 25, 134, 135, 146, 147, 148, 150, 195, 197,
Oral tradition, 11, 120, 121, 132–34, 136
Orality, 32, 81, 104, 120, 130–34, 136, 142, 143, 149–52, 158, 160–63, 165, 166, 170, 171
Organization of African Instituted Churches, xi, xiv
Otibil, Mensah, 66
Ott, Martin, 171

Parratt, John, 111
Pentecostal Association of Ghana, 62
Pneumatological, x, 67, 101, 150,
Pobee, John, 4, 12, 39, 92
Prayer, 19, 21, 22, 26, 31, 35, 60, 62, 69, 71, 73–79, 90, 97, 98, 100, 104, 120, 130, 134, 141–45, 147, 149, 151, 156, 158, 163, 167, 170, 171
Presbyterian Church of Ghana, 62
Primal, 18, 60, 65, 167
Primal religions, 18
Prophets, xi, 44, 51, 54, 57, 58, 100, 128
Prosperity Christology, 66
Protestant, 10, 47, 57, 64

Ricoeur, Paul, 8
Roman Catholic Mission, 30
Ross, Kenneth, 70

Index

Made in the USA
Middletown, DE
16 August 2016